ARMOURED GUARDSMEN

ARMOURED GUARDSMEN

A WAR DIARY
JUNE 1944–APRIL 1945

by

ROBERT BOSCAWEN

LEO COOPER

First published in Great Britain in 2001 by
LEO COOPER
an imprint of
Pen & Sword Books Ltd
47 Church Street
Barnsley
South Yorkshire
S70 2AS

ISBN 0 85052 748 1

A catalogue record for this book is available from the British Library.

Typeset in 10.5/12.5pt Plantin by
Phoenix Typesetting, Ilkley, West Yorkshire

Printed and bound in Great Britain by
Mackays of Chatham plc, Chatham, Kent

Glossary

SOME ABBREVIATIONS OF MILITARY TERMS AND EQUIPMENT

B.L.A.	British Liberation Army, comprised of 1st (Canadian) Army and 2nd (British) Army
G.A.D.	Guards Armoured Division, composed of 5th Guards Armoured Brigade and 32nd Guards Brigade, with Divisional Troops. About 16,000 men, 3,400 vehicles, 246 medium tanks and 48 field guns.
G.A.T. Wing	Guards Armoured Training Wing, Pirbright.
Armoured Battalion	36 officers, 630 other ranks.
	61 medium tanks and 11 Recce tanks.
Squadron	19 tanks, with 4 Troops of 4 tanks.
'F' Echelon	Tanks and Scout cars.
'F2' Echelon	One petrol and one Ammunition 3-tonner wheeled truck per Squadron.
'A' Echelon	1st line Petrol and Ammunition trucks, fitters and stores.
'B' Echelon	Stores, Cookers and officers' mess trucks.
R.A.P.	Regimental Aid Post, normally a White Scout Car where the Battalion Medical Officer was to be found.
L.A.D.	Light Aid Detachment, part of Brigade workshops for limited repairs to tanks.
'O' Group	Orders Group.
H.C.R.	Household Cavalry Regiment – Armoured
G.G.	Grenadier Guards
C.G.	Coldstream Guards
S.G.	Scots Guards

I.G.	Irish Guards
W.G.	Welsh Guards
A.G.R.A.	Army Groups Royal Artillery. Medium and Heavy regiments allocated to Corps Commanders.
R.E.	Royal Engineers, Sappers
R.A.S.C.	Royal Army Service Corps
C.M.P.	Corps of Military Police, M.P.s, Redcaps
E.N.S.A.	Entertainments National Service Association
C.I.G.S.	Chief of the Imperial General Staff
G.O.C.	General Officer Commanding, the Divisional Commander
M.S.	Military Secretary
G.1, 2, 3	General Staff Officer, Grade 1, 2, and 3. Brigade Majors were the former.
A.Q.M.G.	Assistant Quartermaster-General
L.O.	Liaison Officer
L.O.B.	Officer left out of battle, usually in 'A' or 'B' echelons.
R.S.M.	Regimental Sergeant-Major
S.S.M.	Squadron Sergeant-Major
T.Q.M.S.	Technical Quartermaster-Sergeant
D.R.	Despatch Rider
L.c.t.	Landing craft tank – carried five tanks
L.s.t.	Landing ship tank
M.t.b.	Motor torpedo boat
E-boat	German torpedo boat
Monitor	Shallow draft warship with two 15 inch guns for bombarding shore installations.

Tanks, mostly described in text.

Cromwell	Main tank of Reconaissance Battalion
M.10.	Armoured self-propelled anti-tank guns on a Sherman hull with 3 inch or 17 pounder gun
A.R.V.	Armoured Recovery Vehicle. Sherman tank without a turret, carried fitters and gear.

Bren Carrier	Universal infantry carrier. 3 men with Bren gun, 30 m.p.h.
Flail tank	Sherman tank with minesweeping flails revolving in front
Honey	Stuart light tank, with 37 m.m. gun, used by Recce Troop.
Scout car	2-seater Humber, armoured, exceeded 55 m.p.h.
White scout car	Large, half-tracked, lightly armoured

German weapons

Spandau	Standard German 7.92 m.m. m.g.
Lüger	German 9 m.m. automatic pistol
Panzerfaust	Hand-held anti-tank rocket launcher, often called by U.S. name Bazooka
88 m.m.	German mobile dual purpose flak anti-tank gun
105 m.m.	German fixed heavy dual purpose flak anti-tank gun
Nebelwerfer	German six barrelled 150 m.m. rocket launcher
Mortar	German 81 m.m. infantry mortar, and 120 m.m. 7½ and 35 lb bombs
Teller mines	German heavy anti-tank mines, 20 lbs.

H.E.	High Explosive
A.P.	Armour piercing shot
u.x.b.	Unexploded bomb
O.P.	Observation Post, artillery
i.a.	immediate action
T.e.w.t.	Tactical exercise without troops
D & M	Driving and Maintenance
K.R.s.	King's Regulations

centreline	Central axis of an attack along roads or across country
laager	Armoured or other vehicles after dark behind the 'line' drawn up in two or three lines, sometimes with infantry protection
harbour area	generally out of the line where armoured

	vehicles were drawn up along hedges and camouflaged
brewed-up	tank set on fire
Stonk	a specific gunners' term that became a slang army word for all shelling, enemy or friendly, and other excesses!
T.C.V. or L.	Troop-carrying vehicle or lorry. Soft, 3-ton vehicle without protection.
15 c.w.t. truck	Standard small truck, carried officers' mess.
Scammel	Heavy recovery vehicle
Sprocket	Toothed driving wheel on tracked vehicles.
'A' set	Longer range part of No. 19 wireless set, carried on all armoured vehicles, used for battalion 'net'. The 'B' set short range we never bothered with.
I.C.	The crew's inter-com part of above set.

British Weapons

Browning point 5	Heavy 0.5 inch m.g. for A.A. carried on top of Sherman, soon discarded.
Browning 300	Standard 0.3 inch m.g. mounted coaxially in turret and in hull of Sherman.
M.g.	Machine gun
A.A.	Anti-aircraft
Bren	Standard .303 inch light machine gun carried by infantry sections
Sten	9 m.m. sub-machine gun
Pistol	0.38 inch revolver
P.I.A.T. or Piat	Hand-held anti-tank weapon with projectile
Mortar	2-inch and 3-inch infantry mortars 2½ and 10 lb bombs
5.5	5.5 inch medium field gun, 100 lb shell
25 pounder	Standard field gun, drawn by wheeled or mounted on tracked vehicle.
17 pounder	Heaviest anti-tank gun on tanks or wheels
S.P.	Self-propelled guns on tracked vehicles of a wide variety

INTRODUCTION

Written as my diary was, mostly in a hurry, and when out of the 'line' in a 'Rest Area', covering part of 1944 and 1945, I have no pretensions about it. It was none other than a mere personal record of my experiences, hopes and fears, and of those with me, done to occupy my mind and of interest perhaps only to myself. It was just one's own story, because no two people, I believe, however near they are, even as close as within a tank crew, see things quite the same in battle. Confusion, monotony or sudden shocks take charge. Much military detail could of course not be written down at the time and had to be added when all was over and time was on one's hands. At the time too it was never intended to be published. That somebody one day might want to know what happened as I saw it did not really count. Total war is sordid and dreadful beyond measure, but my account was most certainly not written as a cautionary tale. Today I just hope that the record of those Coldstreamers with whom I was proud to serve, who rose superbly to each occasion, and especially for those who gave their lives, will speak for itself.

By 1941, within a fortnight of leaving school aged eighteen – we were not allowed to join up before – I had signed on and passed my medical at the local recruiting office in Redruth, Cornwall. Shortly afterwards, instructions were sent to appear at 3rd Training Battalion of the Royal Engineers in a wartime camp on the edge of Newark, Nottinghamshire, as a Sapper recruit. My eldest brother, Evelyn, a pre-war regular soldier, had been killed in action tragically in the 2nd Coldstream Guards Battalion at Pecq, during the withdrawal from eastern Belgium to Dunkirk in May 1940, as a Platoon Commander. Of my other two brothers, George was also in the Coldstream and Edward in the Royal Engineers, both in training in England.

1

Weeks of drill parades awaited us, followed by initial training for the role of Sappers. We learned such things as bridge-building, mine clearance and demolitions, which were exciting, interesting – and noisy! The very first evening, after a day of struggling into our newly issued battledress and ammunition boots, having been handed out last-war American rifles, we were efficiently put through our paces by the impressive and smart Corporal Miller who was in charge of our squad. Later we were marched off to listen to a homily from the Battalion Padre. One wonders whether such a thing exists today to build morale among recruits.

The Army, I feel sure, has a way of doing the right thing though. One sentence he said to us then I recall so well, "Wherever you serve in the Army, you will always find a friend you have been with before, no matter where you are or when".

Even as he spoke, one of the more cheerful recruits amongst us was Sapper Tony Jones in our squad, whom I had met for the first time that day. He and Corporal Miller himself were to become just such Army friends of mine; both were later to serve with the Guards Armoured Division. The former was to cut the wires and immobilize the extensive demolition charges under and above the huge Nijmegen bridge and so helped to open up the final stage in the ill-fated battle to relieve our airborne forces at Arnhem. He went on to become a most distinguished senior officer in later life. In his last appointment he was President of the Regular Commissions Board in Westbury and the wheel had just about turned full circle. It was a stone's throw then from my Somerset constituency. The Padre's truism was thus to reverberate on me again and again.

After a few weeks we said farewell to our friends there and set off for the next adventure, the first-year course at a University to learn the rudiments of Mechanical Engineering. For me, by good luck, this meant Cambridge. It was an exciting and interesting place to be for a spell in wartime, for there were many such as I was already starting in one of the Services and learning to further our military training doing the first year of a University course – wearing gowns one moment and uniforms the next. I was immensely lucky and proud to be up at Trinity where my father and others of our family had been. I was sharing rooms in Great Court with a future RAF pilot, Christopher Lawson-Tancred, who was destined to fly medium day bombers.

2

Our rooms were magnificent. Above us on our staircase was the then young King Peter of Yugoslavia. A few months earlier he had joined the revolt by Serb officers in Belgrade that delayed the Balkan States falling 'piecemeal into Hitler's power', according to Churchill, and so postponed for a vital few weeks German military plans for the attack on Russia. He had been brought out by a British aircraft after the surrender of Belgrade. Although extremely pleasant, a propensity for playing the drums frequently after midnight did not altogether endear him to his new allies.

Each morning I bicycled off to the Engineering Labs to listen to lectures by eminent dons, including on one occasion by the famed Professor Inglis, Head of the Department. Witty and diverting he, was the designer of the military bridges we had seen near Newark that bore his name. With the rapid increase in the weight of tanks, however, the Inglis bridge had by then to be superseded by the ubiquitous Bailey bridges, hundreds of which were to play a major role in our advance across the waterways of northern Europe. We struggled to understand the principles that lay behind these constructions and learnt how to survey the hills around Cambridge. One moment we might be taking part in an anti-invasion exercise as infantry in battledress, while the next I could be rowing on the Cam in the bumping races in the 1st and 3rd Trinity Eight. By evening the pubs near the College would be filled with off-duty night bomber crews as Cambridge was the recreation centre for many of the Bomber airfields around. We listened enthralled to the tales of their nightly raids pounding the great cities and factories of the Ruhr. So war was never far away. On 7 December 1941 the American Fleet was attacked by Japan in Pearl Harbor, which brought that great nation into the war with us. No one at Cambridge seemed to be in any doubt; we were going to win the war now, however long it might last. Everyone seemed to take on a much more lighthearted view – for a day or two at least. But the bad news was to come only too soon.

My diary note for 10 December '41 tells the tale. We learned that our two great battleships, the *Prince of Wales* and the *Repulse*, had been sunk by the Japanese in the Far East with a dreadful loss of life.

One day I was sent for by the Adjutant of the University Training Corps, a Grenadier Major I recall, who told me the War Office was forming new Armoured Divisions as fast as they could as we had a long way to go to catch up with the success of the German Panzer Divisions.

3

Since I was learning about engines and the like he said that there was an opportunity to consider joining one of these new formations. They had even put the Brigade of Guards into tanks now, and wanted young officers. I could go to the Armoured Wing at Sandhurst as an Officer Cadet, if I was accepted by a Regiment. As I had only seen one tank since I joined the Army, and that was of course broken down beside the road in Newark, I was not too impressed and anyhow knew nothing about them. I was not sure, however, that I had made the right choice in joining the Sappers and, as there might be a chance unexpectedly to join the Coldstream, I agreed without much deliberation. The Adjutant seemed surprisingly pleased.

So soon after off I went for a short and sharp interview with the Coldstream Regimental Lieutenant Colonel, John Wynne Finch, in Birdcage Walk and was gruffly told that my father knew all about steam engines and their like when he was in the Regiment in the last war. I was to report to the Cavalry Wing at the Royal Military College, Camberley, very shortly, and so began the next stage in my life.

Sandhurst, like the Cambridge colleges, was trying to keep up the traditions of peacetime as far as it was possible. At the Old College Building at Sandhurst we still had to wear Cavalry bandoliers across our chests when on parade, polished immaculately along with our boots by a few elderly civilian servants as in the days of the Gentlemen Cadets. Life consisted of drill parades and guards, driving and maintenance of tracked vehicles, learning wireless procedure and gunnery; finally armoured tactical training without let-up for six months through the summer of 1942. We saw little of the tanks themselves and, for the most part, drove about in trucks. At other times we bicycled along the lanes in close groups of four, pretending to be tank crews sitting in the real thing! We were once given the chance to drive the new Cruiser tank, Mark VI, the 'Crusader'. This was great fun and appeared to be a lot better than the Covenanter, its predecessor, and was especially good at bouncing rapidly across country. The Middle East desert battles against Rommel had not been going too well this summer; we heard frequent reports that our tanks were under-armoured and out-gunned by the Panzers, which was a bit of a worry. Nevertheless we met and made good friends there and escaped to London when we could, so morale was high. When the time came to be commissioned we passed out in the time-honoured way before the Commandant, slow-marching up the

4

steps of the Old Building. I well remember Bill Harrington, an old school chum, and myself, side by side, taking up the rear of the troop, ahead of the Adjutant on his horse, with the silver-knobbed Picket Officers' Sticks under our arms, (which was considered to be an honour).

As newly commissioned young officers in the summer of 1942, we proceeded at once to the Training Battalion at Pirbright to be in-oculated with the traditions of the Coldstream and brought up to the highest standards of drill. Although David Baxendale and myself were the only two in the armoured entry, there were many more destined for the Infantry Battalions either in the Middle East or at home. In all there were now six 'Service' battalions in the Regiment, so Pirbright was quite a crowded spot. A highlight was Sergeant Callow's legendary catering in the Officers' Mess, which gave us a taste of a world that for us had seemed to have gone for ever.

After this experience David and I were posted in September to the First Armoured Battalion, then just moving into the modern barracks outside Warminster on the edge of Salisbury Plain. I was told on arrival by the Adjutant to report to Major Michael Fox, No. 2 Squadron Leader, next morning. For almost three years this was now to become the centre of my world and of my diary to follow. I have no hesitation in claiming that this was the best squadron in what was then, and is now, a very fine battalion and I feel sure many whose names appear in this record would wholly agree with me. The Officers and Guardsmen of No. 2 Squadron became comrades and friends for life and when the few of us remaining sometimes meet then it is always the warmest and most special occasion.

Michael Fox gave me a friendly welcome and told me to join No. 1 Troop temporarily while the Troop Leader, Hugo Chisenhale Marsh, was on leave. He duly handed me over to Sergeant Morgan, the Troop Sergeant, to see the men working in the tank park. He and Troop Corporal Fawcett were most friendly and introduced me to each of the Guardsmen who explained what they were up to maintaining their Covenanter tanks. There were three tanks to a troop, each with a crew of four, but, as I was quickly to be made aware, mechanical breakdowns were their frequent lot and some were constantly 'off the road'.

Each tank in our Squadron was given the name of an animal painted on the front and the names in a Troop began with the same letter. It made recognition much easier.

5

It was immediately apparent there was a tremendous difference in attitude between what was known as a 'Service' battalion and the training units I had been with before. The atmosphere was much friendlier, with men of all tanks wanting to be helpful. Everyone possessed tremendous enthusiasm and a determination to overcome problems and learn the new trades in order to become as proficient in their armoured role as possible. Many of the Officers and NCOs had been away on the numerous courses to become the Squadron or Battalion authority on skills such as wireless procedure or gunnery. Our Squadron Second-in-Command, Captain Bill Anstruther-Gray, was even seconded to a Yeomanry regiment somewhere in the North African Campaign, of which more anon. Then there was Tony Watkins, the brother of 'Gino', the intrepid Arctic explorer, tragically drowned on an expedition to Greenland between the wars. 'Watty', as he was called by all, was the second Captain whose job in the field was the 'Rear Link' officer whose wireless set was tuned to the higher formations such as Battalion HQ for orders. He was renowned for his pertinent wit and source of many humorous stories.

I met that day for the first time Val Hermon, who was the No. 3 Troop Leader, several years my senior, but the most friendly and cheerful brother officer one could possibly want to be with. With Michael Fox's immense charm and very considerable Army experience, they were a formidable crowd to be with. Above all, we had our share of those of all ranks who could maintain, when it was most needed, that essential element in war, cheerful, friendly lighthearted laughter, no matter how dreadful things had become.

Exercises at Squadron and Battalion level on Salisbury Plain were the frequent lot of us all during that winter. The featureless and bare hills of the Plain were churned and churned again by the dozens of tracked and other vehicles charging hither and thither. The countryside was ideal for knocking into shape the Guards Armoured Division with its crews and its tanks and long but essential tail of 'soft' vehicles. Frequently breakdowns left a crew spending a bitterly cold and frustrating night beside the tank waiting for the heavy breakdown vehicle, the Scammell lorry, to come and tow one home back across the Plain at four miles an hour. A brandy flask and flying boots were the most valuable possessions one could possibly have. The best mixture for the flask was a much debated issue.

On one occasion the battalion received an appropriate rocket from the Brigadier – our "harbour-drill was disgraceful, there were lights all over the place, I even heard singing coming from the Coldstream harbour". We had developed into brigade exercises by then with the other battalions in 5th Guards Brigade. We were slowly being issued with the latest medium Cruiser tank, the Crusader Mark VI. These at least provided us with a more respectable gun, the 6-pounder, but even these tanks were a product of pre-war Government indifference to re-armament. The Crusader was essentially an outdated design powered by a First World War aero engine and, though improved, still had its cooling problems. British tanks were, in truth, hopelessly underpowered for the weight of protective armour and size of gun they needed to match those weapons the Germans were known to possess. We had never developed an engine in Britain to do this job before the war began and it was now really too late to catch up. It seemed to us, who depended on these machines, that we were always lagging behind.

We moved from the Plain during the major exercise 'Spartan' which finished up for us in Gloucestershire. From there we continued on our own tracks to Norfolk, where 5th Armoured Brigade was to be stationed in the woods north of Brandon, near the Thetford training area.

Shortly after we arrived the first Sherman M4 tanks began to reach us in ones and twos from America, as a result of Churchill's deal with Roosevelt. After our serious setback in the North African desert the arrival of the Shermans there had helped to turn the tide at Alamein. We were in little doubt these would be the vehicles we would be going to war in, so there was immense interest to learn all about them.

One of the first was allocated to us in No. 2 Troop. It caused raised eyebrows and some amusement to find chalked on the armour, by some unknown hand in Detroit no doubt, 'Danger, hammer left in sump'. Although possessing an extremely high profile and being noisy, they looked as if they had a bit more armour around them which was welcome; they were driven by five Chrysler truck engines, bolted together, but seemed much more reliable than before. They were, however, the petrol version, not diesel, and this was to prove one of their principal weaknesses. About their 75 m.m. gun time would tell, but we had our doubts.

It looked now unlikely the 'Second Front' would be made this year, but troop training began in earnest with the new tanks. With these new machines to drive and maintain, with new guns and new types of ammunition, there always seemed an immense amount to learn and practise.

All this time I was getting to know the NCOs and Guardsmen who were now my responsibility. Brough, the Troop Sergeant, a regular soldier, and Lance Sergeant Emmerson, were my two tank Commanders. Both were north-countrymen from miners' families, who thought it very important their Troop Leader should learn to enjoy the right beer from the north.

By mid-summer 1943 we had moved again to North Yorkshire to a new camp in the grounds of Duncombe Park, a large country house, then a girls' school, in a beautiful park at Helmsley, north of York. Here we continued our training with another new Armoured Division, the 11th, with the divisional sign of a charging black bull, and together we were forming the new VIII Corps. The Yorkshire Wolds, despite being the finest agricultural land, had been requisitioned so that we could exercise driving our tanks, willy nilly, virtually unrestricted on ground that was the nearest thing to reality. Such was the madness of modern war. Looking back it seems extraordinary how little of this training took place in close cooperation with our infantry in 32nd Guards Brigade. Vital lessons about our effectiveness were still to be learned the hard way.

Throughout the winter all ranks were still disappearing for courses all over Britain. Our Commanding Officer, Colonel Ririd Myddelton, wanted me to go on a Gunnery course to Lulworth where the pluses and minuses of our 75s were to become only too apparent. Meanwhile a new character had come into our lives in No. 2 Squadron – Bill Anstruther-Gray had returned to take over command from the much-liked Michael Fox who took over HQ Squadron. Bill, who had led a Squadron of Shermans in Tunisia in the last phase, where he had won a notable MC, was to be a great help to the Battalion. Since 1931 he had been the sitting MP for North Lanark. A further change was the arrival of George Dawnay as our Second-in-Command, another war-time soldier – in peace time he was a banker – who was also to play a major part in the months to come. Nigel Pratt also joined the Squadron when we came to Yorkshire, taking over No. 4 Troop. No one could want for more cheerful friends to have in such a war.

Bill was careful not to damage our optimism and morale, but, privately, his concern was that the Sherman was no match for the enemy's anti-tank guns, especially the deadly 88 – 'a sod of a gun', as he used to call it. As an MP, he did not miss the chance of two Secret Sessions held in the House of Commons – sadly and deliberately no record of them was taken – to tell the Government his feelings. We knew that both the Minister of War, P.J. Grigg, and Churchill himself were upset by what he said.

Some of us had had the surprise opportunity to see at the time a German Tiger tank, captured in Tunisia I recall, and found its size and weight of armour and the deadly 88mm gun in the turret quite startling. The Germans had developed an engine almost twice as powerful as anything we had, which propelled it along nearly as fast as our Shermans, even if it was not as reliable.

Good news came in the early spring of 1944. Three officers, one from each armoured battalion in the Brigade, were ordered to report one day immediately to Lulworth tank ranges. Patrick Pollock from 2nd Battalion Irish Guards, myself and another from the 2nd Grenadiers were volunteered. Next morning a Staff Sergeant took us from the Mess to a spot not far away where stood a tank beneath a huge tarpaulin. He pulled it aside as if unveiling some great monument, and there stood a Sherman tank with a magnificent long gun, sleak and gleaming. It was one of the first 17-pounders in a new turret fitted to the Sherman tank, to be known as the 'Firefly'. We were quickly aboard and, after a tour of instruction from the Sergeant, Patrick loaded a simply enormous brass case fixed to a round of armour-piercing shot, nearly three feet tall, into the breech. I took careful aim – we had the range – and pressed the pedal. There was a blinding flash, my beret was whipped off and out through the open turret hatch above. As the hot air and fumes subsided I just caught a sight of the tracer hitting the target and pulling it right out of the ground! A cheer went up from a crowd outside the Officers' Mess and the Staff Sergeant put his head into the turret and called out, "Are you all right in there?"!

An answer to the enemy's superiority of armour had arrived. We had evidently been amongst the first mugs sent to fire it at Lulworth. One of these tanks was soon to be allotted to each Troop – four tanks per squadron. We took ourselves back to London, stole forty-eight hours' leave and went on up to Yorkshire greatly encouraged and immensely pleased with ourselves.

Britain had been at war for five years, bar a few months, and so the war-weary British were utterly browned-off and longing to get on with it, to reach final victory and to 'bring the boys home'. We all knew the invasion could not be long now.

In April our Division made the great move aboard many trains to the South Coast. We loaded the tanks – a tricky business – our kit and ourselves onto the same train in Driffield station one day. The destination was secret – that is until we were just about to leave when an elderly Stationmaster painstakingly chalked up on the outside of the train the word – Hove!

Second Army, which the Guards Division was now part of, were to be crowded along the South Coast of Sussex and Kent, with some of the Canadian 1st Army, part of the grand deception plan designed to show that the landings would be in the Pas de Calais region. South Coast towns like Folkestone and Brighton were packed with troops and guns and tanks, and the harbours were brimming with naval landing craft.

Most of our battalion were now billeted in the smartest houses in 'The Drive', Hove, with our tanks neatly parked with their backs into the pavement. The coastal area had been declared restricted to visitors and only the massed troops were allowed in and out.

We were, of course, not part of the specially trained and equipped assault forces due to land on the first days, but would be taking our turn when there was room for us. We knew nothing about when that might be.

Waterproofing the tanks and soft vehicles up to six feet or so was the principal task. Once completed, they were tested through a local swimming pool. Otherwise there was not an awful lot to do except enjoy ourselves in the town and local cinemas. Air activity had stepped up immensely and we had to play our part in the 'deception' exercises on the wireless, talking nonsense for hours on end. It was all good fun. Great men such as Eisenhower inspected us and there was plenty of time to go to greyhound racing and visit the restaurants and the night club of the town. Very few wives or girl friends were to be found or allowed in the area but the weather was kind and it was a good place to be.

Every morning Jenny Wren drove a smart naval car down the middle of The Drive past No. 2 Squadron Tanks to pick up the Commander of the Navy's Landing Craft Force 'S' which was waiting to embark part of the assault troops in Shoreham harbour. There was the

10

usual chorus of wolf whistles and catcalls, that customary servicemens' salute, to the young women of the day passing by, whoever they may be. It took me a long long time to discover who this particular girl might be. As it turned out she knew the Coldstream and their vulgar ways all too well; she was the granddaughter of our very long-serving and respected Colonel of the Regiment and her name was Mary Codrington – a surname that had been on the Coldstream Roll for quite a few years. Fortune ensured that this was not the right moment for us knowingly to meet, even if we had unknowingly met perhaps at Brighton's only wartime nightspot.

One day we were sent out on a route march around the town to keep us fit and out of mischief. Air force activity had been incessant overhead the night before. Then all of a sudden people came out of their houses and down their gardens to greet us on our march. They cheered and called to us, "Our forces have landed, the Invasion has begun". This was the first we had heard. The day we had all been waiting for had arrived. The intense planning, the secrecy and deception had come to fruition and to their real test.

For us there was no chance to move for several days, as our continued presence where we were was vital to persuade the Germans that the main Allied attack was still to be delivered in the Pas de Calais. Next day the Divisional Commander addressed all officers in the Division in Brighton to tell us the landings had gone well.

In retaliation, the V-1s, the flying bombs, had begun to arrive in southern Britain. It was not long before we saw one coming over straight up 'The Drive', at about four hundred feet up, going very fast. We had a go at one or two of them later with the machine guns mounted on the top of our tanks, but did little more than speed them on their way. This was Hitler's first terror weapon. We had already heard it was doing some damage in London, when the tragic news of the total destruction of the Guards' Chapel during Morning Service on Sunday 18 June came through to us. There were appalling casualties, many of whom were of course well known and related to the Guards Division. As to the effect on morale collectively in the Division, who could say? But it seemed to us minimal. If anything, it may have added to the resolve to get on with whatever job we had to do.

In a few days we were to move westwards nearer our point of embarkation and my diary takes up the story.

11

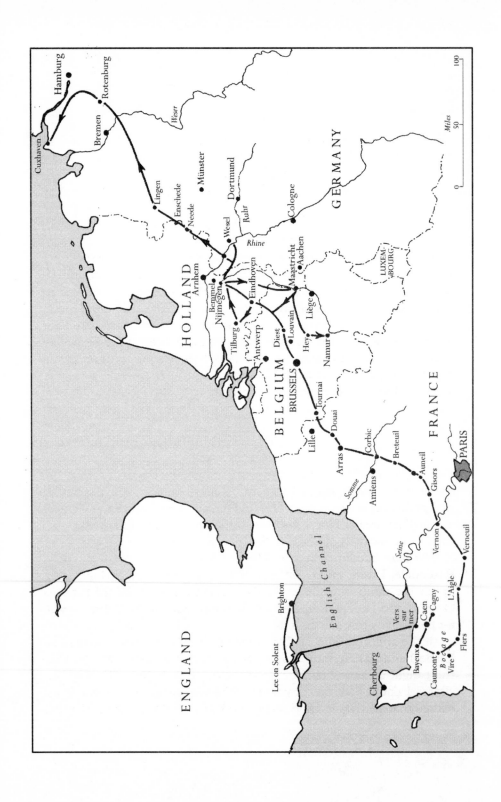

ENGLAND

English Channel

Brighton
Lee on Solent
Cherbourg
Vers sur mer
Bayeux
Caumont
Caen
Cagny
L'Aigle
Bocage
Vire
Flers
Verneuil
Vernon
Gisors
Auneil
Breteuil
Corbie
Amiens
Arras
Douai
Lille
Tournai
BRUSSELS
BELGIUM
Antwerp
Tilburg
Diest
Louvain
Hey
Namur
Liège
Eindhoven
Maastricht
Aachen
LUXEM-BOURG
FRANCE
PARIS
Seine
Somme
Bergen
Nijmegen
Arnhem
HOLLAND
Wesel
Rhine
Ruhr
Cologne
Dortmund
Münster
Neede
Enschede
Lingen
Cuxhaven
Hamburg
Bremen
Rotenburg
Weser
GERMANY

Miles
0   50   100

DIARY

This is started by the sea at St. Aubin in Normandy. I look out from above the sea wall, the horizon filled with ships and landing craft of all shapes and sizes. Opposite, about two miles away and beyond some tank landing craft, lies a monitor, her two fifteen-inch guns point menacingly at the German-held coast around Deauville, now blanketed by a billowing white smoke-screen. Fascinated by this scene and rather sleepy from the hot August sun, I find it difficult to recall from day to day all that has happened in the last two months, but allowing for a poor memory, I am trying to write as truthfully as I can.

18 August 1944
Guards Armoured Division Rest Camp

Friday, 30 June. We set sail for France at last. After months of waiting before the invasion and, when it had started, another agonizing three weeks, this came as a great relief. We moved from Brighton to a dreary marshalling area at Horndean after 6th June, and were stuck there in a large wood away from our vehicles to await our turn.

2.00 pm. Accompanied by Hugo Chisenhale-Marsh and David Baxendale, I went on board L.c.t.534, after we had backed our tanks up on the ramp into the craft. We pushed off from a hard between Gosport and Lee, and moored out in the middle of the Solent to wait for the convoy to carry us across.

All the afternoon the convoy gathered. Bill Gray's (No.2 Squadron Leader) and Val Hermon's craft pulled out and moored near us. They had caught up as we left Horndean the day before them. Through my glasses I could pick out nearly the whole squadron, and parts of the battalion, loaded up in various tank landing craft that swung to the tide.

13

We had a very amusing tea with the skipper and his two young lieutenants. Afterwards we went up on to the deck while the troops finished water-proofing and closing down the tanks. On Val's craft two barrage balloons collided in mid-air, one burst and fell on the deck. There was an immediate rush for it, as everybody seized and tore up his share to use as a cape.

All this time Hugo was telling us how sick he was going to be and being utterly gloomy. This increased when the Navigator came and told us the weather report was black.

7.00 pm. I remember standing in the stern looking across at the hundreds of craft of all descriptions, the battleship *Ramillies*, cruisers, destroyers and masses of landing craft. There must have been two to three thousand ships visible.

I tried to recollect the last time I saw the Solent; perhaps it was sailing there on the *Sheldrake* seven years ago with all the family off Osborne, whose towers I could see clearly. No, I was wrong, the last time was during the first week of the war on the *Aquitania* returning from America with my brother Edward. It was quite empty then.

Hugo and David joined me, and we discussed yachts and ships and sailing after the war, when there was a commotion on the bridge. It appeared we were off at last.

About 8.00 pm. We went on to the bridge and watched the convoy form up. It amused me that they had not had any orders, nobody knew where to go, nor who was convoy commander. Such things happen even in the Navy. We eventually pulled out to lead the right-hand column. In our convoy there were about twenty ships, all L.c.ts. On the bridge leading the left-hand column I saw Peter Hunt and John Sutton from No.3 Squadron, so we waved frantically. Meanwhile the craft behind yawed up and gave us a good bump in the stern, followed by frenzied signalling. This was a big joke amongst our naval friends, all the better for the looks on our faces, no doubt. Slight relief at last, an M.t.b. came out and took control. We were turned right round towards the shore and put at the back of the convoy. Anyway we should not run into the mines first.

The skipper ordered us, in the event of an E-boat attack, to traverse our guns outwards and to let off a broadside from our seven tanks, a popular idea.

It was then that Hugo made the obvious remark on all our minds –

14

"I wonder if any of us will ever see England again". I turned and looked towards Spithead and the 'Island' which were fading on the horizon. I determined then that such sentiment must be avoided at all costs, and this I succeeded in doing until after the battle of Sourdevalle.

David and I turned in and left Hugo. He was starting to feel ill and had decided to spend the night on deck where he could lean over the side at will. The ship heaved and rose in the sea and it had started raining, so I lent him my greatcoat, since I have never seen anyone look so miserable. David and I went to sleep on the wardroom seats.

Saturday, 1 July. I went out early on to the bridge expecting to see the French coast, but there was nothing apart from the two long lines of landing-craft, pitching and rolling. Hugo was sitting on the bridge. He had been there all night, poor man, and was looking very green, but said he felt better. There had been quite a swell earlier on and I was thankful I was a good sailor. I must admit, as it is five years since I have been on the sea, I was not sure at first whether I had lost my sea legs; however, all was well.

"We should sight the coast at about nine o'clock," the cox'n told me.

I went down and aroused the men; only a few had been ill, but they had had a very uncomfortable night I am afraid, and were only too glad to cook some breakfast. I posted anti-aircraft sentries on two tanks, rather dubiously.

09.00 hrs. We sighted the French coast and then began an excited search on the map and charts as to where we were. Soon we managed to pick out church towers and villages, and made out the white lighthouse of Ver-sur-Mer. The scene off the coast was unbelievable. There were more ships than off Portsmouth, each with its balloon up. To the west at Arromanches there was a mass of sunken ships forming a prefabricated port, and to the east was the familiar grey outline of the battleship *Rodney* and its screen of destroyers. A corvette passed us at great speed with a dark green flag to show it had a hoard of German prisoners battened down below.

We pulled into 'K' for King beach below Ver, and went full speed towards the shore opposite a man waving a large yellow flag. There we sat in about four feet of water to wait for the tide to go down. This infuriated us because we were waterproofed up to six feet, but a truculent beachmaster insisted on making us land dryshod, so we just waited. It did save a change of precious gearbox oil afterwards. 'K' was a sector of Gold Beach almost directly below the Ver lighthouse where 50 Infantry Division had led the assault.

There was great competition amongst my crew for my binoculars, but when I managed to get hold of them I had a good look round. The houses along the front were battered to pieces, the fields studded with enormous craters and the beach littered with debris. All along the beach were landing craft piled up ashore, some overturned, others smashed up, caused by the great gale just after 'D' Day. As well as this the beach was covered in stakes and nasty iron spikes, forming part of the German defences. It is remarkable how the craft got through them on 'D' Day. Perhaps they were not really as formidable as might have been expected. The opposition to the British assault generally had been surprisingly light. Our skipper told us that they had all lined up under a smokescreen about 5,000 yards out, and just charged in firing everything. I saw a picture of our boat on a news-film before we came over; it had a Sherman tank on fire inside it.

The skipper was determined to take his motor-bike ashore while waiting for the tide, so there were frantic efforts to get this started and find a pump for its tyres, which we provided out of our scout car.

1.30 pm. At last the tide dried out and I led my tank down onto the beach – rather an exciting moment. In fact 'Cheetah' was the first tank of the whole convoy ashore. I went on to the beach not knowing where to go but eventually found a beach control officer who remarkably enough knew my name. He told me to lead the column off along the shore and thence to our concentration area. I led on for miles and miles following the Div. arrow with the black dot on a white background (stencilled on small discs stuck in the ground). We went along the devastated beach on a dusty road between it and a minefield beyond in some swampy ground, then turned south near Arromanches through the village of Asnelles. Here the first French we saw waved as we thundered past.

Within ten minutes of landing I was nearly decapitated by a low-hanging signal cable which caught me by the neck. By now every road seemed festooned with these menacing wires.

We went on, winding about the French cornfields already stacked with ammunition and supplies and passed the 'dewaterproofing' area. Here we should have been halted by George Dawnay, but he was asleep in a cornfield, so on we went, until fortunately I found a D.R. who led us to the battalion concentration area at Esquay-sur-Seulles near Bayeux.

There, standing in the road, was Nigel Pratt with his unforgettable smile ready to guide us into our harbour area, looking like a civilian on holiday, in grey flannel trousers and white shirt. He had arrived a day before in a L.s.t. with part of the squadron, a U.S.-built ship, much larger than ours. I collected my troop, parked them in a corner of the small field and settled down for what turned out to be a not unpleasant fortnight.

I start again, sitting on the sands at St Aubin. Oliver Heywood, the battalion Signals Officer, arrived last night, so I accompany him out on to the beach, while he sketches the wrecked houses and sunken L.c.t. to the west. The monitor HMS *Roberts*, after firing a few broadsides last night, has gone this morning. Instead a flotilla of destroyers have appeared and look a fine sight riding silently at anchor and showing up white in the sun. No, I am wrong, she is hidden behind a tramp-steamer. Soon, while I am still watching her, a massive orange flame and dirty smoke-cloud bursts from the barrels of her twin 15-inch guns as she continues to pound German positions to the east.

R.S.M. Knowles, also resting here, appears and we engage in conversation but nothing of interest is said, and he continues striding down the shore.

Sunday, 2 July. We began our stay at Esquay and stayed here until the 18th, during which time we had many small experiences and learnt a lot. But the great thing was it gave us time to get accustomed to war. The squadron was harboured in a very pleasant field with the rest of the battalion in neighbouring ones. Typical Normandy fields, small with densely leafed hedges or banks that gave the cover from the air we needed for our vehicles. We had the squadron officers' mess out and got comfortable, and I slept with my crew beside my tank in a corner of the field. The day started with a gentle breakfast followed by a short while working on the tanks; dewaterproofing at first was the main item.

From here we watched the progress of the war. It was going slowly then in Normandy. Cherbourg had only just been taken by the American 1st Army, but Caen was still firmly held by the Germans, and our bridgehead was nowhere more than twenty miles deep.

On the 3rd. I took the jeep out with Squadron Sergeant-Major Robertson, and David, to tour the battlefields. The roads were very full and David disappeared to try and clear the traffic at Bayeux. We could not find him again and after waiting some time had to go on without him.

We went and saw an undamaged Panther at Jerusalem, a flattened village at a crossroads on the Bayeux to Tilly-sur-Seulles road. Here I met Nigel with some men doing the same. The Panther is a very impressive-looking vehicle with a long and powerful gun. From first sight I realized it was, head-on, a much superior match to the old Sherman. With five inches of sloping front-armour, and a long 75 m.m. gun, it was not surprising that hardly anyone had been allowed to see a captured Panther in England. The German Mark V tank, the Panther, had been introduced in 1943 to deal with the famous Russian T34. The Sherman, the main Allied tank, was turned out by the ten thousand in the U.S. and so with a short 75 m.m. gun of lower power than its counterpart in the German Mark IV tank, and with only three inches front-armour, quantity had taken precedence. At 32 tons the Sherman weighed 11 tons less than the well-protected, hard-hitting Panther. Shortly before the Invasion the 17-pounder gun Sherman arrived. The Firefly, one allotted per troop, was our big hope to redress the balance.

We went on to Lingèvres where there had been a fight between Panthers and Shermans, and we had knocked out six Panthers in and around it. The Brigadier, a Welsh Guardsman, whose brigade had captured this village, was looking at the mess, and he explained to us what had happened.* One Sherman crew had done extremely well, fighting their way right into the centre of the village, but their tank was now to be seen riddled with holes standing a few yards from a Panther.

From there we drove along a deserted and rough cart-road littered with carnage and sordid scatterings of war to Tilly where there had been fierce fighting. It was only just captured, completely devastated, and smelling strongly. Bulldozers were clearing a road through. Firing was going on quite close and with difficulty I dissuaded the Sergeant-Major

---

* This was Brigadier Sir Alexander Stanier, commanding 231st Infantry Brigade in 50th Division. I was mistaken, for, many years after, he told me Lingèvres was taken by the brigade immediately to his right. His Brigade had captured the strongpoint of Le Hamel and Arromanches on 'D' Day.

from climbing up a Château and having a look. What would be the point of getting killed at this stage? So back we went. Dead cattle were still lying in the fields and all was rather gruesome, but it was a gentle breaking in for things to come. Bulldozing proved a good method too of burying distinctly dead cattle and Germans alike. I noticed many knocked-out Shermans littering the countryside. Beside some were the last resting places of the crews. From the very beginning we learnt that our tanks were an easy victim to the German gunners.

The S.M. and I arrived back gasping, grey with dust, and hungry for some lunch.

This evening I went for a long walk with Nigel through Esquay. We tried to talk French, not with much success. Back at my tank I was very excited to find a note on my pillow from Dermot Musker* telling me to come on board the *Rodney* next day, and if I could, to be at Brigade H.Q. at nine o'clock.

Tuesday, 4 July. I drove down to Le Courseulles in a scout car with Dermot, John Yerburgh, Irish Guards, and Peter Chance, all from 5th Guards Brigade H.Q., to be met there by a midshipman on the beach and be taken off on a launch. The *Rodney* was about three miles out.

We were met on the quarterdeck by the Captain, Oliver Fitzroy, Dermot's father-in-law. Preceded by an excellent hot bath – I was given the Admiral's bath – we spent a very amusing day on board. Before lunch in the wardroom Captain Fitzroy broke the news gently to us; we were in for a shock. General Montgomery, then commanding the whole shooting match in the bridgehead, was coming on board. After lunch we toured the ship and gun turrets. Unfortunately they did not do a shoot, as their target near Caen was already taken without their assistance. They were ready to fire on a target at a range of 39,000 yards, spotted for by a Spitfire. The ship was leaking 900 tons of water a day, they said, before they started to bombard the coast, but this had since gone up to 1400 tons; and, as they had used up nearly the complete supply of 16-inch shells in the Navy, were hoping to go home for good soon!

Monty arrived for lunch. He addressed the crew first, followed by the

---

* Dermot Musker was detached from 1st Coldstream to Brigade H.Q., but would be rejoining No. 2 Squadron later on.

officers in the wardroom. This was the first time I have ever seen the little General, and I must admit in spite of all adverse reports I could not help being impressed.

He told us a great deal. The main points were that 2nd Army was to contain the German armour in the east around Caen, while the Americans were to attack south down the Cotentin Peninsula. In fact, he said, they had already started attacking this morning, but, with a slight smile, he was a little anxious as to their sober state since today was the Fourth of July. He was very confident and spoke without any trace of self-advertisement. He looked a real soldier, absolutely in his element, and my estimation went up a lot. At the end he said, "Gentlemen, I have the greatest hopes that by today week Caen will be liberated." Then he saw me sitting there and remarked on a 'soldier' being present. On a closer look he said, "Ah, Guards Armoured I see," adding quickly as his eyes flashed, he had something in store for us.

We came back loaded with white bread for the Squadron. The army's mobile bakery had not yet been given the priority to embark so it was a welcome change to hard biscuits. Altogether we had a most enjoyable day.

Later Comment.

Until the breakout from the Normandy bridgehead, Monty commanded both 21st Army Group and the 1st U.S. Army. I could not write down then that the most morale-raising remark he had made on the *Rodney* was that once Cherbourg had been cleared of mines and wrecks there were twenty-six American Divisions ready to be shipped in direct from the United States. This would be the turning point. With the information we had been told, of course, I realized after, we should never have been let off the ship.

The next few days were spent touring the battlefields and gaining as much information as we could. On July 6th tragedy overtook my troop. Guardsman Neary, who was Sergeant Brough's Operator, was killed in a truck accident north of Tilly. It was such very bad luck. Guardsman Neary, whose parents were from Moss Side, Manchester, was hardly twenty; he always had the most cheerful and nice nature. It was a real blow and he was a real loss to us as he was a good Operator. With the rest of the troop and our Padre, I attended the burial service that evening, which was a very gloomy affair in a corner of a field near Tilly.

A French farmer was very kind and made a lovely cross out of honey-suckle for the service.

Sergeant F. Brough, aged 23, a regular soldier, had been my Troop Sergeant since Salisbury Plain days in 1942. From a miner's family in Adwick le Street, Doncaster, he had already seen action at Dunkirk in No. 2 Company under Michael Fox. A wireless instructor, he commanded '2 Able'; my other two tank commanders were Lance-Sergeants N. Emmerson, a 34-year-old miner, who had been a Trade Union representative from Blythe, Northumberland, and a gunnery instructor who now had the 17-pounder gun, '2 Charlie', and R. Caulfield, at 27, a regular from Proudhoe, Newcastle, in '2 Baker', and a champion long-distance runner who often represented the battalion.

I went with Bill on the 7th to see the six knocked-out Panthers at Bretteville L'Orgueilleuse close to Carpiquet airfield, still in German hands then. The tanks had been caught by surprise by four 17-pounder anti-tank guns while advancing in the open and were all 'brewed-up' still in formation over a small area. So far we had seen only one knocked-out Tiger in the bridgehead.

Later Comment.
The Tiger, Mark VI, was the German heavy tank weighing 55 tons and armed with the deadly 88 m.m. gun; it was greatly held in awe.

Incidentally the 32nd Guards Brigade were then fighting or, rather, holding part of the line there. The 5th Coldstream had had a few casualties from mortaring, including Mark Howard, a company commander, killed. They formed the lorried infantry brigade at that time in our division.

On Saturday 8th we went for a gentle but dull route march round some hot and dusty cornfields. In the afternoon Nigel and I bought butter and cream in Bayeux. Bayeux is about the only town undamaged and has quite a lot of things in the shops. It was full though with very untidy British troops. There is no discipline at all in the army over here except in the Brigade. A great showdown I think, and they look even more scruffy than the Americans.

The dust is terrible out here and will get worse. They do a good thing by making all tanks go across country and not on the roads, though these dirt-tracks are like driving in a sandstorm. Most of the roads before the invasion could have been hardly more than cart-roads. Goggles are an essential, although the ones the army provide are almost useless.

In the evening the S.S.M. and I drove down in the scout-car to the artificial Mulberry port at Arromanches to try to find some bread for the squadron off a ship. Ships were continuously unloading now. We ventured out on the pontoons to the floating piers a mile or so offshore, but our quest was unsuccessful. All the same it was one full of interest and we enjoyed ourselves.

Previously air activity overhead was limited. The landing strips were already working well, a remarkable feat, but were only sufficient for Typhoons and Spitfires, as well as Dakotas for the wounded. Every night we had a small air-raid, everything was shot into the air and the noise was very unnecessary, as they never hit anything. I watched a most exciting dog-fight between a Spitfire and Messerschmitt overhead, which was eventually and inevitably, it seemed, sent down nearby in flames. It pleased us all a lot.

On Friday there had been an incessant rumble of artillery to the south-east and that evening we watched 450 Lancasters bomb the outer defences of Caen, a truly remarkable sight. I only saw one come down. They seemed to lead a charmed life as they steered through the mass of bursting flak, and then turning through a wide circle made for home, while fighters streaked and twisted over them. Above Caen the sky was darkened by a tragic pall of drifting smoke and dust.

Next morning the Canadians attacked Caen and by Sunday evening, according to what Monty had said on the *Rodney*, it was in our hands. A devastated town indeed, except for the Cathedral, L'Abbaye aux Hommes, where five thousand French people were sheltering. It was untouched. This sent up our esteem with the Normans a lot.

Sunday, 9 July. I went to church this morning early, held by Tony Weigall in a French farm building. There were few attendants and Michael Hamilton and I were the only officers supporting. I think this is because Tony never tells anybody when it is.

The rest of the week passed without real incident until Saturday evening. We remained happily in our field entertaining and sleeping. Derek Wigan, our former adjutant, came to dinner one night from 30 Corps H.Q. with all the big shots' news. We fed extremely well under Hanson's catering, and really had nothing to complain about.

On Sunday I took a party to fire the Piat at a knocked-out Panther near Carpiquet, rather a boring morning. A rough and ready, dangerous anti-tank affair, the Piat was fired from the shoulder and could penetrate enemy armour at short range, if you were still around to know it. We walked down a French railway, a terrible mess, a wonder the Germans managed to make the railways work at all; everything was rotten on them.

We had various 'tewts', route marches and the inevitable vehicle maintenance during the week, while a course on the 17-pounder for the 2nd Welsh Guards had to be run. Rex Whistler came, and I had great fun instructing him. He was killed sadly the first day in action near Caen by an 88 mm. A tremendous loss to the world of art as well as to his many friends, he was both a very talented individual and the greatest fun. Far too old to be still a subaltern, such a versatile, original person should never have been allowed to be thrust into the front line, although I am sure he wanted it that way.

On Wednesday 12th Dermot came round in a jeep and we went off to Verson just over the River Odon, a village four miles west of Caen which the 4th Armoured Brigade had just taken. An interesting afternoon, I saw John Althorp, a school friend, in Verson quite unperturbed by anything. In command of the recce troop of the Scots Greys, he had just had a spoke knocked out of the idler-wheel of his Honey tank by an 88. He told us we would be heavily shelled in five minutes as the Hun had a regular timed programme. Quite enough for us, so we jumped into our jeep and shot off leaving John sitting happily on his tank. As we left the town and crossed north of the Odon, Verson was 'stonked' good and proper. We were out just in time. I hope John was all right.

We sat on the next hill behind and watched the shells land amongst the tanks of the Greys below us, until we thought they were landing rather close. The bursts of smoke and dust erupted with a vicious angry force and then the tearing raucous crrrump, crrump, crrumps. We were green to shells then and thought it much too close when they were several hundred yards away.

We visited their brigade H.Q. near St. Mauvieu and saw Ralph Cobbold from the regiment, gaining the local news; they had a new very young Brigadier, Michael Carver, who appeared for a moment. We came home well satisfied.

Thursday, 13 July. We had an exercise, or rather a demonstration, for all officers in the division in a nearby field. It was really a social meeting, the 32nd Brigade had pulled out and were back near Bayeux. I saw Harry Graham-Vivian there. He had had a nasty shelling at Carpiquet with the 5th Battalion, but was none the worse. He came to tea with Nigel and me.

The rest of the week passed with no particular excitement. I had a very good bathe in the River Seulles with David, and also a pleasant walk with Nigel to Vaux-sur-Seulles, where we had a drink of café cognac in an estaminet. It was a very nasty drink. Nigel was in his usual good form, his dry sense of humour cannot fail to keep one amused.

I had various letters from the family, but they still do not know whether I am in France or not. They have not got any of my letters yet. The post is very slow at the moment. My sister Mary seems to be enjoying the Wrens, and Mummie appears to be on her way to Cairo; I hope she goes as she needs a 'holiday', I think.

We were a very happy crowd in the squadron mess. Bill kept us well informed on all subjects and managed to create a strong squadron spirit, while George kept us permanently alive and amused. His slow pedantic way of speaking now and then became almost a mutual language especially amongst Nigel, him and me. Hugo, our Second Captain and Rear-Link, of course is the least happy in the field; comfort is always his main want. I don't blame him, and how extremely adept he was at securing it.

Our dinner parties became rather a social event and the officers' servants produced bigger and better meals. George Dawnay was in great form and never stopped talking. Ian Jardine came to tea one day. We had visitors to dine in the mess including the Navy and RAF and one of the Prime Minister's parliamentary private secretaries. Bill Anstruther-Gray had been commanding a squadron of the Lothian and Border Horse in Tunisia. No doubt thought most unfair by the Germans, he took his squadron of Shermans into the sea to outflank them to force the surrender of Hamman Lif.

The four Troop leaders in order were David, myself, Val and Nigel. We had been the same, on and off, for the last two years so we all knew each other well. Sergeant-Major P. Robertson was a character, strict but with ample sense of humour. His enthusiasm for everything to be correct was tremendous, and he was the mainstay in so many things. I had very many good friends in the original No. 2 Squadron especially in No. 2 Troop, nineteen strong, who were a selection of some of the best of them. In all we were nineteen tank crews, and with the men of the 'soft' transport, we certainly could not have started with a better feeling and confidence in everyone than we did.

We had several standing jokes in that field; the chief being the ack-ack fire put up when a Hun came over with not the slightest effect, despite every firearm in the neighbourhood loosing off. The word Bocage, or 'Bockage' as the Guardsmen called it, caused considerable amusement, although nothing could be more unpleasant than fighting in the Bocage, our enthusiasm hadn't paled by then. We thus upheld our share of the unbeatable quality of the British soldier to spring a funny remark out of the dreariest occasions, setbacks or successes – that most basic essential for winning a war – which is why the Germans lost it.

Next to my troop in the field was a covey of young partridges which I watched with interest and some clean nice-looking cows belonging to the old *fermier*. Each evening he came out and cut a small patch of hay for his donkey and *les lapins*. In all it was a pleasant stay, but towards the end one felt it was high time we got going – the inevitable question, when?

Returned now back to the battalion. I find it harder to write and only in short bursts.

Saturday, 15 July. All officers were summoned before the 'Commander'. From that moment we knew our ordeal had started.

"Well," he began, "the great day has come at last. On Tuesday we go into our first battle. It is going to be a big show and ought to be a very good party."

Lieut-Colonel Ririd Myddleton; under him the battalion had trained in armour. A shy man, he was well liked and trusted by all ranks. He then gave us the plan.

The position was that rather a deadlock had taken place all along the front. Caen had been taken, but the American advance in the west had made little progress. So in order to draw the German armour away from the Americans, to enlarge the bridgehead and to place us in a good position 'for further operations', the British were to put in an attack in the east.

30 and 12 Corps, both infantry, were to attack on Sunday and Monday respectively west of Caen, to draw the enemy away from the main attack. On Tuesday 18th, preceded by a terrific artillery barrage and the 'heaviest aerial bombardment of the war', 8 Corps, consisting of the Guards Armoured Division, 11th Armoured Division, 7th Armoured Division and 3rd Infantry Division, were to attack south from the new direction east of Caen. The Canadians were to occupy the suburbs of Caen east of the Orne and 51st Highland Division were to take Troarn on our eastern flank.

The plan was that after the barrage 11th Armoured Division would advance almost regardless of loss due south as far as the main Paris railway at Cagny some five miles, the furthest limit of the bombing, and then turn due west to take the high ground on the right flank near Bourgeubus. John Rodney, a fluent French-speaking officer, raised a good laugh when asked by the Commander to put us right on the pronunciation. The G.A.D. were to follow led by 2nd Grens, followed by 1st Coldstream and 2nd Irish, to reach the railway at Cagny and then turn east to take high ground by Vimont, and so protect the east flank. The 7th Armoured were to follow us and continue south as far as they could get, directed on Falaise. The armour was to smash straight through without its infantry, and this was to follow by lorry in rear; 'flail' tanks and flamethrowers would be in support.

All the towns and villages as far as Cagny were to be plastered by the heavy bombing, and our route was to be covered with fragmentation bombs from the 'Mediums'. The opposition was expected to be feeble after the bombing. A few tanks, we were gaily told, and the only thing in Vimont was the 'tailor's shop of 21st Panzers'.

It sounded a big plan and excited us all a lot. To us then it seemed as if it might be the big offensive towards Paris, but little did we realize what wishful thinking that was. We left that little barn where our orders were given anticipating great things.

On Sunday all officers in the division went to listen to the divisional commander, Major-General Allan Adair. We learnt of the wonderful tank country beyond Caen, flat and open cornfields; and that we had 700 tanks to be let loose on the enemy's possible 30. He was impressive and cheering. He told us the plan and encouraged us with his dramatic voice to shoot straight. Good straight cool shooting, he bawled out. Exactly the thing one expects a General to say before battle.

26

The Brigadier, Norman Gwatkin, spoke to all the men in the evening, a very short speech and to the point, but much as everyone else had said. In the evening we had a short church service in the corner of the field, where we sang the troops favourite hymns followed by a good little sermon from Tony.

Monday was spent feverishly preparing for the battle. Yesterday and today we listened to a continuous rumbling of artillery in the distance that showed us 30 and 12 Corps were attacking. The weather had suddenly turned good, though the early morning was misty, a perfect excuse for the Royal 'Advertising' Force to call off their bombing tomorrow. We spent the afternoon folding maps, studying aerial photographs, receiving and giving orders, and cleaning our guns. For this occasion George would not be with us, he had the disappointment to be the officer left out of battle, or 'L.o.b.', in the echelons. It was a day of anticipation and I was glad when we set off for a night drive north of Caen. With a slight feeling of regret we left our old field and trundled out down the road.

It was an awful approach march, cross-country on a very dark night with only tail lamps, and, worst of all, a thick cloud of dust everywhere. The dust was appalling. I had made my co-drivers drive as I thought it would rest the first drivers, but this turned out to be a mistake. The visibility was so bad that it needed the best possible driving to keep going without running into everything. Because of this I lost one of my tanks, 'Cobra', which went into the ditch, and Brough was not seen again until after the battle.

'Cougar', Sergeant Emmerson's tank with the 17-pounder, also broke down due to dust in the petrol filter. This disappointed me a lot. My own tank, being driven by Liddle, the co-driver, hit something, but no damage was done. Eventually we arrived at about one in the morning drawn up in a long column in a field west of the bridge over the Orne and a few miles north of Caen. We filled up with petrol, shook the dust off and got down under a blanket for a few hours' sleep.

Many people have written about one's feelings before one's first day under fire; baptism of fire and other such rubbish, they call it. But I must admit that evening I had no real reaction at all. Tomorrow was going to be just another day and I did not think it could be anything other than rather disagreeable. A clear starry night. I lay gazing at Orion the Hunter for a time before going to sleep.

Operation Goodwood

Thursday, 18 July. It was a clear grey dawn with no mist. I woke up about six and lay waiting for the day to start. Suddenly the silence was broken by the crash of a nearby medium battery, followed by a rising crescendo of guns, soon breaking into a roar all along the line. A minute or two later the heavy drone of bombers could be heard. And there they came, hundreds of them, sweeping in from the coast in an endless untidy stream, protected by a few Spitfires, flashing and wheeling like hawks high above them. Soon they were over their target, red sparks and white puffs of flak were going up all round them, and then one heard the muffled crumps of their bombs. The air boomed and the ground shook as these showered down, while a dense cloak of grey dust rose slowly over the battlefield. Soon nothing but a continuous roar could be heard. The game was on, the umpire had said 'Play'.

For a few minutes I lay and watched them going over, and then threw my blanket off and got up, encouraging my crew to make some break-fast and wash. I saw Hugo and the Sergeant-Major, all slightly staggered at the size of the bombardment. On and on came the bombers, Lancasters and Halifaxes, then one fell victim to the flak; with an orange flame and black smoke it fell like a stone to the ground.

Bill told me 'Cougar' had turned up during the night, so I walked back down the column to look for it. There were tanks, guns, carriers, half-tracks and other vehicles as far as the eye could see, hundreds of them, head to tail, rank upon rank, arrayed behind a small ridge. Beside each was a little petrol fire and around this a small group of men cooked or washed and shaved. I passed No. 3 Squadron and spoke to Henry Allsopp, commanding No.3, and Peter Hunt, and further on to John Sutton and Ian Jardine; all expressed incredulity at the bombers and guns. Bill, however, was not so sure; he made the wary observation to me that despite the bombardment enemy 88 m.m. flak did not seem to have quietened down that much. How right he proved.

After nearly an hour the heavy bombers stopped and Fortresses and 'mediums' flying in tight swarms took over, sprinkling fragmentary bombs on our centre line.

Later Comment

I am positive we had not time then to spare the enemy another thought. They would be blasted to pieces, that is all that mattered and our morale was much heartened by it. From a ringside seat, four or five miles away, we were witnessing the most concentrated destruction yet devised, perhaps unsurpassed until Hiroshima. Two thousand British and American aircraft, manned by many thousands of aircrew, delivered this fury, all in two hours. What the cauldron was like inside was not our concern. Of course it must work. Yet the enemy, in far inferior numbers and without air cover, survived, regained their poise and, equipped with a superior gun, offered the most stubborn resistance and struck back. Gone were any doubts, if they existed, about the stamp of foe we were against; surely 21st Panzer Division were among the most remarkable soldiers anywhere. The lessons were all too clear. To me the most fascinating account of the battle is told by German officers from this Division who fought us here. An article on 'Goodwood' in the Household Brigade Magazine long after includes their story of the battle to the Staff College. The receiving end of the bombardment makes terrifying reading. But, as this account makes clear, the Germans had warning of the British attack and organized their defence in great depth.

I found my lost tank 'Cougar' and Emmerson, who was eating break-fast, so told him to join me when he had had it. Brough had not yet appeared. I looked hopefully for him; however, Nigel had been back in a scout car for his own tank and had passed him three miles behind well and truly ditched, so I took it we should not see him for some time.

Breakfast of two sausages and tea, then we cleared up and got the tank ready. At a quarter to eight we broke wireless silence and 'netted' the sets. Whittle, my operator, had switched on and I could hear Oliver H. checking the battalion net. Then came the familiar whine of the starter-motor, one or two coughs, a bang, and a roar as Jepson warmed her up.

Around eight the 11th Armoured moved forward and the barrage slowed down. A couple of shells landed quite close, so we mounted our tanks ready to go. Soon after eight the battalion moved off in a long column line-ahead.

We crossed the Orne on a pontoon bridge called 'Pegasus' and made across country for our start line. Even on a large-scale map I found it hard to know exactly where we were then, but we just followed blindly. Through the wrecked gliders of the 6th Airborne Division where they had landed on D-day we moved up to the start line.

On the air the Commander told us that already the first villages, Demouville and Cuverville, had been cleared by the 11th. No.1

29

Squadron were leading, followed by Battalion H.Q., ourselves, and then No.3. When No. 1 reached the start line they said they were held up by the troops in front so we waited there.

Later Comment
Throughout the campaign, except when a Squadron was detached, each tank's wireless was tuned in on the 'battalion net', so every tank crew could listen to all that passed.

Then the shelling started. Our leading Troops and Battalion H.Q. were shelled quite hard and continuously while a few landed near us. Not really knowing the effect of H.E. on our tanks then, we sat tight, hoping nothing would hit us. It was there we had our first casualty. Our attached gunner Battery Commander of the Leicester Yeomanry, Peter Buxton, was called up on the air, but there was no answer. Oliver H., who, as Signals Officer, travelled as the Operator inside the Commanding Officer's tank, tried several times. Someone answered that he was knocked out followed by the call for '6', the doctor, which was countermanded with the word 'understood' from Oliver. So we knew he was killed. A few minutes later I passed him, caught by a shell while out of his tank. I was glad this did not upset me and I very soon got used to such. We had to steel ourselves to the many that would follow.

We eventually crossed the start line through our own minefield and, still line-ahead, moved south. To our left was a battalion of the 11th, the Fife and Forfar Yeomanry, in Shermans, firing at some houses. What at I do not know, but they were all milling around firing shots at a blazing farm, so I traversed my gun vaguely in its direction. We passed over a lot of slit-trenches and pits full of dead and 'bomb-happy' Germans offering no resistance, though I had a grenade ready in hand to chuck in if anyone was truculent.

The country was a flat open plain of corn land, bordered on the right by shattered and burning buildings with Caen and the Mondeville steel works in the distance. About a mile wide, the left flank of the plain was thickly wooded and slightly higher ground, good going all right, but the flanks suited our enemies well.

We passed Cuverville and Demouville on our right and crossed a railway line running east to west, having done about two miles advance, a single line from Troarn to Caen, by a small signal box. I felt uncomfortable crossing that line, as anything could fire straight down it from a long way off. However, all was well.

Then we stopped. The Grenadiers in front had been held up somewhere, no one knew quite what was happening. Later we discovered about eight of their tanks had fallen victim to 88 m.ms and other anti-tank guns, and Sir Arthur Grant, their No.2 Squadron Leader, had been killed. Our No.1 Squadron spread out in front and No.2 to the left flank. On our right was a blazing Sherman and a little further on some German Mark IVs, the most numerous and reliable of the enemy tanks. Oily black or white smoke poured out of the turrets and every joint in the armour. Panthers had been reported to our left and, as my troop happened to be on the extreme left, I turned them in that direction and kept a good look-out. Our tracks were nicely covered in the tall corn but we were a sitting target to any Panther in the woods. Vehicles of all kinds were crowding up behind, the 1st Motor Battalion Grenadiers, Harry Stanley's No.4 Company, in their halftracks, and some carriers of heavy machine gunners, the Northumberland Fusiliers. No.4 Company were attached to us to provide close infantry support, the practice during training and until the end of this battle. Mixed up too were a few odd tanks of the 2nd Recce, Welsh Guards. It was a lovely target and soon the shells and mortars started landing heavily with their tearing crumps.

No.1 Squadron came up with reports of three Panthers moving on the left. I scanned carefully with my binoculars but could see no movement in the trees about eight hundred yards away. Then Malcolm Lock reported a Panther opposite him and he got it with his Firefly, the 17-pounder Sherman. He did very well getting it, I heard afterwards, having stalked close; with one shot it 'brewed up' nicely.

Later Comment

According to the German Officers' account no Panthers were in this area at the time, but the survivors of a battalion of their even more respected big brothers, the massive Tigers and Royal Tigers, mounted with 88 m.m. guns, were playing hide and seek with us on the flank. This is interesting because I believe at the moment we thought there were numerous Panthers around. No less interesting is the remark that their tank gunsights had been thrown out of adjustment by the bombing, an unexpected dividend I am thankful to confirm from experience later that day.

31

It was a cloudless day and extremely hot, but there was a large amount of smoke and dust about, and in the tank everything was covered with a layer of grey dust. The noise of bursting shells and m.g. fire was continuous. Just then a shell hit a Grenadier halftrack near me, and I am afraid hurt several of them. A long grey line of prisoners with their hands up came sauntering past escorted by a couple of men. They looked a dejected crowd, very shaken by the bombing, some still wearing what Nigel aptly described as their evil-looking steel helmets.

By now the situation was far from clear. It was about 11 o'clock and it was obvious things were not going to plan in front. The Grenadiers appeared held up and all was confused, so, in order to get on, the Commander ordered us, No.2 Squadron, to move round the right flank and try to push on to our first objective, Cagny.

Nigel's and Val's troops led off cautiously to the right, while I was left behind for a bit to protect the left flank from these Panthers. One of Val's tanks put a burst of m.g. into a ditch and out got thirty Huns with white flags. A tank on my left was firing away madly at a ditch. What at I couldn't tell, but when I passed out came four more Huns which Emmerson took prisoner. All the time tanks and guns were firing, but as one could never tell what at, this made everything very confusing. In the distance a tank vehicle of some sort was moving across our front in the direction we were moving and there followed a long argument as to whom it belonged. No one could tell and we were ready to shoot when it turned and could be identified as ours, a Welsh Guards Cromwell. This is half the trouble, when there are so many vehicles, one never knows what to shoot at.

Later Comment.

From the German account it appears we were amongst the remnants of the battalion of 125 Panzer Grenadier Regiment at this moment, an infantry battalion 'utterly destroyed' by the bombing.

About this time the Commander was told to get a move on as the farm to which we were advancing so cautiously was where Brigade H.Q. already were, such is the confusion of war. Dermot, the Brigadier's protective Troop Leader, told me afterwards that all the big shots of brigade had been walking about, talking and giving orders next to the farm when he thought he saw something move in it. He put a shot or two into the buildings. A few minutes later over a hundred Germans came out and surrendered. If they had chosen to fight, brigade would have looked very silly. This farm, called Le Prieure, we shall come across again.

We passed Le Prieure to our left and went on towards Cagny. A number of burning Grenadier tanks were about; evidently they had run into some trouble from 88s or other anti-tank guns in the trees near the farm. One of these could be seen abandoned in the corner. The Shermans were crackling like burning timber as their small-arms ammunition went off. One, a flail tank, a Sherman with a mine-sweeping arrangement on the front, had the sinister round hole of an 88 shot through its side that had lifted the turret half off.

Val and Nigel were leading. I was on the right flank now, and David left. We pushed on south through the wide cornfields towards the railway. It was not known whether Cagny was in ours or enemy hands, or where anybody else was, but the squadron came round the corner of a small wood and there we saw a sight that rather shook us all.

Eight hundred yards to our front was the railway on a steep embankment, almost a tank obstacle. This side of it and to our left front was the remains of Cagny lying beside a wood; it appeared empty with a few burning tanks. But beyond the railway the horizon was covered with burning Shermans. I could count nearly twenty, a whole squadron, burning in one field alone. More were hidden behind the black smoke of others brewing up, while yet others were still being hit and bursting into flames. Someone reported an 88, but, though I had a good look at the enemy slope, I saw nothing that stirred and the only objects to be seen were the regular heaps of drying hay in some fields. A number of men were crawling towards us through the corn, or the large open patches where it had been blown flat by the bombs, some German, some English, who had escaped from their burning machines, some of them wounded.

A few Germans were walking openly, coming in to surrender and we waved them to the rear. Beyond was gently rising ground, evidently housing a barrier of 88 m.m. anti-tank guns. The railway was the end of the bomb line, so the 88s were unmolested. Someone had run into the hell of a packet.

The Commander decided then "we must not add to this disaster" so must move under cover of the railway embankment round Cagny ready

33

to push on to Vimont, our main objective. The Grens were engaged north of Cagny, it appeared, with some Panthers, so we were to move south of it through a bottleneck between a wood and the railway. Nigel led through, followed by the remainder of the squadron and me, who remained in the bottleneck to cover them. It was a horrid place, a battered little railway station with a signal box and level crossing on my right and a wood surrounded by a stone wall on my left. I was being continually sniped at, since one always had to have one's head out of the top, from a building on my right, I think. The tiny village of Le Poirier lay just over the line.

Further up the line, where Nigel was, something was going on. A Panther had put its nose round the corner of a wood and shot at Nigel's and the Sergeant Major's tanks. I think it was firing down the railway, anyhow a few minutes later there was a bang on the top of my turret or somewhere as something hit my tank. 'Driver Reverse', a heave and a jerk as we jumped back for cover as the dust set up inside settled. I quickly reversed away as I could see nothing and put down some smoke. Typically, it failed to go off. Luckily, the tank appeared undamaged and reversed back to the wall round the wood. Caulfield's tank 'Caribou' did the same. I remember asking Jepson, my driver, whether anything had come through, but he said it was all right in front. Here something knocked the bin off the back of my tank containing all our blankets and greatcoats, so Liddle and I jumped out and heaved it on. Even so it fell off again later and we lost the lot including the crews' best 'Paris' battle-dresses. It comforted me somewhat, while I was up against the railway, when another troop of tanks crossed it behind me and bravely went round to my right flank. However, they soon came back over the level crossing. Ian told me afterwards that this was his troop, he had no idea what was over the railway but was very glad when ordered back. If he had known, he said, he would never have dared to go over.

Meanwhile Nigel's tank had been hit by an 88 m.m., H.E. luckily,* which only knocked out his driver. The co-driver managed to lean over and reverse away. Nigel had a shot at the Panther but missed as it went into some trees. The Sergeant-Major had been hit a glancing blow too, but got away with a groove in the armour, that he proudly displayed to everyone afterwards. Something firing at us from the other side of the railway had been spotted by Emmerson. I believe the trouble was coming from a partially hidden Château I could see in the trees. For a

34

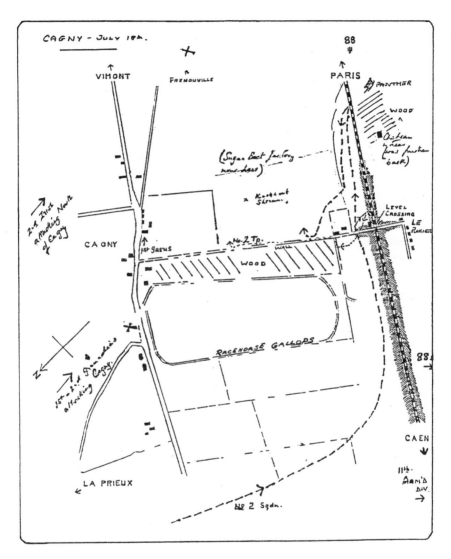

July 18th. Cagny ". . . full of craters from bombs of a large size . . . one had to twist and turn to avoid falling into one". The wood with the wall surrounding is prominent. Over 600 tons had been dropped on this village in the morning, but the inhabitants had all been removed by the Germans a few days before. The map shows the route No 2 Squadron took between the railway and the wood, which was surrounded by a stone wall.

few minutes all was chaotic until Bill eventually ordered us all back to the wall round the wood between the railway and the village of Cagny.

It was extremely difficult to move there as the whole place was full of craters from bombs of a large size. Everywhere one went one had to twist and turn to avoid falling into one, but we eventually sorted ourselves out with our backs along the wall. A horrid place as we had no cover at all, but it was no good going on as we should run into quite a lot of 88s and have a similar fate to those south of the railway.

It was getting on for seven o'clock in the evening now and brigade was agitating for us to push on. The Commander rang up Bill and asked him if he could, but he answered rightly that if we did we would only run into disaster. This was confirmed a few minutes later when one of our planes flew over the Germans and a volley of 88 m.m. flak went up at it quite close showing there was plenty of 'stuff' there. We learned after that the Irish were having a stiff battle trying to advance round the north of Cagny, but the Germans were now dug in in strength, and without the infantry to deal with the anti-tank guns in the woods, progress bought serious trouble. So we had to sit and wait in this horrid place to hold Cagny until dark when the infantry would take over from us. Up till now I had not felt frightened, but sitting on that wall for four hours was a very disagreeable experience and I longed for darkness to come.

The whole Squadron was spread out along the wall, my troop on the left nearest the village, a shocking position but there was none better. Harry Stanley's infantry were mopping up the village. Sniped at continuously, we replied with ineffective bursts of m.g., as we could not tell where the shots came from. We did not sit still but managed to move about a few yards from time to time between the bomb craters. I found cover at one stage half in a crater behind some bits of a wrecked Lancaster. In the middle of the space before us lay one lonely smouldering Sherman.

Soon the enemy got our range and we were mortared and shelled heavily and continuously. They landed all around us, mixed with many airbursts. No damage was done but they were very noisy and

---

* The enemy tanks had quite possibly run out of armour-piercing shot here for these were high explosive shells that did not penetrate the armour.

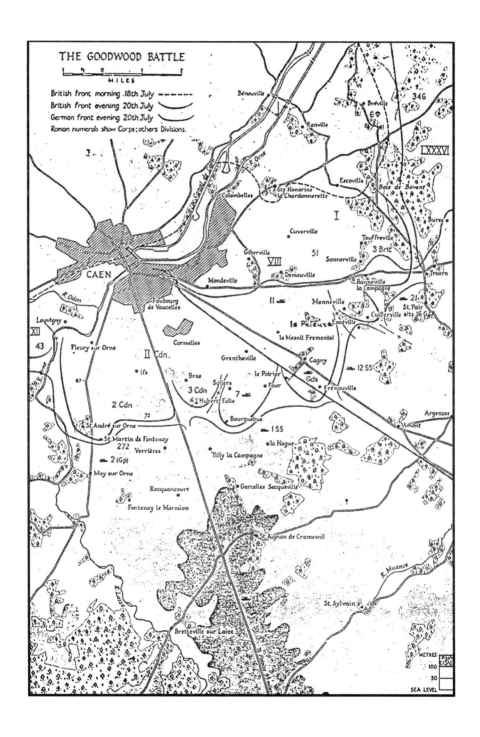

THE GOODWOOD BATTLE

MILES

British front morning 18th July ———————
British front evening 20th July ‿‿‿
German front evening 20th July ‿
Roman numerals show Corps; others Divisions.

Bénouville
Bréville
Ranville
346
6
LXXXVI
Escoville
Bois de Bavent
Côte Honorine
Colombelles
la Chardonnerette
Bures
I
Cuverville
Touffreville
3 Brit
Giberville
51
Sannerville
VIII
CAEN
Mondeville
Démouville
Troarn
Bannerville
la Campagne
Faubourg
de Vaucelles
11
Manneville
21
St. Pair
Cuillerville elts 16 G
le Prieure
emieville
R. Odon
le Mesnil Frementel
Louvigny
XII
Cormelles
Cagny
43
Fleury sur Orne
Grentheville
12 SS
II Cdn.
le Poirier
Gds
Frénouville
Bras
Ifs
Soliers
7
Four
Argences
3 Cdn
Hubert Folie
Vimont
2 Cdn
87
Bourguebus
St. André sur Orne
1 SS
72
St. Martin de Fontenay
la Hogue
272
Verrières
Tilly la Campagne
2 (Gp)
May sur Orne
Garcelles Secqueville
Rocquancourt
Fontenay le Marmion
St. Aignan de Cramesnil
R. Muance
1 SS
St. Sylvain
Bretteville sur Laize

METRES
100
50
SEA LEVEL

discouraging. Every now and then the horrible roar like a tube train of the nebelwerfer six-barrel rockets came over and stonked us. Six hundred yards to our front was a thick hedge running across and beyond in the distance was the village of Frénouville with its church tower a target for our guns. It could well have been the enemy O.P. It was noticed that every time one of our spotting planes, an Austercraft, flew over we were shelled. Later it was discovered that this was a captured British one used by the Hun O.P. We heard that all our own were ordered to the ground, and sure enough over it came, only this time every gun let off and it was soon shot down.

In my tank we were bored, tired and really fed up on that wall. As we had had nothing else to eat, we ate chocolate hard and drank water. But worse was to come. Two planes came low over us and I realized they were Huns just as one was in front of me. I saw him release a bomb which came spinning down towards my tank and Cougar. I took cover on the floor of my tank and hoped for the best. It landed at the back, but bounced away harmlessly and was crashing through the wood as I looked out of the top again, a U.x.b!

Then what we feared most of all occurred. We were being steadily mortared and bombed when I heard that sickening whizz and crack of an A.P. shot and saw a neat round hole appear in the wall behind. A beastly Panther or something was shooting at me but I could not see where from. It fired several shots at Cougar and me. Why none of us brewed up, I don't know, but they missed and after a while the Panther went away. It was easy for him to waddle up in the wood or hedges opposite, unseen, and pot us.

During the evening, Johnnie Gull, our splendidly enthusiastic Technical Adjutant, had been trying to bring up the three Armoured Recovery Vehicles with the Squadrons' fitters to Battalion H.Q. Unable to find them, he drove into an orchard where there were three Panthers already sitting. After a short and one-sided skirmish the battalion had lost one of its three A.R.V.s, that of No.2 Squadron. Of the fate of the crew nothing was heard. Johnnie himself rapidly curtailed his unfortunate excursion and escaped with the other two A.R.V.s with only a shot through the watercan at the back of his scout car to show for it. We heard some of the confusion going on over the air over a description by the Commander of our position as being near a 'roundel', an unfamiliar sign on the French maps.

38

Later Comment.

For more than twenty years I never really knew what happened to any of our squadron's crew until I chanced to meet Briscoe, the Driver of the A.R.V. at a memorial parade in Wellington Barracks. He told me how he was taken prisoner and sent to Germany. The actual armoured scout car that Captain Johnny Gull was in is to be seen today in the Tank Museum at Bovington in Dorset.

I was relieved when about eleven o'clock the infantry appeared. Small lines of men crawled out and dug in to the front of us, and we started to pull out. It was the 5th Coldstream.

They would have a noisy and uncomfortable night, having followed up behind in their T.C.Ls, and that could have been no fun. Owing to the bottleneck at the start the infantry brigade were not used in the attack.

We were given a parting stonk of shells as we picked our way back between the craters. Two of No.3 Squadron's tanks had already to be abandoned at the bottom of bomb craters. We formed into a long line and were led off back to laager for the night. On the way Sergeant White's tank from Nigel's troop stopped and would not restart, so I offered him a tow. While we were shackling on our tow rope a Hun plane was machine-gunning something quite close with a spectacular display of tracer.

It was now pitch dark, we were left behind and we spent an anxious half-hour looking for the rest, during it I cursed Sergeant White several times to myself. I ran into a scout car with Tony Jones, a sapper friend with the division, an old friend who was in the same squad with me in the Royal Engineers, when we first joined at Newark. Surprisingly he was attached to the battalion and was able to tell me it was quite close. So I walked about and at last found them next to a stinking burnt-out Sherman. After considerable 'chos' we got into a laager position, drawn up in two lines, just east of La Prieure and about a mile back from Cagny. There we filled up with petrol after a search for the truck. I posted sentries and immediately lay down with the crew under my tank in the corn. It was nearly one a.m. and reveille was at four to break laager. After sixteen hours in a tank I was pleased to get out and soon went to sleep. A long and unsatisfactory day, we had done all we had been asked to do, but of course were still a long way from our objective.

Before I leave the first day of the Caen battle, I must say briefly what happened in the 'big' picture. It was heralded by all the press as the great breakthrough towards Paris and other such nonsense. This was more than premature. Some seven thousand tons of bombs were dropped at the beginning, and the 11th Armoured Division pushed on quickly to the end of the bombed area, or 'bomb-line'. There they met the 88 m.m. anti-tank guns and, being told they must push on at all cost, they lost one hundred and four tanks, about sixty per cent. Ourselves did the same, but not being told to push on, lost perhaps another thirty altogether. We could only have destroyed twenty German tanks, if that; the division got about five. The 7th Armoured Division were never able to pass through the leading divisions. Vimont, our objective, was not taken for another six weeks.

So this was not a real success, and by no means a breakthrough. It lost us a lot of confidence in our Shermans. We knew that their armour could stop nothing serious and their guns, except for the 17-pounder, could not knock out enemy armour. This attack, though no losses were mentioned, caused a good deal of criticism in the papers and even amongst ourselves about the command. Armour without infantry may be all very well in the desert, but it was not the drill for Normandy.

Wednesday, 19 July. A short and noisy night. During it one stonk of nebelwerfer landed amongst us. I was anxious that night, only lying under my tank there was not much protection. Not above two hours' sleep. Around five we were woken by the guard to move our tanks out of close laager into a defensive position. We moved out to a very nasty place on the forward slope, overlooked by the enemy, a few hundred yards from where we slept. However, nothing happened, and when it got light we cooked some breakfast, the inevitable 'swanks' and tea.

We were reserve battalion during the day, so hoped for a reasonably quiet time, but after yesterday's disaster to 11th Armoured nobody was inclined to push on to our original objectives, and court another armoured débâcle. Shelled intermittently, we lost a few men wounded in Battalion H.Q., including No. 3 Squadron's Sergeant-Major. We passed the morning in the same place until we had an order to move to a defensive position as enemy tanks were reported behind. We moved only to be told to come back again. Yet a second time we moved back to this position, followed immediately by being sent to the north of Cagny behind the 2nd Irish Guards in case of a counter-attack. I met Nigel on the way; he merely repeated the rhyme about the young lady of Spain who it was 'changed not once but again, and again and again, and . . .'. When belting along between these positions, I suddenly saw an aeroplane engine lying hidden in the corn in front. Had we hit it we would have overturned at that speed. I shouted "Right" at Jepson, who swerved just in time and ran into the next tank on my right. It was Bill's. Luckily we only hit a glancing blow and did no damage. He swore voluminously at me above the roar of battle. I heard something about two horses colliding out hunting.

A shocking position. We ended up on a forward slope in view of the enemy, as usual. Suddenly an M.10 tank in front of us was shot by a Panther and it brewed up at once in a cloud of smoke. I saw some of its crew running away in the corn so I hope they all got out. It was disheartening to see these tanks burn up so quickly. The Germans called our Shermans 'Tommy Cookers', a fitting name. The generals and senior officers were angry if one called them this, and we were not meant to know what the Germans thought of Shermans. They were definitely no good for the job of attacking tanks. We needed a heavily armoured tank with a big gun like the German Tiger to do any good.

The rest of the day we spent sitting uncomfortably on the slope inside the tanks. Shelled all day, we could not get out. I managed to get hold of the bulldozing tank to dig in my 17-pounder, or 'Charlie' tank, 'Cougar', in a good dug-in position. Orders had come to the leading troops following this brew-up in front of us to protect our main weapons, but it was an unsatisfactory and difficult job to push up a mound of earth on a receding slope and I am not surprised it was never suggested we did it again.

No. 1 Squadron tried to advance a little in a wood on the left. To our right there was a large amount of stonking and smoke as our infantry went forward to capture Frénouville. From time to time the 'moaning minnies' or nebelwerfer rockets shrieked into the air. An abandoned battery of the six-barrelled launchers for these horrors lay beside my troop's position here and I had a good look. Still loaded, their shells were an alarming 5-inch calibre at least.

It could be called a fairly typical day in the line. We were fast beginning to learn how to live under these conditions of shelling. With headphones on and the wireless crackling all the time, we talked little. I shaved precariously on the floor of the turret and Liddle cooked, or rather 'did' a meal, in the front seat. We felt unsafe all day and were glad to move back in the evening.

I learnt how dangerous small mistakes in war can become. This evening I had a short but unpleasant experience. We moved back to the spot where we spent last night, but David's and mine were sent forward as protective troops well in front of the battalion. David was on watch first. Nothing much happened, so I left one man on sentry on the tank and the rest got out to cook, while I sat on the floor of the turret and tried to read.

We were sent to a forward slope overlooked by the enemy, I thought. After a time I had an uncomfortable feeling. The Boche could easily waddle up an 88 m.m. and pot us. I walked back and told Bill, but he assured me all the Grenadiers were in front of me and I was not overlooked. He came up to have a look as I was far from reassured. The open ground, more or less level for about a mile to the railway embankment, rose up gently beyond to some wooded country held by the enemy around Borguébus.

Bill climbed on my tank with his telescope. Just then there was a loud bang. I thought at first we had been hit, but then realized Corporal Arnold, my gunner, had pressed the firing pedal and let the '75' off. Dreadfully easy to do, when all guns had to stay loaded in the line, but it had an after-effect.

While we were still looking through our glasses about thirty planes appeared flying low and quite slowly across our front. They seemed a bit odd for a moment until I saw the black crosses. Bill jumped down under my tank and lay flat, and I jumped on to the 'point 5' A.A. gun. One plane was a lovely shot but the something gun would not fire. It had become clogged by the dust. I made frantic efforts to get it going to no effect apart from single shots, and gave it up. I saw the planes circle round and come towards me. All was well. They were halfhearted when the flak of the other tanks went up, and did no damage. As the planes flew away I did another stupid thing.

Bill was walking back to Squadron H.Q. after assuring me my position was O.K. I stood on the turret of my tank and tried to wrestle with the A.A. gun; I was facing the wrong way too. Suddenly I heard the sickening whizz and saw the tracer of an A.P. shot bounding away

42

behind me. It must have passed close, luckily too high. It went near Bill and I heard him shouting at me to come back.

Later Comment

An alert enemy had probably spotted the flash of our 75 m.m. a few minutes earlier.

It took seemingly years disentangling myself and getting Jepson into reverse. Shots were whizzing over. An armour-piercing shot goes so fast I saw it bouncing half a mile behind just as I heard the whizz. A Sherman can only reverse very slowly and now it seemed like a snail.

Whittle, my operator, caught the enemy gun-flash through his periscope two thousand yards away. He tried to put us on to it, but it was too vague. The 'overs' were bouncing in Battalion H.Q., so frantic calls for smoke were sent out by them which amused me. Luckily I wasn't hit, so put out smoke, a good screen fortunately (to the consternation of the Grenadiers ahead) and withdrew behind a small ridge.

In the middle of the firing an extraordinary thing happened as a Guardsman, on foot, completely oblivious of the battle and missiles, threw some earth at me in my tank to attract my attention, and said, "Will you take the squadron mail sir and the bread ration?" I almost burst out laughing. Rather shaken, I was handed a welcome letter from my brother George, serving with 2nd Coldstream in Italy. He thought the war would end by October. It cheered me up a lot.

Ian Jardine got a Panther today. He was sent to lie in wait for it at dawn, a lucky chance.

We dug in under our tanks and spent a noisy but not too bad a night. Anyhow I was too tired to worry. I took my turn on guard, slept well and remembered nothing.

Thursday, 20 July. Quite quiet. By now it was obvious that the much vaunted breakthrough had completely fizzled out. We spent the day in the same place sitting in our tanks. I dug a slit trench outside mine and sat there reading, amongst other things, Hugo's *Tatlers*. My crew were dubious about my digging, until we had a heavy 'plastering' at one moment. In the afternoon the rain started. It poured and poured, and soon there was a quagmire. We moved back to where we spent the night and I put my tank over the same, now waterlogged, trench.

I soon went to sleep only to be woken by a great tragedy. About 1.30

43

I was woken by Nigel who told me simply that David had been shot. I did not quite take it in properly and asked him if he was bad. Nigel replied, "Yes, I'm afraid so". I then realized he was dead, but it did not come at all as a shock yet. It was too sudden to comprehend. I got up quickly and found Nigel who showed me what had happened. At first I was more concerned whether the Germans were still about until Nigel told me that David was shot by a sentry of Nigel's tank. I remembered then I had heard two shots in my sleep. Nigel had done well and was brave and calm about it. He had had a very unpleasant few minutes as David did not die at once. He was lying out in the open, so we carried him back close to the line of tanks. He and I then woke up Bill and told him; he was very calm and sorry. I sent Nigel back to bed and remained myself on guard for the next hour. It was then I began to understand and feel. I thought of my brother Evelyn in 1940. How frightened I felt standing near David's body in the rain seeing the telltale blanket lying over him. He was a great friend, and I had known him since I first went to Eton.

It was the most dreadful hour I had experienced. Total darkness and incessant rain added their dismal worst, with sporadic firing going on all round. David had been coming across the open ground in the laager between the lines of tanks to wake me for my turn on guard. The sentry fired two shots with his pistol. When the hour was up I was greatly relieved and woke Val, the next officer on sentry. He was taken aback. I went to bed and thank goodness was too tired to think any more.

Friday, 21 July. It continued to pour with rain. The papers gave the rain as the excuse for holding up the so-called breakthrough, but this was rubbish; it had been stopped two days before. The place had turned into a swamp nearly, a tank leaked like a sieve, and we were all soaking. We rigged up sheets, buckets and mugs to no avail. It was a most depressing day. David was buried in the morning, but I did not attend. It was at Battalion H.Q. and we had had to move out at daybreak to take up a defensive position. I did not really want to, and seeing it going on in the distance made us upset. I felt better as the day wore on and, though we were shelled a bit, I went and talked to Nigel and we managed to laugh over something which was a tremendous relief.

During the afternoon we were ordered to move out of the Caen plain to the suburbs of the town for a few days' rest and regrouping. With difficulty the squadron started to pull out, for the rain had found its

44

way into several engines and some were disinclined to work.

I was very pleased to leave that horrible plain. Bleak, grim, dreary, soaking with no cover, like all battlefields, it was a horrible place to those who fought there. The attack had succeeded in bringing the enemy armour over to the eastern flank and had contained the enemy's main forces, so, as it turned out, it wasn't wasted. Now we would have to keep them here by displaying ourselves as far as possible in range of the enemy, we were yet to discover.

We went into a field at Faubourg de Vaucelles, the S.E. suburb of Caen. When we arrived it was still mined and a fifteen-hundredweight truck blew up on one just in front of us. It caused a complete wreck of the truck and it surprised me how much damage. The whole of the back was smashed and the people in the back were badly hurt, one lost a leg. It sickened me, but luckily an ambulance column was passing at the time, so saved their lives.

We dug in deep, the rain stopped and all felt much happier. Ian came round to say how sorry he was about David. He told me then about his Panther which had pleased him a lot.

The rum ration was issued that evening and we had a good meal. Then Val and I attacked a bottle of whisky. It did us a lot of good and we cheered up. I had a really good sleep, the first for several nights. Thank God the battle of Caen was over.

Saturday, 22 July. We remained in the field, tidied up and maintained the tanks. Brough returned to me with his tank after being in the Forward Delivery Squadron. A party of men went and 'looted' some German equipment in nearby fields. Headed by that notorious Squadron wag Guardsman Looker, they had rounded up and captured for the pot all sorts of stray ducks and tame rabbits that were wandering about the deserted rubble and battered allotments of this city suburb, the only sign of life in all that tragic devastation.

We moved that evening a mile further back to Giberville.

Giberville

Sunday, 23rd July. We spent almost ten days in this desolated spot. It is not a place I like to remember. In a dingy and scraggly cornfield we were drawn up in squadron lines. One side was the sordid remains of a bombed and deserted village, on the other ran a high railway embankment broached by craters with tangled rails sprawling over it. Just below the field was a ruined church and graveyard. The contents of the houses and the graveyard, furniture and refuse were spewed around indescribably and overall hung the smell one would expect. The only outlook was the awful remains of a factory a mile away, the Mondeville steel works, which formed a fitting background to this gloomy scene. I never saw the sun shine there once, I don't think. We lived dug-in under our tanks as there was intermittent and stray shelling. Under these conditions people at home might assume one would have constantly to watch the morale of one's men. Yet such was the stolid character of the Guardsmen that we had no qualms on that score. Their high morale and humour could be taken as read. Indeed, to anyone outside it might have appeared that war to Guards Armoured was one huge joke.

The Officers' Mess truck arrived up, so we began to settle down for a few days in reasonable comfort. In the morning there was a church service and the rest of the day was spent in cleaning up. Some English papers arrived and we had a good dinner provided by Hanson and Kershaw, our two faithful retainers. We had the sad business too of dividing up and packing David's kit. Ian lent me *Alice in Wonderland* to read with great pleasure; books like this were a help. We passed the evening periodically diving under a tank or into a trench whenever we heard the telltale whistle and 'boomph' of a distant gun. A sharp, noisy, air raid during the night but no damage was done in the battalion. 'A' Echelon had not been so lucky. On the first night of the attack they had been accurately bombed, causing several casualties and trucks damaged. All were shaken badly.

Monday, 24 July. Our stay was to be cut short. We had orders to support the Canadians in another attack south of Caen the next day. We studied maps and photographs and prepared for the attack. It was to be a searchlight attack by night at first and we followed next day. All were rather depressed about this and we knew the opposition was heavy there and the same exactly would happen as last week. In the afternoon I took the squadron into Caen to have 'mobile' baths but these were mortared just before we arrived. The place was chaotic with several casualties. An extraordinary sight seeing a crowd of men with nothing on taking cover in all directions. The 2nd Grenadiers lost an officer and a few others, I'm afraid. Quite possibly a fifth columnist gave the

46

position away to the Germans somehow, since it happened again when the baths were full. Nigel was with me. He bravely had a bath but I had to take our men back before it occurred again.

All day medium and field artillery round us had been getting ready for the attack. A battery of 5.5 inch guns in the next field went off from time to time with a deafening crash. Once we were surprised by a peculiar wet whoof from one of these guns. Before any of us had time to look up, there came an instantaneous roar, "put the bloody shell in next time", from the Battery Sergeant-Major across the field, and a roar of laughter from us. The Canadian infantry would do a moonlight, or rather a searchlight, attack to broach the so-called line south of Caen. When they had taken their objective we were to push through and take the high ground beyond, to complete what we had not done before in the previous battle. Opposition was expected to be heavy, and it was.

No sleep; the guns 'belted' away all night for the preliminary, and now customary, Normandy heavy barrage. The 5.5s made an awful row, added to innumerable 25-pounders. A small air attack too, no damage but every vehicle fired some automatic weapon into the air which did little good and caused a lot of noise, that's all.

The Canadian attack went in that night and they took their first objectives, but with very heavy casualties. Waited all morning to move forward, but no order came through, until, about midday, it was re-alized our attack was off. The Canadians, as foreseen, had struck very heavy opposition: dug-in Tigers, as well as a minefield. They had lost a lot and been driven back, or in kinder language, withdrawn to almost where they started from.

We were all relieved when that attack was called off; it certainly wasn't 'on'. It was a job for a Churchill tank, though even these had not really enough armour or a big enough gun. Every man knew now to go into an attack like this with a Sherman needed a great deal of cool courage. Unless one spotted the enemy first, a difficult thing when advancing, one stood little chance. An 88 m.m. in a Tiger or a Panther's 75 could go straight through us at 3,000 yards, but the Sherman's 75 could not penetrate either except at close range. The 17 pounder was our trump card, but we did not have enough of them and then they were not much good if shot at first. If we had had a really big 'infantry' tank, like the Panther with more armour on its sides and as fast as a Sherman, I am

47

sure we should have defeated the Germans in Normandy at much less cost and in much shorter time.

The higher command seemed to be relying entirely on numbers and they came in for a great deal of criticism from all ranks lower down. The names of Montgomery and our army commander, Dempsey, stood low then. Unfairly, as responsibility for the weapons we fought with was not theirs. The Prime Minister in the House of Commons said that our tanks were more than satisfactory and in every way superior to the Germans. To the men who had to fight the tanks this made them wild and lost a lot of confidence. As we saw it then we knew these tanks were inferior to the enemy and an easy prey in a role in which the enemy had the advantage of lying up and surprising us. We knew that inside them were the best trained and probably the best selection of men in the world. But what we did not know was that these and subsequent apparently fruitless attacks won the war in Normandy. We were wearing down the flower of Von Kluge's 7th army.

During these few days an event occurred in Germany that raised our morale a great deal, though it did not come to anything. It was the German generals' attempt to kill Hitler. We knew nothing of course of the terrible retribution and bloodbath that Hitler's anger was to perpetrate.

So we settled down again in the field, the trucks and officers' mess arrived and we tried to get as comfortable as possible. Shelled every day sporadically by a single enemy gun we thought was an 88 m.m. from a Tiger that waddled up. We knew it as the fast bowler of Giberville, the shells were very high speed. Every time we heard the 'boomph' of the gun we dived underground; one shell landed within five yards of me but I was lucky, and no harm done. The battalion and the 'Micks' (the Irish Guards) had a few casualties from them, a number did not explode. The only other enemy action was the bombing every night. A few enemy planes came in low and generally managed to hit something. One night a Grenadier tank and two of their ammo trucks made a great blaze. It made the nights noisy while the 5.5s periodically let off with their deafening crash without any warning.

When the weather permitted the Typhoons or 'Tiffies' came over and shot up enemy tanks. They are the most encouraging sight and must be one of the most successful weapons of the war. Later on they proved more than their worth. We watched them dive literally through a cloud

48

of flak to release their rockets which shoot down leaving a trail of smoke, followed by a loud thud. They could deal with any Tiger or Panther and blew them to pieces.

On the 26th I lost my Driver, Guardsman R. Jepson, who broke his arm when the engine door fell. I was very sorry to lose him as he had driven me for two years; a nice man from near Sheffield, as well as a first class driver. He would anticipate my orders and knew exactly what I wanted, ideal for a tank driver achieved by working together for so long. I was fortunate too in his replacement, Guardsman Berry, another experienced driver, dark haired and smiling.

Ian and Nigel had dug themselves a nice deep dug-out so I spent a lot of time there being entertained by them. We sped the days quicker reading, talking and laughing. Dermot walked over from brigade one afternoon and we discussed the yacht we were designing or had tried to design back at Helmsley. The officers' mess was in action but shells always seemed to land near it. With shouts of derision from Bill and Hugo, I set to and dug a slit trench there eventually. They were the first to use it when the next stonk came over. The place was alive with escaped rabbits that helped out the larder. No 3 Squadron kept one as a pet and still have it, I think, called 'Gibers'.

Saturday, 29 July. We all went for a route march by troops this morning. This was the order and of course caused the regulation grumbling. I went for a short one round the ruins of the Faubourg, a gloomy walk but nowhere else to go. Met Ian coming the other way round, rather angry as all his squadron had been made to wear 'tin hats', while we had not. In the bigger picture, the Americans had been attacking down the west of the Cherbourg peninsula and were making great progress. They had reached Coutances and were making for Avranches, the key to the peninsula and to Brittany. It looked as if it was going to be a big breakthrough. This was only possible because nearly all the enemy Panzer divisions, especially the S.S., had been drawn over to the Caen sector by us and the Canadians. The Canadians were still prodding in the east so as to keep the Germans tied down.

Today the American attack appeared to be a great success and the plans were changed in order to exploit it.

We, in fact all 8th Corps, were to move quickly over to the west next to the Americans in the Caumont area to try and protect their left flank and break through ourselves if possible. This news pleased us a lot, as

49

it sounded like a better party than the last one and we thought we would get away from some of the S.S. Panzers for a while. 11th Armoured Division had already moved over there today ready to attack south from Caumont tomorrow. Caumont incidentally was captured on D plus seven and had been held ever since. So we prepared to move this afternoon.

Maps were now a problem. We had sent back to 'B' Echelon all our maps of the American sector and No. 1 Squadron had even burnt theirs. It never pays to be certain of anything in war. I went back to 'B' Echelon in the scout car to get Bill's maps of the area, the first time for a fortnight nearly I had left that gloomy Caen area, and it was very pleasant to find oneself in the undulating clean countryside N.W. of Caen where 'B' Echelon was harboured.

I saw Oliver Heywood there, come to do the same thing and taken the opportunity to have a peaceful afternoon's sleep in the sun.

Orders were given out and we prepared to move this evening, but it was changed and we left early next day.

Sunday, 30 July. Leaving Giberville was like leaving the valley of gloom. We passed out of Giberville through the rubble that was Caen. Much of Caen was flat literally, the worst I had seen or have seen since. "There was not *one* stone standing on another," as George Dawnay remarked; far worse than any town in England, the only thing that wasn't hit was the Cathedral.

We left Caen, passed the aerodrome at Carpiquet out into the rolling cornfields towards Bayeux. The sun was shining and I felt happier than I had done for weeks. At lunchtime we ended up in the field near Bayeux we had been in for a fortnight before the battle of Caen. It had not changed a bit; the covey of partridges were there grown larger. I hoped we might come back again on September 1st. We put our tanks in the same places and Bill put his chair under the apple tree as before. Bill's tubular steel chair from our billet in Brighton was a squadron feature, strapped on the back of his tank, he was easy to see in battle.

This was the start of our next campaign and fittingly it began in the same field at Bayeux as the last. It was a more successful one, but many of us were not to see the end of it.

Sunday, so we had a church service in the evening, in the corner we had it in before Caen. Since then a great deal seemed to have happened.

That evening we moved out of the field and had a night drive to the

50

south-west of Bayeux. A tedious and dusty drive, but as we were possibly going into battle next day I thought it best to rest, so travelled and slept closed down in the co-driver's seat. We spent the remainder of the night in a field just north of Balleroy called Le Tronquay, a comfortable and quiet night, the best for weeks.

The Bocage

Monday, 31 July. Spent the day maintaining and lying in the sun at Tronquay in a nice clean field surrounded by thick woods, I wrote a long letter home in the afternoon. The attack south of Caumont had started, with the 11th Armoured, the 15th Scottish Division, and the independent 6th Guards Tank Brigade in action for the first time, and was going well. The Americans had pushed further south. We were to move south to Caumont that night ready for the division to attack with the 11th Armoured Div.

We moved to a farm just north of Caumont, arrived just before dark after a dusty drive down a cross-country track. Passed through Balleroy which has a beautiful Château. It was a most memorable sight as the column drove slowly down the long broad avenue of the village street towards this focal point in the red evening's sunlight. Slept in an orchard where the squadron harboured near the village of Cormolain.

A mass of stuff was pouring south, the whole of 8 Corps was rushing after the 11th Armoured who were doing very well.

Tuesday, 1 August. I woke up remembering it was the first of August, rather wondering whether I should see the month out. It was a misty morning, and a damp one, as we had not put the bivouac up that night. We moved out of harbour early and passed south through Caumont, a badly damaged little town on top of a hill and not very attractive. On the way I saw David Rasch, a Grenadier, standing at a crossroads directing traffic as he is in the Provost Company. The Corps Commander Dick O'Connor passed us on his way up looking tired but pleased, and was acknowledging everyone's salute with a friendly wave. We made slow progress down the only road to the south and ended up in a cornfield just south of Caumont and a village called Sept Vents. There we stayed the whole day while news of the situation grew more and more exciting.

In the west the Americans had now definitely broken through at

Avranches and were speeding on into Brittany. The sands of time for the 7th Army were now undoubtedly running out. Further east the American Corps, on our right, were pushing south parallel to us. The 11th Armoured had pushed on ten miles to Beny-Bocage and the 'Galloping Grocers', 2nd Household Cavalry Regiment, in their armoured cars had patrols in Vire, ten miles further south again. It was now a breakthrough centred on one narrow road down which vehicles were flooding the whole day. The 6th Guards Tank Brigade had attacked a heavily wooded area (the Bois du Homme) on the east of the gap and had done well, though they had lost a few tanks.

Later Comment

At our level we only had the sketchiest outline of the confusing battle that had already begun. We knew nothing of a stroke of luck on our right flank that 11th Armoured Division had been quick to exploit. A troop of Household Cavalry armoured cars had pushed along a path through the Forêt L'Eveque during the early morning of 31 July. They found to their surprise the Germans had left a bridge undefended across the River Souleuvre that led to the village of Le Beny Bocage. Tanks from 2nd Northants Yeomanry were sent immediately to secure this bridge and a few hours later the 23rd Hussars carrying the infantry of the 3rd Monmouths were attacking Beny Bocage. From there on 1st August the 11th Armoured had gone on to threaten the other important bridge at Cathéolles from behind and capture the steeply wooded high ground above the valley of the Souleuvre. This was on the Centreline of the Guards Armoured Division and was a bridge which carried the main road from Caen to Vire. Before daylight next morning the 3rd Irish Guards infantry had walked down the hill from Le Tourneur and found this bridge at Cathéolles intact and undefended.

The story of 11th Armoured's coup, that caught the Germans on the hop, and may have changed the course of the battle, is well told in *The Charge of the Bull* by a Frenchman, Jean Brissot, who was living nearby in the Bocage under the Occupation. A full account of the 11th Armoured's part in Operation 'Bluecoat' based on Official War Diaries is given by Major J. J. How, M.C., in *Normandy, the British Breakout*, 1980.

The battalion itself was attached to the 32nd Guards Brigade and Squadrons were split up under command of infantry battalions. No. 1 Squadron were attached to the 3rd Micks, and No. 3 to the 1st Welsh, No. 2 were in reserve with Battalion H.Q.

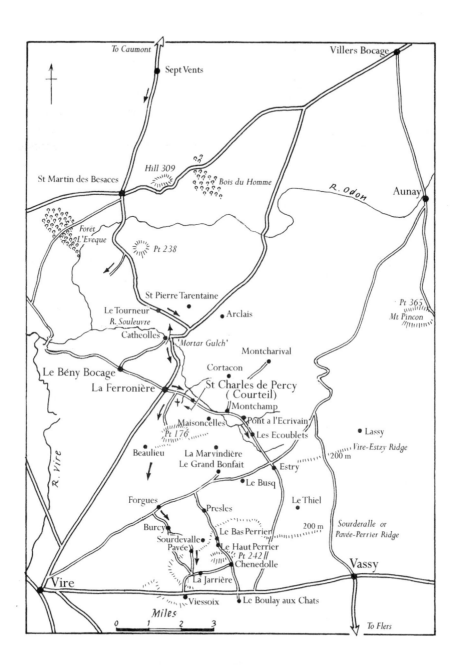

To Caumont

Sept Vents

Villers Bocage

Hill 309

Bois du Homme

R. Odon

Aunay

St Martin des Besaces

Forêt L'Eveque

Pt 238

St Pierre Tarentaine

Arclais

Le Tourneur

R. Souleuvre

Pt 365

Mt Pincon

Catheolles

'Mortar Gulch'

Montcharival

Cortacon

Le Bény Bocage

La Ferronière

St Charles de Percy
(Courteil)

Montchamp

Pont a l'Ecrivain

Maisoncelles

Les Ecoublets

Lassy

Pt 176

Beaulieu

La Marvindière

Le Grand Bonfait

Estry

Vire-Estzy Ridge

200 m

R. Vire

Le Busq

Forgues

Presles

Le Thiel

Burcy

Le Bas Perrier

200 m

Sourderalle or
Pavée-Perrier Ridge

Sourdevalle

Pavée

Le Haut Perrier

Pt 242

Chenedolle

Vassy

Vire

La Jarrière

Viessoix

Le Boulay aux Chats

Miles

0   1   2   3

To Flers

53

Our old friends 21st Panzers were reported in the area, also 9th S.S. Panzers.

We made ourselves comfortable, slept most of the afternoon and had a good meal, all the time expecting to move. A regiment of S.P. 25 pounders were in the next field, who made a devil of a noise but they went later on. Near Battalion H.Q. a German prisoner was found in a hedge, one of these S.S. 'Supermen'. He had been there three days and wouldn't give himself up in spite of being badly wounded.

Wednesday, 2 August. We spent the whole day sitting in the same cornfield feeling rather left out of it. A lovely hot day, Nigel and I sat and talked most of the morning, and I went and saw Michael Hamilton at Battalion H.Q. in the afternoon.

The battle seemed to be going well, but now started ten days of heavy fighting for the division north east of Vire in the closely wooded hills of the Bocage. It was most confused and we had a lot of bitter fighting and casualties. The division did well, but it would be tedious to describe anything but what actually happened to me personally. No two troops, no two squadrons, not even two men could have the same experiences in this close fighting.

Bill had great news this evening. The Americans had reached Rennes, the capital of Brittany and had broken right out into Brittany itself.

That night at dusk we moved south of St. Martin des Besaces to a farmyard near St Denis Maisoncelles, one of the many little villages round here with fascinating names. The Germans had been there the day before. My tank 'Cheetah' broke down on the way, the throttle stuck wide open through not being oiled. It was bad and annoyed me, so I changed into Caulfield's tank and went on. The farm we came into was littered with German equipment and I was nearly shot by Michael Hamilton in the dark who was looking for this equipment and ran into me. I was walking into the harbour on foot ahead of the tank. We expected to find Germans in the hedges. I stayed up waiting for my tank to arrive, but gave it up at midnight and slept with the crew of Caulfield's tank 'Caribou'.

Thursday, 3 August. Moved out in early morning ready to support the Micks. My tank had arrived in late, but it was not right so I left it in the field. We went up as far as Le Tourneur, but were halted by Colonel Ririd, turned round and came back to the same field as before, order and counterorder. . . . We spent the rest of the day here. Peter Towers-

Clarke, in H.Q. Squadron, came and saw me and we bought some excellent butter off the local farmer, a very nice man; in fact I rather enjoyed trying to make myself understood. Slightly shelled in morning and a dud landed in a bank a few yards from the S.S.M. and me; we thought ourselves lucky.

We heard in the evening that Reggie Batt had been killed by a sniper while getting in his tank. He commanded No. 1 Squadron, an able and brave officer; he was our first senior casualty. A sniper jumped up on a bank in a narrow lane and at a few yards range shot him in the head. No.1 were advancing in close support of the 3rd Irish Infantry, west of St. Charles de Percy, and he had been forward on foot, when they lost a couple of tanks in front on the way up to point 176, east of a small place called Beaulieu.

Friday, 4 August. Still in reserve in this field. Wild rumours were coming in, but it was evident that some pretty sticky fighting was going on. The initial breakthrough impetus had been slowed down, but the Americans were pushing on fast into Brittany. For us an eventless day, we felt rather out of it, though our turn was certainly to come.

The Bocage country we were fighting in during these and subsequent days, known by the papers as the Norman Switzerland (was causing a great deal of trouble). Steep rolling hills rather like the Yorkshire Wolds in contour but covered with tiny fields. They had no ordinary fences but thick Cornish banks, often two together, with dense untrimmed trees and foliage all along them. It was a close wooded countryside with visibility limited from one field to another. Steep valleys penetrated it and dominating hills (lay in successive lines across our front) while the roads were more like narrow Cornish lanes with high banks. The farms were small and poor, set in thick orchards. Bocage is the best description of it, pretty country to look at but a nightmare to advance in.

Later Comment

"But the nature of the resistance was changing." This significant factor as recorded in the battalion News Letter may not have reached back to us in reserve. I did not mention it, but those already engaged in this confused and disconnected battle would have been aware of the change. "At Caen," continues the News Letter, "we had run up against strong enemy positions which depended on some sort of 'line'. 88 m.m. guns supported by infantry in fairly large numbers were backed up, there, by strong groups of armour and were sited in depth. Here the enemy had not had time, or the material to construct any such defensive position. Small groups of five or six tanks, possibly including a Panther or two, worked with a platoon or a company of infantry, but each group was an entity and seemed to have no fixed position in the general scheme of defence." Even so these tactics were highly effective for the country, while the S.S. men remained as stubborn, and their shelling as intense as ever.

From *The Story of the Guards Armoured Division* whose joint author, Colonel Roddy Hill, was in a few days' time to take command of the 5th Coldstream, it is clear "the Germans were equally doing some quick thinking and had by now become fully aware of where their danger lay. The commander of 21st Panzer Division also correctly appreciated the importance of the bridge at Cathéolles, a mile or so south-west of Le Tourneur, "and the suitability of the area for defence, and in the event we seem only just to have forestalled him by a very short head. . . . The Germans had indeed failed in the primary object of preventing us crossing the river Souleuvre through being forestalled at Le Beny Bocage," on the centre-line of the 11th Armoured to our right. By August 2nd resistance had stiffened in the steep hilly country beyond the Souleuvre and ". . . the arrival of another reinforcement of first-class calibre that day in the shape of the 9th S.S. Panzer Division made a halt to capture it essential."

It was thus between the Souleuvre and the ridge four miles south along the top of which ran the important secondary road from Aunay-sur-Odon south-west to Vire, through the villages of Estry and Le Busq that our division were now engaged.

"The 11th Armoured Division also",* continues *The Story of the G.A.D*, "came up against increased resistance that day and though it succeeded in penetrating to the main road from Vire to Vassy at one point near Viessoix about four miles east of Vire, reported that opposition was becoming extremely strong in all directions. Further west XIX U.S. Corps after advancing almost as far as Vire found the German 3rd Parachute Division dug-in in strength on the outskirts."

I went for a short walk with Nigel in the evening. Val's troop were sent out during the day to shoot at a German O.P. but were unsuccessful and returned. Late in the evening news came that No.1 Squadron were

---

* Until 9th S.S. Panzers arrived on the scene enemy reaction was not as rapid as usual and so 11th Armoured continued to advance unchecked into the maze of Bocage country during 2 August. By that evening they had formed a strong narrow salient with the Fife and Forfar Yeomanry, armoured, and 3rd Monmouths, infantry, battalions on the right and 23rd Hussars and 8th Rifle Brigade battalions to the left on the Pavée-Sourdevalle-Perrier ridge five miles east of Vire. This seriously threatened the enemy's important lateral communication, the Vire to Vassy Road. But more of the story of this salient is to come.

having a sticky battle so we stood by to help them, but they did not need us. David Martyn was killed when his tank was hit by a Panther around Point 176, and No.1 Squadron lost another knocked out. No news from No.3.

We moved up later that evening to a steep field near St Charles de Percy village called Courteil to support the 3rd Irish if they needed anything. We moved in after dark and dug in.

On the way up in a deep, wooded valley just south of Le Tourneur we halted while the 4th Grenadiers in their Churchills, part of 6th Guards Tank Brigade, came back to harbour out of the battle. The photograph of my troop at this moment appeared in *The Sphere* shortly after. We were by the bridge at Cathéolles where the main Caen-Vire road, now Route D.577, crosses the small river Souleuvre and enters this unforgettable wooden defile. James Higgins, a Sandhurst friend, I saw in one of the tanks. We waved and he pointed smugly at the thickness of his Churchill's armour.

There was a lot of small-arms firing all round and very close, so we spent an uncomfortable night stood to all the time. A search party was sent along the neighbouring hedges to look for snipers, but none were there. We were mortared slightly. I let off a 4-inch smoke bomb by mistake and caused a lot of anger from Hugo as he expected a stonk of mortar at once, but none came fortunately. Two smoke canisters were kept in cups, cocked and ready to discharge in emergency, on the off-side of the turret. They were too easy to kick and trigger off as one climbed up. A noisy night and we were glad next morning to be able to see the situation by daylight.

Later Comment

The name St Charles de Percy was a bit of a mystery. We referred thus to the small string of battered houses at the crossroads where we turned off from the main road to Vire that evening, two miles south of the bridge at Cathéolles. I possess a map reference and code-name 'Husky' attached to this name neatly copied down in my hand before the battle to prove that Brigade and Division must have thought the same. Most likely it was due to the way the map was printed. But these houses are called La Ferronière.

With so many small villages, many destroyed or their names misplaced on British maps, it may help to explain in detail where we were. From this cross-roads at La Ferronière the then narrow road signposted today to Montchamp and Vassy leads east about a mile to the next small village known by us as

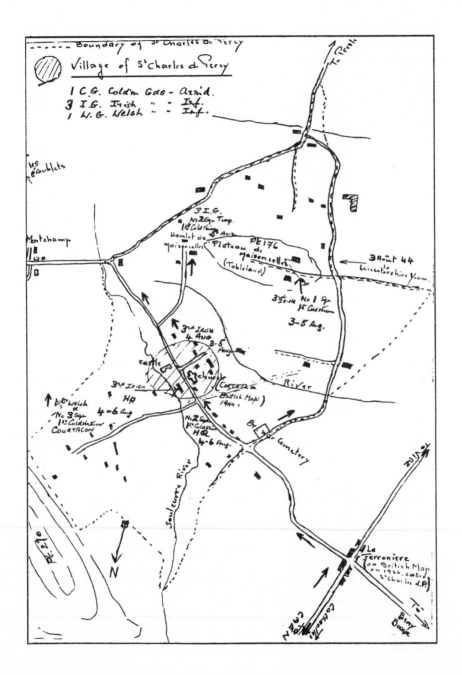

Map by the Mayor of St. Charles de Percy, Monsieur M. Leteinturier. October 1983

Corteil. Courteil as a name no longer appears but this place was, and is, St Charles de Percy, now with rebuilt church, Mairie and Château. Just before reaching this church a side lane turns north down a steep dip to a stream and leads up towards the high wooded ground around Courtacon. Our field that night of the 4th at Courteil remains quite unchanged. It lay to the left of this side lane before crossing the stream. Today the road at the top east from the church is a wide modern road, it passes a concrete pipe works and goes on for about a mile to Montchamp.

The infantry battalions of 32nd Guards Brigade supported by our two Squadrons, 1 and 3, were hotly engaged on either side of this same road. No. 3 with the 1st Welsh to the north around Courtacon and the 3rd Irish having run into heavy fire at Courteil had turned south-east to Maisoncelles with orders to enter Montchamp. No 1 Squadron with the Irish were still in contact with the enemy around Point 176. The 5th Coldstream/2nd Irish Group were having a hard time around La Marvindière, a couple of miles to the south-east. The 15th Scottish Division supported by the Churchills of 6th Guards Brigade were coming from the north to enter Montchamp and then push south towards the Estry ridge.

The British Military Cemetery of St Charles de Percy, where many friends and Guardsmen lie amongst the 788 killed in this battle, is a quarter of a mile east of La Ferronière.

Saturday, 5 August. We had a rather disturbed breakfast as some A.P. shots came bounding across our field quite close like high-speed cricket balls. They were only 'overs' but rather upsetting to one's sausages and tea. A bit early to open the bowling I thought, most unfair. Apparently these came from a Panther withdrawing from a tight spot, deeply resented by Battalion H.Q. who were right in the fairway.

We were expecting to be put into the battle going on all round but we were not called on that day. Nigel's troop and Bill went off to protect a company of the 3rd Micks near Montchamp. They had quite a good time but rather disappointing. This was X Company, Scots Guards, at Maisoncelles under that unique and seasoned soldier 'Feathers', Patrick Stewart-Fotheringham.

I was sent out at lunchtime to protect the Mick Battalion HQ, just across the side-lane leading to Courtacon. Rather a dull job but the Mick Commander seemed to think if he had a tank sitting round him he was quite safe. On recollection he soon had my troop at work in an orchard around his Battalion HQ co-ordinating defence with some

59

heavy machine gunners and knocking down several trees to clear their field of fire.

Later Comment

He was, of course, Colonel Joe Vandeleur, no less, and how glad I am to have seen at close hand this legendary soldier in battle. His HQ was full of events. The orchard and scattered farm buildings still remain much the same, close behind the fine rebuilt château.

An amusing thing happened when a Mick kicked over an empty barrel in a house nearby and out came a Hun. He was a Russian-Pole, terrified he was going to be shot and burst into tears, though it turned out he was most frightened of being shot by his own officers. There were many such incidents during these days.

Heavy and difficult fighting was going on all round with other battalions in the division, but we again had little to do. The 5th Coldstream were cut off near Le Grand Bonfait, actually around La Marvindière a mile or two south-east of us and had lost all their senior officers; in fact Billy Hartington was commanding the battalion. The 2nd Irish, the armoured battalion with them, had had a bad day and lost a lot.

Sunday, 6 August. A peaceful morning in the orchard and I was sorry when we were moved back to the squadron at lunchtime. The battalion then re-grouped in a field back near St Charles de Percy.

We all went back to this field and both 'A' and 'B' Echelons arrived up. A moment of relief! One knew one was quite safe then. We were told we would be regrouping there for a couple of days' clean up and rest, while the division got sorted out. After the recent fighting all formations were confused. However, this was only a breather in the campaign.

In the bigger picture the Americans had swept right through Brittany as far as Brest and were starting to turn east to Le Mans. Round Vire and north-east as far as Villers Bocage very heavy fighting was still going on. This must have been some of the hardest fighting of the whole invasion campaign.

Spent the afternoon cleaning ourselves up – a dead cow in my troop area needed a lot of removing.

The Officers' Mess truck and the squadron cooker were up and gave us a good dinner. After attacking the whisky we all felt a great deal better and more cheerful. I went to bed in my sleeping bag, kept in the mess truck for such special occasions, determined to have a good night and long-lie next morning.

Monday, 7 August. Not a bit of it! I was woken about 12.30 a.m. for orders. I fell asleep at once and had to be re-woken. We assembled in the back of the 3-ton cooker truck.

The gist of it was the squadron were to move up to a village called Les Ecoublets near Estry to protect a company of the 3rd Irish already there, prior to an attack on Estry the next day. Reveille was at 3 a.m. and we moved out about 4.30. Raining hard.

We moved up through Montchamp, taken only yesterday by the 1st Welsh Guards and 15th Scottish Division and on to Les Ecoublets.

George went on in a scout-car to find the Micks. Typically enough they did not know we were coming and did not want us a bit, in fact were all asleep when we arrived. We went on through the village, missed their forward platoons and were shot at by a Spandau and some A.P. shots, so we withdrew sharply. We were not wanted and no attack was planned, and went back to the next village Le Pont à L'Ecrivain about 600 yards behind.

I continue this while resting again in the divisional transit camp near Beringen, Belgium, just east of the Albert Canal.

The difficulty I had turning my troop round when we withdrew sticks in my mind; with Sgt. Brough's tank in a boggy field on my left and Sgt. Emmerson's 17-pounder in a thick orchard to my right in case of any sign of the S.P. that had fired at us, I was rather anxious. Some Teller mines were hanging on the apple trees. However, the years of training showed. Sgt. Brough saw the bog in time and Sgt. Emmerson dismounted and guided his tank in reverse. With all our guns traversed to the rear, Sgt. Caulfield remained covering us while we went back through Les Ecoublets.

I thought I had built up a really efficient team if only we had a fair chance to use it.

Later Comment

The Story of the Guards Armoured Division shows that the Germans were now determined not to yield on the Estry-Vire ridge. "Although the 3rd Battalion

Irish Guards occupied Les Ecoublets without opposition, the 15th Scottish Division found Estry defended with tremendous determination by the 9th S.S. Panzer Division the next day, August 7th, and was only able to establish itself on the northern outskirts after severe casualties. It was obvious the Germans did not intend to let the Vire-Estry line go without a bitter struggle – their decision to launch the now historic Mortain counter-offensive that day made it, as we now know, even more imperative to hold on."

Unknown to us then about a mile to our right the 5th Coldstream supported by the 2nd Irish tanks had met devastating fire the day before, August 6th, when they advanced from La Marvindière to attack Le Busq across the Vire-Estry road on top of the ridge. "Both forward companies started to lose men heavily. . . . Lt. Colonel Hill drew his men back to the line of the road content with an important if limited gain of territory."

"The enemy's temper and disinclination to yield any further was even more positively shown on the sector of the 11th Armoured Division" – immediately to the right of the 5th Coldstream – "where a vicious counterattack was launched that evening, August 6th, on the salient – across the road – jutting out to the Vire-Vassy road.* It was led by the 10th S.S. Panzer Division", the close partner in crime of the 9th, "but included other troops of first class quality also and its intention was at least to eliminate the salient completely. Losses were very heavy on both sides, but it was eventually driven off after gaining only a few hundred yards of ground". The head of this salient was the notorious ridge at Sourdevalle a couple of miles south of the Vire-Estry road, but as yet of course we knew nothing of all this. So back to our field behind the 3rd Irish at Les Ecoublets.

---

* This counterattack against positions on the right of the Salient was at Pavée, held by 29th Brigade of 11th Armoured. By a stroke of luck, it took place at the moment of the arrival of the infantry of 3rd Division to take over from them. The 1st Royal Norfolk Battalion had just relieved the hard-pressed 3rd Monmouths who with the Fife and Forfar tanks had held off repeated attacks on the previous day by the 9th S.S.

This renewed attack in the evening of the 6th by German infantry and Tiger tanks of 10th S.S. Panzers was thus met by greater force than expected. In bitter and costly fighting, often hand to hand, the Norfolks, and the Monmouths, who had returned to their positions, supported by the Armoured battalion, and with massive help from the whole 8th Corps Artillery, stopped the enemy. Meanwhile their soft transport that had brought up the relief battalions and that waiting for the Monmouths in the orchards behind the ridge was caught by the heavy shell fire and was all in flames.

This was one of the several ferocious battles on the ridge known to them as Pavée and Le Bas Perrier to the left and is vividly recounted by some of the survivors in Jean Brissot's book. As will be seen this same ridge was known to us as Sourdevalle.

The 11th Armoured Division had reached the Pavée-Perriers ridge on 2nd August and formed a salient. For a brief time they advanced beyond to Le Haut Perrier and to the village of Chênedollé, while a troop of tanks even crossed the Vire to Vassy road. This lovely country of dense apple orchards and numerous small farms was then untouched by war and some of the families were still anxiously living among them. It was possible at first to identify correctly the names of these farms and hamlets, such as Pavée, but after a week of heavy fighting, intensive shelling and mortaring, most of the buildings were burnt out piles of rubble, trees smashed down, and banks ripped out. When the G.A.D. arrived to take over, we only knew this area of devastation as Sourdevalle, although that actual name belongs to a farm or small hamlet some way behind the ridge and to the left of the road up to the positions we took over at Pavée on 9th August.

Confusion over the name of this infamous battlefield needs an attempted explanation. It may well lie in the maps we were issued for these operations, based on pre-war French. This showed one name only on the ridge west of Le Bas Perrier, and that incorrectly spelt, Sourdevalle. The Guardsmen who were there always knew it thus, and will continue to do so, inaccurately maybe, but Sourdeval as the name should be spelt, will remain our battle.

We spent the morning sitting there with no particular event except a little shelling and small arms on our left. I handed my troop over to Brough and armed with a rifle and grenade went off with Caulfield, one of the best shots in the battalion, to patrol the hedges on our left for snipers or any Germans who might have crept up. I enjoyed that, rather like the stalking games we used to play in the grounds of our home at Tregothnan in Cornwall, but the 'coverts' were empty.

Two o'clock, Colonel Ririd came up to see if we were wanted there. Feathers, the Mick Company Commander, splendid with his enormous feathery moustache, a rifle always slung from his shoulder and collar clipped together like a guardsman, said we only brought shells down on them. But the authorities said we must stay. The mobile baths had come up to the rest of the battalion, so we were to be relieved by No. 1 Squadron while we went back several miles to the harbour area and then returned. Ridiculous. No. 1 were furious and we got dirty again on the way back, but orders is orders.

While the men bathed I cleaned up my things and had a wash in a bucket, almost enjoyable. We had a good meal off the mess truck and I was pleased to see Ian and John Sutton at dinner. Michael Fox, who commanded H.Q. Squadron and 'A' Echelon, also appeared, pessimistic as usual, talking about "two years' trench warfare when we reach the Siegfried Line".

We took over again from No. 1 that night and pulled all together in a field.

There was a lot of firing and shelling at one time and I thought we might be counter-attacked. A German Spandau, unmistakable owing to its high rate of fire, fired bursts all night. It was so close it made us anxious and we kept a good look out.

Next morning, when we found the Spandau was a captured one being used by the Micks just in front of us, we all felt furious, a dangerous thing to do, and not to be encouraged.

Tuesday, 8 August. Very early, about four o'clock, a battalion of the 15th Scottish Division, the K.O.S.Bs, formed up in our field. When daylight came they had all dug in and were having breakfast. Supported by a squadron of the 4th Grenadiers, in Churchills and flamethrowers, they were going to put in a brigade attack on Estry.

It was only then we discovered what was in Estry, as there had been so many and various reports, and the squadron had gaily set out to attack it alone the day before.

Bill sent me down to find the Grens and get any news from them. For some reason he always sent me to find out semi-military and personal news from other units. It is extraordinary how one always finds friends in the Army. Down the road I found the squadron of Grens, and met a Sergeant with me at the G.A.T. wing* at Pirbright last year. He told me all their news. I was very sorry to hear that Jim Marshall-Cornwall and Oliver Fitzroy† had been killed by snipers.

We dug in well and prepared for 'overs' and shelling from the attack. I watched the faces and feelings of these little infantrymen carefully, as this was the first full-scale infantry attack I had seen. It was interesting to compare them with our own feelings. I sat with Nigel and their most splendid looking R.S.M. was dug in just by the tank. Nigel had lent him his cooker and he was calmly cooking his meal, a real old-fashioned spectacle.

Some of the younger men looked nervous waiting, others slept. The officers were having their final 'O' group and were too busy to show any outward signs. It is one of the great advantages an officer has, plenty to keep his mind occupied before an attack, whereas the men have little.

The usual barrage started and at twelve the attack went in. The infantrymen were quickly lost to view in the bocage ahead. Certainly a

---

* Guards Armoured Training Wing.
† Both contemporaries of mine at school and at Sandhurst. Oliver was the son of Captain Fitzroy of the *Rodney* and the brother-in-law of Dermot Musker.

lot of stuff came back, bullets whistled overhead all day and a good deal of shelling, one nebelwerfer stonk landed in our field.

The attack was a partial success only. I never heard exactly what happened, though I think they took Estry. But the usual tragic parties of wounded, stretcher bearers and ambulances came filtering back. A few prisoners returned and one was put under guard in our field, a poor specimen, not an S.S. man, a Pole I think. Nigel and I talked to him; he had little to say but that they thought our Shermans reliable; one could set little store by him.

The S.S. youths were fanatical thugs. Nigel told me then how, when he was away with his troop a few days ago in support of X Company on the southern edge of Maisoncelles, he saw a German crew cross the road in front of him to a house for a drink. Not wanting to give his own position away he jumped out of his tank and moved up with a sten gun. He shot at the man about five yards away, but the sten jammed and the German rushed into the house firing at Nigel with a revolver. He ran back to his tank fired at by a Spandau at ten yards range, got in and sprayed the road with Browning. The Hun was wounded and lay groaning. Nigel let him groan. He refused to let anyone go forward, as the man was an S.S. and it might have been a trap. When eventually some Irish Guards brought the Hun in he turned out to be the most brutal horrid-looking devil: "more like an animal than a man", those were Nigel's actual words. Despite being badly wounded he remained arrogant and proud.

Nigel, who was a quiet and mild individual, was rather brutal I thought then, but these S.S. men are such complete beasts, I know I would do the same. He was very brave, Nigel, though never showed it. He said to me that afternoon he did not really mind whether he was killed or not. I did not quite know how to answer, but thought to myself and said that, at this stage of the war, I minded the hell of a lot .

An amusing story came from the 1st Welsh. When interviewing four S.S. thugs they could get nothing out of them, so their R.S.M. went out, came back and laid four crosses on the table. After that they talked their heads off.

The night was disturbed like the last, but by now one did not worry. I did a guard with my troop. It is always a nervous business going round sentries at night in the line. One never knows who is on guard and whether he is a windy sentry or not. I used to whistle between my teeth to attract attention, but I don't think anyone had forgotten David Baxendale yet.

Later Comment

But Estry had not fallen and the enemy did not finally withdraw from there until two days later on the 11th. An infantry brigade, the 6th Guards Tank Brigade, 8 Corps artillery and an air bombardment failed to dislodge the Germans from this village, who fought until their supplies ran out.

Sourdevalle

Wednesday, 9 August. In same field and same sort of day with a number of 'overs' from the front line, bullets and shells from the direction of Estry. By now we were doing no good at all and felt it was high time to move.

I heard a sharp crack out of hundreds in the morning and Whittle came out of the tank and up to me with a bullet hole in his arm. One of the stray bullets I thought and I took him off to the R.A.P. at once. Walking him back holding his arm in my hands we were able to joke on how soon he would go back to England. It wasn't very bad, but it meant a six-week job, in other words I would lose him.

It made me especially angry when he told me at the R.A.P. that he was shot by my Gunner Lance-Sergeant Arnold who was cleaning his revolver inside the tank. A thing one could not conceive possible. It is incredible how stupid some men can be. Whittle I considered was the best Operator in the squadron. He was an 'old soldier' of the best kind, a steadying influence on all of us, in fact in Michael Fox's platoon when Michael was an Ensign. Always completely calm, I never had to bother about the wireless at all which was a tremendous help. A bad Operator can make one twice as tired. I shall always remember this Yorkshireman's smile in the turret when a shot landed too close for comfort.

This had more far-reaching results. Although I had had this particular crew for a long time, and it was my aim to keep my tank crews the same from the early Norfolk days, I felt we needed a change. This must needs be if one has to live day in day out in a confined space like a tank. I put it to Brough who knew exactly my feelings and we devised a change, though he was determined to keep his crew the same as he

66

always had. It was a tremendous asset having a Troop Sergeant who knew what was wanted but by far from being a yes-man.

I took Channon as my Operator, a good Operator, cheerful, keen and kept a cool head though young. Meadows came as my Gunner, a quiet and cheerful person too. Channon hailed from Shepperton, Middlesex, while Meadows was another South Yorkshireman. These two were great friends. I left Berry and Liddle the Driver and Co-Driver as before. Emmerson was rather angry at losing Channon but I gave him Arnold instead.

A letter from Father said that Mummie was now in Cairo on Red Cross business and was going to see Edward wherever he was. I supposed somewhere there in the Middle East. Wrote a letter home and one to John Corbould telling him all the Coldstream news. While reading some of Hugo's papers, I had to dive into his vast slit trench when a crump of shells came down on us. We had a fight to get to the bottom of the trench first and I ended up sprawling on top of him causing some acid comment.

A word about the bigger picture. The Americans had spread well out all over Brittany and cut off the peninsula. They had turned east towards Paris and were slowly leading Von Kluge's army into a bag with the British on the northern side. The Germans had counter-attacked at Mortain with four armoured divisions towards Avranches, but all the British and American air forces had turned on them and the attack had led to disaster. The Hun had lost a great number of his priceless tanks.

I now come to what we knew as the Battle of Sourdevalle and will describe those two fateful days in as much detail as I remember.

At six o'clock in the evening, 9th August, Bill was summoned back to Battalion H.Q. for orders and returned a good hour afterwards. We knew by then we were going to move, but his orders were an unpleasant surprise. The 11th Armoured Division, who had had some very heavy fighting slightly to our right, were to be pulled out for a rest and we were to take their place. During the night 3rd Irish were to move up to the Sourdevalle ridge (in a salient beyond the Vire-Estry road) and take over from the Monmouths who were supported by a squadron of Hussars.

Later Comment

The battalion Newsletter shows them as B.Squadron, Scots Greys, not the 23rd Hussars, and the Irish Guards History says that the Monmouths were by then a weak composite battalion formed with the Norfolks after having lost so many men there. On 6 August Corporal S. Bates of 1st Royal Norfolk Regiment won the V.C. in this battle on the Perrier Ridge in which he was mortally wounded.

The Squadron was to be in support of the 3rd Irish, while the rest of the battalion were to remain in reserve below the hill with some S.P. anti-tank guns.

The position we were told then was horrible, in fact most disagreeable. It was overlooked by a hill opposite, and by another hill on the left flank, being heavily shelled all the time. The Micks were to move in soon after dark and take over. Until they were well dug in, we were to wait before we came up in case we brought down shelling on them. That's all we knew then, but Bill was going off to recce the position now and we were to move back under George towards Montchamp and pick him up with fresh orders on the way. He went off in the scout-car with the Sergeant-Major.

I went back to my troop, told them what was happening, folded maps and warned them we were going to have a pretty sticky day or two ahead. We then cooked ourselves, and ate, as good a meal as the pack ration could provide, and got ready to move. About eight o'clock No. 3 Troop, Val's, led out, followed by George and Hugo in Squadron H.Q., then my Troop, followed by No.4, Nigel's, then No.1, Anthony's, back down the road to Montchamp. Anthony Gell had now come up and taken over No.1.

We covered this road for the fourth time, turned west towards St Charles de Percy, halted and closed up in two lines at the top of the field at Corteil where we had spent last Friday night.

Bill had come back and we went over to him for orders. It was a bloody place. Much worse than Bill had thought, and he was certainly not the man to over-estimate unpleasantness. We were to move up to the hill behind it straightaway, sleep for a few hours and, at three, to go on up. Bill had seen the Squadron Leader there and they had arranged to leave guides for us. If the tanks were too far forward, or too far to the right, they would be shot up from the hills in front and to the left as soon as it was light. Already five burnt-out Shermans were there to justify this. As they had only three troops up, Val's was to remain in reserve with Hugo at the bottom of the hill. I must say I rather envied him. As we had four tanks my troop was to be on the right, Nigel's four on the left of the road and Anthony's three were to be in a sunken lane to the left flank. There was nothing else, so we were to move off as soon as we could.

Back to my tank, told the three tank commanders where we were going to, and off we went in the same order. Brough led, as it was considered one should have somebody in front as a buffer, also Brough was an extremely good map-reader. I followed, then Emmerson in the Firefly, then Caulfield, and that was what we nearly always did. On as far as St Charles de Percy, then we turned south across country along a tank track passing near Beaulieu. It was rather boggy, though only the fitters in their scout-car stuck, but they soon got out. About twelve we reached a good field, the squadron bunched up close and got down to sleep straight away. It was a horribly lonely place and deathly silent. The prospects of tomorrow seemed very disagreeable and I imagined the worst, which is perhaps a good thing.

Thursday, 10 August. Some shells landed quite close and I do not think I slept much. At 3 o'clock, when reveille came, I was wide awake. After another brief 'O' Group we set off. The Sergeant-Major led the way in a scout-car, as he had just come back, off the track, onto a road, across the Vire-Estry road at Forgues, and then down into the valley below Sourdevalle. The road was steep and narrow down to the stream and again up the hill we had to get to. Thick with at least three inches of dust, we were putting up a great cloud, so I expected shells to come down on us at any minute. Under direct German observation from Le Bas Perrier on the next ridge, it was being shelled all yesterday whenever any dust was shown. I had my tin hat handy. I never wore it until we were actually being shelled, then always put it on. People who wore berets whatever happened I thought were stupid.

The road was dark and we had to go slowly. I lost sight of Brough's tank in the dust. Then to my great relief I saw a white cloud enveloping the valley beneath, a thick fog down there, and we would be spared shelling on the road at any rate.

Bill was into the fog and came up on the air to tell us to dismount, if necessary, and walk in front of our tanks. I went on slowly and, as we moved into the thick bank, it went suddenly cold and dark. I shivered. I don't know how the driver could see, as I could not see a yard or two

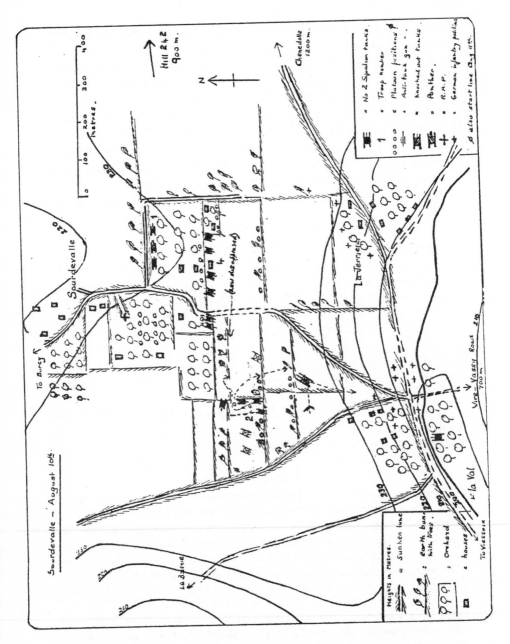

Sourdevalle – area marked 'A' on p.85. Position of No 2 Squadron during 10 August when attacked by Panthers. The knocked-out Panther found by Bill Gray is in the orchard at bottom left in front. We passed through a small village I remembered to be Burcy on the map, then came to a fork, but had passed it before I realized it was there, so halted. I knew we had to turn right but could not make out whether this was the track or not. I search the ground with a rotten little pocket torch for tracks and decided to go right.

Just then a D.R. appeared in the fog completely lost. I told him I thought we were in Burcy. He turned out to be an officer from the 3rd Micks going up to Sourdevalle and he knew the way from there, saying he thought it was Burcy church on the corner to the right. I walked over and was surprised to find the church a few yards off the road.

We knew exactly where we were now and he said he would lead me up the hill, but Bill came over the air ordering us to halt as they too were lost in front. So I told him not to bother and go on. I think he was rather reluctant to go alone and wanted company in the fog.

Nigel came up to me and we decided to back the tanks to be ready to move on down to the right. Just then three or more S.P. guns appeared going back and had to try and pass us in this very narrow lane with walls on either side. Somehow or other we got them past; it was tricky. Nigel walked down to the bridge over the stream at the bottom, found the Sergeant-Major, came back and led our column down with a torch. I walked on and found Bill coming back to the bridge too. A nasty situation over, lost in the fog in no-man's-land, one was liable to be in trouble to say the least.

Val and Hugo were dropped off at the bottom of the hill in a field and we moved slowly up to Sourdevalle. As we came up to the top we came out of the fog and could see the road ahead.

Later Comment
It was easy to miss that sharp left turn just after crossing the bridge over the River Allière below Burcy, as Bill Gray had done. After this turning the lane swings round to the right again before starting the long pull up to the top of the Sourdevalle ridge. It is about one and a half miles from the bridge to our forward positions, much longer, narrower and steeper than I remembered before I went back eleven years later. Although we did not know this at the time we had been quite right to be anxious about losing the Squadron in the fog for the enemy were still holding Le Bas Perrier in strength. This lies only a few hundred yards to the left of our lane leading up to the head of this narrow salient. Half way up off a turning to the left is the farm called Sourdeval. It was an area of small farms and numerous little houses up to the next ridge.

71

I had a sinking feeling going up to that hill, rather like going to the dentist to have a tooth taken out, knowing when one comes out all will be well again, but it was soon to be forgotten.

We halted, someone jumped on to my leading tank and led us off through the village, turned right off the road across a field and halted in the next one. I went up to the guide, the Troop Sergeant there before. He told me where to put my tanks. I did not like the positions, but could see almost nothing in the dark. If I went further to the right, he told me, I would be shot up from the hill on the left. I could already see a burnt-out Sherman to justify this, so I could only follow his advice until dawn. The guide talked quickly and seemed anxious to get away. He was evidently shaken and had had a terrible day. Before I had finished talking to him he had disappeared in the darkness. Poor man, he must have been pleased to leave that spot.

My tank was in the left-hand forward corner of that small field, a bank in front of me and on my left, Brough in 'Cobra' was ten yards to my right along the hedge. Caulfield, in 'Caribou', I tucked in the left-hand corner of the field behind facing our right.

The night was sinisterly silent, but it was nearly five o'clock. I called the Tank Commanders together and told them to camouflage the tanks all round at once, then to dig a slit trench. I wanted them to cook breakfast in it directly it got light and have had some before any shelling started. Two men were to remain on watch in each tank all the time.

The men were keen to camouflage and dig then, and we managed to get all done by dawn when they started to cook some breakfast. Tin hat and sten gun in hand, in case there were snipers lurking about, I walked round the position through the neighbouring fields. The field to our left was in full view of the enemy and it was covered with shell holes. A dud shell lay in the open and there was a brewed up S.P. gun. Obviously no one could live there. I looked at my camouflage and decided to thicken it up on the left.

To my front along the next hedge was the forward platoon of the Micks well dug in behind the bank. It was under Peter Doyle, a contemporary of mine at school. They were twenty yards ahead of us and the enemy not far beyond.

Another platoon of Micks was along the hedge to the right of Brough and their Company H.Q., No. 1 Company, just behind 'Cougar'. Further up the field were three knocked-out Shermans, hit from the hill

72

to our left. Beyond them was a little sunken lane full of dead Germans. In fact the whole area was littered with the carnage of war when the hill was taken a couple of days before and counter-attacked many times, twisted and burnt-out carriers and trucks, abandoned rifles and equipment and above all the smell of decay. They had not even had time to bury our own dead, and from the look of it they had had a costly battle.

By now I could see the enemy hills opposite and to our left, though they were indistinct in the morning mist. My tanks were hidden by camouflage, but I did not like the position at all. We were on the forward slope of the hill and had little view or field of fire to support the infantry, but if we went further back, hull-down behind the ridge, the infantry were completely out of sight. The banks were thick with the trees and bushes of the Bocage, making it not only difficult to see far ahead, but we were even unable to see into the field on our immediate left, let alone have any chance to fire our guns there.

Later Comment
When I returned eleven years after and found this position exactly, it was really right on the crest of the ridge. The ground sloped away gently at first in front and then fell more steeply beyond the forward platoon's position.

Bill walked round to see me and I told him all this. It was the best we could do for if I started moving the tanks forward or back now they would see or hear us and start shelling heavily. We did not mind so much, but the infantry would be rather uncomfortable. Squadron H.Q. were in the orchard two fields to my left and Nigel across the road beyond. Back to my tank and had a very enjoyable sausage and mug of tea.

Up till now only occasional mortars had landed around and odd bursts of m.g., but about nine o'clock, when the Boche had had his breakfast I expect, he opened up on us. I climbed into my tank and must have been seen doing so above the hedge, for I was greeted by a burst of Spandau around my head.

There we sat all morning; the shelling and mortaring went on at varying intervals. We kept watch in turns. During the lulls I walked round the tanks and sat in their slit trench. There was a gap in the bank between me and Brough and I collected a burst each time I crossed it. Caulfield's trench was in a comfortable position and I spent quite a while sitting there and was glad of it when some nebelwerfer rockets landed on us. The Commander came round to see us during a morning pause and realized what a bloody place it was. It did us good to have him with us. Going across the open field between us and Squadron H.Q. was a harassing business and he ran faster than I could have thought possible.

By the time I had had a refreshing mug of tea at the Company H.Q. behind me I began to feel that the place was not as bad as all that. But war does not go away for long. An Irish guardsman was brought back badly shell-shocked. It was difficult to make out whether he was pretending or not and they had already had one man making false pretences that morning. The Company Commander, Desmond Kingsford, was suspicious, but decided to send him back. It is difficult to tell whether a man is genuinely shocked or showing cowardice on an occasion like this.

In the event of an attack I foresaw we could do little to support the Micks against Panthers. We should have to move off the forward slope if they appeared, otherwise they would get us cold, and if we showed ourselves at all we should be shot up by the 88s on the hill on our left. If infantry attacked us we could do good work. They understood, and we arranged if the Panthers attacked they would get down to the bottom of their slits and let them pass over onto us. This was the best we could do. I could not understand why there weren't any anti-tank guns up there, as they could have done our job far better.

I was anxious too about our right flank, which we had to cover. There seemed nobody there and a Panther might waddle up and get us from behind. Visibility was only to the next field, so I sent Caulfield and Emmerson off on a patrol telling them to be cautious. I do not think they went further than I had that morning and only came back with a German revolver and no more information. However, we should hear a Panther getting over the sunken lane. There were no troops of ours on our right flank that day. The 1st and 2nd Grenadiers held the village of La Bottrie, a mile behind to the north-east.

The day passed wearily on. We sat and watched and changed our positions inside the tank. One man sat in the Commander's seat and another alert in the gunner's. I saw Brough in his trench peeling potatoes, so sent Liddle into ours to give us some lunch. I read *Blackwood*'s when not on watch. Father sent it out to me and this one

74

had some good stories. By now I did not mind the shelling. They were landing at intervals all round, but I could tell by the sound of the gun which were going to be close and when to duck below the cupola. What annoyed us was that we had practically no artillery support all day, most unusual.

I scanned the enemy hills through the glasses continually, but nothing moved. The hill on the left was Point 242 and the village called Chênedollé was just over it. The small hamlets of Le Haut Perrier and further behind us Le Bas Perrier were on this ridge that overlooked our position all along our left flank. From this strongly held flank the Germans could observe and sweep the crest of our hill with impunity. I only hoped the enemy could see as little of us.

It became a beautiful clear evening. I was getting rather tired by watching and was hoping for darkness to come. Tomorrow, Bill told me, we were going to attack the hill opposite, but we would get plenty of support, he said.

It was now about six o'clock and I think our alertness had fatigued a lot. Our wireless was switched off, necessary for saving our batteries and for listening for enemy tanks. Bill was permanently on the air as we had arranged to ring him up when anything happened.

Fortunately I was watching in the Tank Commander's seat, but the Operator, Channon, was in the Gunner's and Liddle, the Co-driver, was in the operator's. The Driver, Berry and Gunner Meadows were out in the slit trench. Brough's crew all seemed aboard, but Emmerson was cooking in his slit.

The mortar fire suddenly increased and the shelling became a barrage. To our front the chatter of machine guns suddenly broke out. I could hear the quick-firing Spandau and the slower Bren working up to a crescendo. Soon the machine-gun fire burst into a fusillade. An attack was coming in. I shouted to the Driver and Gunner to jump in, and switched on the wireless. There was no time to change the crew into their places, but Channon I knew was a good Gunner. We had all trained in each other's jobs, something I had insisted on and now was to be amply rewarded. I seized my headphones and binoculars; inevitably they got entangled. An agonizing moment was spent straightening them out. I rang up Bill as soon as the wireless had heated up and told him an attack was coming; he was already alert to it. Emmerson was slowly packing up his kit and still out of his tank. I roared at him to hurry up. I now tried my tanks on the air, but they were slow and "off-net". But there was no time to get tuned in and Liddle was not an Operator, so we had to do as best we could. Switching off the wireless was not a good idea, and we weren't really ready half quick enough.

Meanwhile I heard the sickening whizz of an A.P., the most frightening of all to a tank crew. It makes one's blood surge round inside. We must be attacked by Panthers.

I was trying vainly to catch an infantryman to tell me what was happening in front, we could see so little, when one came up and told me their Company Commander had just been killed by shrapnel. Desmond Kingsford was hit while in his slit trench at his H.Q. just behind me. Peter Doyle was now in command, but being forward with his platoon could not be got at. The leading platoon was heavily engaged at the moment. They had only one other officer left and the Company was rather disorganized.

My troop was remaining doggo without switching on engines, to try and listen and find out the position before committing myself. Several more A.P. shots went somewhere, but not at me, and I could hear tanks close. On the air I heard Bill and Nigel saying they were being shot at and someone had been hit. Being in the dark like this when things were going on so close was an anxious moment. I thought of going forward on foot to see for myself when a runner came back from Peter. He was unperturbed by this attack, and sending me a scrap of information was a tremendous help.

The runner, frightened, shouted something at me. Being harnessed up with headsets etc, I could hear nothing, so after my repeating the performance of undressing, steel helmet, goggles, headsets, he managed to say there were tanks in between the forward platoon and us. I knew this was untrue, as I could see that distance, but evidently the enemy were very close up. Before I could say anything he had disappeared. He had done extremely well though, bringing the message, standing up to give it to me in the top of my turret while shelling was intense all round us. I had a feeling the enemy could be coming up on our flank to the left and making our position impossible. Now was the time to pull back off the forward slope. I rang up Bill and asked him if it was all right to move back. This was stupid and unnecessary, and he answered, "Do what you can". I felt unhappy leaving the infantry, as one stretcher after another testified to the trouble the Micks were in, but ordered Brough and Emmerson back.

All this seemed like hours, but really the attack could not have gone on for more than ten minutes by then. With difficulty I backed my tank without running into "Cougar" behind and also the Company H.Q. carrier behind him. Brough had started to pull back across the field when he came up on the air. "Hello Two Able, Panther moving across front from left to right." He always spoke calmly on the air. I had just time to acknowledge him when I saw some dust moving across the front from right to left. Brough had it the wrong way round. "Driver Halt," just in time to prevent us backing into the carrier.

The game was on. I'd spotted the whereabouts of the stag and we were now to fight it out. "Seventy-five traverse left slightly, on, 200, fire at the dust." Channon loosed off a round into a cloud of dust. It was only a reckless shot as I could not see the tank. However, I hoped it might frighten him a bit. The shot went low and kicked up dust in the bank ahead, but I was not worrying about that.

We were all now in a huddle at the left-hand back corner of the field and Caulfield, 'Two Baker', was still stuck in his field behind. I came up on the air to Emmerson: "Hello Two Charlie, Panther moving across front from right to left. Move up into the field on your left and up to the next hedge, but do not go on to the forward slope. Two Able, stay back against the hedge where you are now and keep a look out to the right. Two Baker pull out from where you are, ready to move over to the left." I noticed, thank God, I was speaking slowly and calmly on the air, a great relief, especially as I was on the 'A' set and everybody else could hear.

Emmerson moved through the hedge on my left and went forward to the next bank. I followed, but it needed a lot of backing and turning to get through the only gap in the bank, and wasted a valuable minute or two. I couldn't see where Emmerson had gone and had now lost trace of the enemy so I came up on the air: "Hello Two Charlie, is there a good position for me beside you?" I had to repeat this, and the answer came back to my surprise, "No". I wanted to get up to him to observe his shots. I had sent him as his 17-pounder was my answer to the German tank but it kicked up such a dust when it fired that its own gunner (Bodsworth) could not observe his shots and it needed another tank close by to do so.

When I got through the hedge I saw that Emmerson had gone much too far, in fact off the ridge and was two fields ahead. Either he had not listened to what I said or I had not made myself clear, but he was always inclined to go bashing off like that. It was too late to stop him now, so I moved over to where he should have gone. I turned my tank to the right to face the enemy and took a look forward.

Just as I got there a cloud of smoke came out of the top of Emmerson's tank. Some men jumped out of it and lay rolling on the ground, one I saw had his clothes on fire, another ran for cover, two stretcher bearers from the Micks raced over to them. A cloud of white smoke now poured out of the turret. I heard Channon say over the I.C., "Poor old Two Charlie's had it".

There, not three hundred yards away, slightly to the right of the burning tank, I saw the turret of the Panther behind a hedge, his gun pointing at me. I could just see the round hole of its muzzle. "Traverse right". My gunner saw it at the same time. They could not have seen more than my turret either.

It was a desperately exciting moment. The stalk was over, it was them or us. My job was over. All I could say was "Fire". The first shot went off and at the same time I heard the roar of the A.P. as the Panther's shot whizzed past my head, while a sinister smoke ring appeared out of the black hole of its muzzle. My shot went low and kicked up a cloud of dust in the bank beyond. The next was also low. The third I saw hit fair and square on the front of the turret. But it appeared not to have the slightest effect and was greeted by another "whoozz" like the roar of an express train as it passes another. It could not have been far off its mark.

There seemed a long pause before the next shot and I looked down to see Liddle having difficulty with a round. It had stuck on the way into the breach and he seemed to be taking an unearthly time to find the rammer. Both Channon and I shouted at him to hurry up. I cursed the bloody little pop-gun for just bouncing off. Just then I heard an agonizing yell from outside the tank and saw Bodsworth, the gunner of Two Charlie, standing covered in blood. He was in a terrible state. I could see he was horribly burnt and wounded. I was in a dreadful dilemma, he desperately needed morphia, but the enemy was in our sights. I knew I was too engaged to leave the tank. There was nothing I could do then except throw out the first-aid box and come to his aid later. I had a tremendous struggle with it as it was jammed in the chaos of the moment. He picked it up and, still squealing,

78

staggered off. I did not think there was much hope for him.

Meanwhile Channon had got off another three shots and the first had hit the Panther again. It did not fire now and disappeared from view.

I had been conscious of hearing on the air that George's tank had been hit and I heard Bill say, "For God's sake someone give us smoke before the bloody Tiger gets the lot of us". Other tanks had come up, I thought, and were hitting Squadron H.Q. about a hundred yards on my left. I started to put down smoke. I fired the two dischargers on the side of the tank and hoped it was covering the right place, but could not see. To load these one had to get right out of the tank, exposed to any shrapnel. I leant out, got the top one reloaded and fired again. I was now in view of the hill on the left and shots were coming over from there, so I gave it up and started to move back into a more covered position. Squadron H.Q., I learnt afterwards from Bill, were under fire from an 88 and a large tank some distance away on this left flank. Brough came up on the air and said he thought he saw the dust of a Panther to his front again. I told him to move over to the sunken lane on our right and move down it, and he might see the Panther I had shot at and get a go at him on his flank. He went off. However, the Panther had had enough and disappeared. Caulfield was disappointing. I could not get him to move from his first position and he did nothing much.

We were now to the right of the orchard where Squadron H.Q. had been and in front of the Mick Battalion H.Q. I tucked myself behind an old farm building and there we sat. Again a threat of Panthers to the right flank was reported, so we kept a good look-out. Shelling and mortaring started heavily again and were landing all round us.

George came walking up to me. With blood on his tunic I thought he had been wounded, but he was unhurt. His tank had been hit on the gun, now twisted like a corkscrew, from the hill opposite, so he had abandoned it. He told me he had found Bodsworth and had taken him to the R.A.P. at the back of the orchard, but he did not think he would live.

George had taken over another tank, Sergeant White's from Nigel's troop, who had been wounded when an 88 struck the top. He was a few yards away from me on my left. We smiled at one another and then burst out laughing. We both looked pretty shocking sights, I think. I saw a Mick walking through the orchard and asked him to go to the R.A.P. and find out what had happened to the crew of "Cougar". He came back and told me. Sergeant Emmerson had died, Bodsworth and Sergeant Arnold were badly wounded, Entwistle their driver was only shaken.

Several days later, when the area had been cleared of enemy, Bill found a Panther at the bottom of the hill below us. Two shots had hit it, one had hit the gun and had gone down into the driver's compartment and killed him. It looked as if the crew had slept by it, then abandoned and fired it. I don't make any real claim but it is possible that this was the one. I like to think so anyway, and no one else claimed it. If so, it was one of the few Panthers knocked out head-on in Normandy, certainly by a 75.*

The sun was very low now and shining into us. We cursed it and longed for it to disappear, expecting a Panther over the ridge at any moment. We had reason too, for something came up quite close and put a shot through the already knocked-out S.P. in the field ahead of us. It went up with a loud bang. A cow moved across the skyline and in the sun it looked like the turret of a tank, but with relief I saw its legs move. Poor pathetic animals, I could not but spare a thought for their misery, and I hoped that a swift end had come to the old white carthorse that had sunk to the ground and died a few yards from my tank.

Inside the tank the floor was covered with all sorts of things, and with sheets of bumph. We laughed over this and I told Channon to get out my bottle of whisky I always carried in my brown case to recover our spirits. I handed round a good drink and we all felt much better.

Later Comment

Channon and Liddle had done especially well handling the gun, and my crew fully deserved their brief respite. So had Brough and his crew, but we all felt downcast at the loss of the fine crew and friends of our fourth tank, Two

---

* This burnt-out Panther is to be seen in the aerial photograph, opposite page 00, nearest the bottom left-hand corner. It is almost directly below the slope where the action described took place in the evening before the photo was taken and adds credence to the probability this was the tank we hit. It was Bill Gray's belief that it was. We shall never know why the Panther which a few moments before had put two fatal shots through Sergeant Emmerson's tank turret and then turned his gun on our tank, did not continue until he had finished us off too. Something had made him stop firing, and back away out of sight. Could it be that one of Channon's shots I had seen hit the German, had penetrated through a 'chink' in his armour? The driver's hatch above his seat where the armour was thin could have been that 'chink'.

Charlie. Only Channon could say much; until yesterday he was one of that crew and now he could not believe how fortune had treated him. Sergeant Arnold died of wounds a day later, and soon I would be writing to tell a wife in Blyth and a mother in Birmingham how two brave men had died face to face with the enemy. I would try, I know inadequately, to bring a little comfort to their shattered homes. Bodsworth recovered remarkably and we had a great meeting at Wellington Barracks many years after. Their turret was pierced twice, but I shall never know for sure whether it was the Panther or an 88 from the hill on the left who had fired, although they must have been close to the former when they moved forward. The 3rd Micks with our limited help had not given an inch of ground. For us the day's loss included three killed and at least one Guardsman severely wounded with two tanks gone, while the Irish had lost a company commander killed and two officers and seventeen Guardsmen wounded by shell splinters or machine-gun bullets. In a truly laconic understatement their official history, recording yet another incident among a thousand such, simply remarks, "Early that evening the Germans attacked the two forward companies, Nos. 1 and 4. The Guardsmen beat them off easily."

The shelling got much heavier now and my tank was hit. I don't know quite what happened but I must have been briefly knocked out or concussed. Channon picked me up off the floor of the turret and from that moment I became rather dazed and cannot remember much. An H.E. shell had hit the top of my turret a few inches from my head apparently. The crew was all right and the tank appeared undamaged.

I sent for Brough and told him to take over the rest of the evening, as for the moment I did not know what was what. Bill called me on the air and I told him. There was a carrier near my tank, a Company H.Q., and I sat talking to their Company Commander while he revived me on whisky and tea. We talked very nearly to midnight on all sorts of things. Every two or three minutes, bang, and we both dived under the carrier. He had lost his best friend, Desmond Kingsford, that afternoon and needed someone to talk to. We discussed shooting grouse for one thing, prompted because, true to Brigade form, the code name for the attack tomorrow was Operation "Grouse". Although then I had not taken in his name, this agreeable Mick officer must have been Desmond Reid, commanding No. 4 Company, with a distinguished record already in this campaign. One of his platoon commanders came over to join us, but was not quick enough getting down and was hit in the back. He was taken away in a poor state, although I believe he was not seriously hurt.

81

Brough had arranged guards and watches, so I got into my tank, lay on the floor of the turret and went to sleep. I had heard we were going to attack tomorrow with an aerial bombardment first, but was too tired to worry.

I saw Nigel by the orchard for a brief moment. We sat down on a tree stump and talked for five minutes. He also had had an awful day. His Operator, Sergeant Banks, had been killed by a direct hit from a mortar bomb just beside him. We finished with some little parting joke, said goodnight, turned and walked away. I never saw him again.

Later Comment

"The next engagement about 11th August, was probably the most bloody of all those fought by the 3rd Battalion," wrote Colonel Joe Vandeleur in *A Soldier's Story*. Only this book and the *History of the Irish Guards* give other than the thinnest accounts of this devastating day. All the rest do less than justice to the torment and gallantry of these Micks and the few Coldstreamers. "To cut a tragic story short . . ." is the brief dismissal of this attack in *The Story of the Guards Armoured Division*, not untypical of several accounts. It could be that some felt the least said the better, but those few I occasionally meet who fought that day at Sourdevalle know otherwise. They would never hesitate to endorse Colonel Joe's opening words and his postscript: "The steadiness of the men in the Sourdevalle Battle can be very largely attributed to the particular brand of discipline of the Brigade of Guards. Although the task was hopeless, they remained steady as rocks."

Friday, 11 August. It was an uncomfortable night. We all slept in turns in the turret, while one was on watch in the commander's seat. My head felt terrible this morning, and was dazed still. When "stand-to" came about 5.30, I was glad and encouraged my crew to get breakfast as soon as it was light. George came and told me the attack was to be about 9 o'clock. Anyhow I would come to him for orders at 7.30, but it was hoped the attack would be put off.

A little later Bill told me to come with him to recce a route to the back of the village* to take my troop to fill up. John Baddeley had dumped the petrol in a field at the back. I found the way, told Brough to bring the tanks and moved over there. I had not been to the back of the village

---

* It was not really a village at all, but a jumble of small farm buildings, all devastated.

82

before, but it was the most complete devastation of burnt-out vehicles and equipment. The Unit before must have lost about fifty vehicles there and it was the most gloomy, tangled, twisted orchard I have ever been in. "Sourdevalle, a tiny village utterly eradicated by the battle which the 29th Armoured Brigade had in its vicinity" it was so described by the battalion News Letter.

I found the petrol and the tanks started to fill up. Val and Hugo had just moved up from below and were also there. I saw and talked to them, and they produced mail and papers. Amongst these I found a welcome letter from Mary, and I began to read the *Daily Express*, but felt too ill.

Then the shelling started again. I did not mind what happened now and was pinned down under a bank by this shelling for several minutes with Hugo. Val was in his tank and very condescendingly threw out a tin hat to me. My tank had filled up and gone forward through the village to our old position, so I decided to run after it before the shelling got worse. I picked my way through the tangled mass of burnt vehicles and started to run as fast as I could. Shells were landing too close, so I dived for a slit trench. There was a Mick Officer there, William Hardy, whom I did not know, and I sat talking to him about the attack for a bit, laid flat on the bottom as shells were landing only a few feet away. At the time I thought this was his name, but most probably it was William Harvey-Kelly. It was getting on for 7.30 now, so I had to get back to George for orders. I ran as fast as I could, every gun in the world seemed to be aimed at me then, straight into the Commander, who was running back to his scout-car with the R.S.M. Out of breath, he shouted a message to give to Bill.

I got back to my tank and called for my map. They handed it out, but they were very shaken. The tank had just been hit again by an H.E.

Over to George for orders. They were – 1st Welsh Guards supported by tanks of 2nd Irish were to take Hill 242 and Chênedollé on our left, and so clear our left flank. When this had been done, and not before, 3rd Irish supported by the Squadron were to advance straight forward and take the main Vire-Vassy road on the hill opposite, about 2,000 yards away. The main weight was to be on the left. In the first phase the 1st Welsh would be attacking the villages of Le Bas and Le Haut Perrier on our left rear with the Churchills of 2nd Scots Guards. They were then to take Hill 242. The 5th Coldstream were to capture Chênedollé in the next phase, and the 2nd Irish tanks to move on to cut the same main road as us. The two Grenadier battalions were to advance on our right and cut this main road at Viessoix.

Our centre line was straight down the lane which ran from Le Pavée, a company supported by two troops on either side of this road. Anthony and I were on the left under George, with No. 2 Company, Anthony Eardley Wilmot, and Val and Nigel on the right under Hugo, with No. 4 Company, Desmond Reid. Bill was to remain with Colonel Joe Vandeleur. Anthony and Nigel were to support the leading platoons, Val and I the rear ones. We could not easily get over the banks, but Anthony had a tank fitted with a "Rhino", a device like a huge fork for cutting through the banks between every field. His troop was to lead and cut a hole for the rest of us.

Later Comment

An error occurs on page 86 regarding the positions of the two Irish Guards Companies on the start line. They should have been the opposite way round. No. 4 Company was on the left of the lane up from Le Pavée farm, which was the Centreline, while No. 2 Company was on the right between the Centrelines and the next sunken lane on their right. No. 1 were to remain where they were the previous day under Peter Doyle and not move forward.

Very soon the intense fire from Spandaus on both flanks forced No. 4 Company, together with No. 2 Company's two platoons, into the sunken part of the lane on the left. A forceful account was written by No. 2 Company's Reserve Platoon Commander, Brian Wilson, who, with William Harvey Kelly, whose platoon was near the right-hand lane, were the only two officers in these two companies to come through unscathed. Brian Wilson's story, written within that year, is the best account of the infantry at Sourdevalle I have seen. I should also mention a letter from Eric Udal, the Micks' Intelligence Officer, and an account from Dennis Haydock, Co-driver in No. 3 Troop, on his experiences in the battle. But this is essentially my own account and I am loath to borrow from the recollections of others.

The attack was to start at 9 o'clock and we were to form up at 8.45 provided Hill 242 had been taken. There was still a chance of it not coming off, as, even if they took 242, there were a mass of 88s and things on the hill opposite, and we were in full view apart from mines at the bottom where there was a small stream.

However, George came back to say the attack was definitely on, so I called Brough and Caulfield and told them the plan. I was still badly

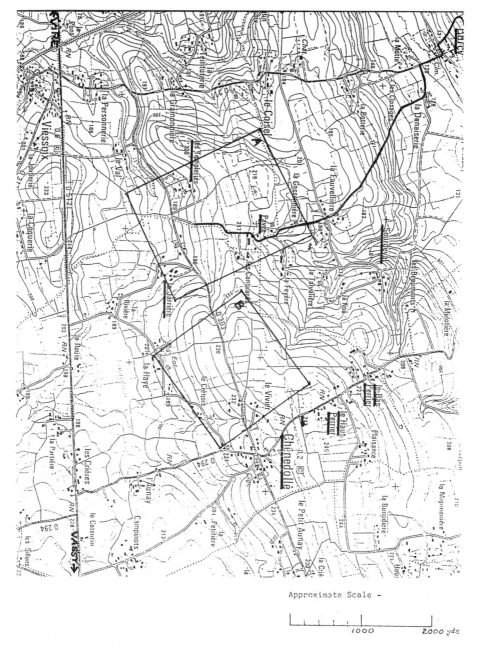

Approximate Scale –

1000   2000 yds

The areas marked 'A' and 'B' cover the two days, 10 and 11 August, when we were engaged on the notorious Sourdevalle–Perrier–Chênedallé Ridge.

dazed and I told Brough he might have to take over, so I took him forward to see the platoon commander we were supporting and to look at the ground. I saw David Ryder and we decided the only thing was for me to keep close behind him, my tank being in the centre if he wanted me.

Later Comment

The start line was the tree-covered bank right along the crest of the Sourdevalle ridge. It had been our front line all yesterday. Brough and I peered anxiously over this bank with the platoon we were supporting. With an open cornfield we had to advance down to the stream, and then rising ground on which the Germans were entrenched, we would eagerly endorse the description of it in the Irish Guards' History: "The vista in front of them was appalling. A man on this rise could see a mouse move on the forward slope opposite him."

Colonel Joe's book explains the situation we faced, vividly.

"The centre attack by the Irish Guards was considered to be the least important. Nevertheless, in the original plan we were to be supported by an air strike on the Vire-Vassy road, and the artillery support of one complete field regiment with additional smoke.

"We . . . had very good knowledge of the German positions. We had up against us elements of the 10th S.S. Panzer, 9th S.S. Panzer, and 3rd and 5th Para; all good soldiers." Eric Udal had identified these two paratroop units for the first time from the dead lying in front of our positions during the night.

"The Irish Guards had the most appalling ground to attack over. They had to advance down a forward slope under complete observation by German tanks and infantry. There were no covered approaches. The attack would have to be 'head-on'. Just before zero hour, I was informed that the air strike had been cancelled and that our artillery support had been reduced to one field battery, with no additional smoke. I protested, but was informed that we had to play our part in the Viessoix – Le Bas Perrier operation. Upon these occasions a commander must realise that the battle he is about to fight is only part of a larger operation, and that throughout the course of a campaign he must expect to be given nasty assignments. It is no good taking a parochial view."

At 8.30 I started to get ready my tank and crew and "jockey" for the start line, but my tank had been damaged and its wireless knocked out by the shell hits. So I had to change horses into Caribou. Caulfield took mine, but as he had no wireless I told him to follow behind and conform to me. Changing over tanks at this eleventh hour was a hectic business and I left all my kit behind.

By now our own artillery barrage should have been going down but I had not heard a shot yet, except enemy shells pouring overhead and bursting at the end of the village. At a quarter to nine we moved up the lane and out on to the top of the ridge on the left of the road behind Anthony. Directly the enemy heard the tanks move the shelling and mortaring increased to a barrage. Still no sign of our own artillery and no reports as to whether 242 had been captured yet.

My watch said nine, but the start line was a cloud of seething dust from mortar bombs and airburst shells. I glanced up and could actually see the shells and mortar bombs raining down, and had the extraordinary impression that the sky was darkened by them. The infantry got up to move forward but were driven back into their slit trenches; their platoon commander rallied them out again and they pushed forward down a hedge. The leading troop went over and now everything opened up in all directions. Hill 242 had certainly not been taken and 88s and machine guns were whistling and slicing across from the left. From the hill in front, too, A.P. came tearing over.

George told me to move up now as the leading infantry had disappeared. I went forward to the next hedge down the forward slope and was greeted by volleys of A.P. and mortar all round. The air was thick with deadly missiles, shrapnel and smoke. The tank in front of me went up and white smoke poured from the turret, stretcher bearers were coming back with their burdens. Slightly to my right I saw Anthony's tank moving up and down. On the right of the road progress had been better, but they had lost several tanks and all seemed confused. The infantry I was supporting had disappeared into the sunken lane that ran down on my right. I was completely exposed now to fire from the flank and George told me not to go further forward. There was no real plan except just keep behind the infantry. I had fully expected the battle to go like this.

Nigel's tank and several others had been hit on the right. Wounded and unhorsed crews were crawling and running back over the ridge now. I saw one figure race back, dive over a bank turning a somersault and running on over the ridge safe from the machine-gun fire. I recognized him as Nigel and felt very relieved.

The position after about an hour on the left was that we had made little progress, one tank was burning, another hit; the infantry had had to pull over to the right into the sunken lane, they had lost their officer and could not be moved. It was obvious we could do little with the hill on the left untaken, so Brough and I tried to move up to the left to engage it. Each time we moved we were blinded by a smokescreen and "belted" at by some A.P., so it was no good.

On the right Nigel's troop had all been knocked out, they had reached nearly the bottom of the hill. The infantry could go no further as they were being "belted" at by m.g.s and mortars from a farm on the left called La Jarrière.

Later Comment

From my position less than a hundred yards to the left of the lane it was impossible to know what was going on beyond the hedge immediately to my right. I could only guess from occasional calls over the '19' set which was 'netted' into the infantry '18' set for the battle. I could see virtually nothing through the hedges, despite the Tank Commander's line of sight from a Sherman being over nine feet above the ground. Many years elapsed before I learned that none of our infantry reached the bottom of the hill or anywhere near. Neither of course did Nigel's tanks nor anyone else's. When his tank was hit it was about the position shewn in the aerial photograph a hundred yards forward of the start line. C.S.M. Larkin was found next day not far ahead of one of our own knocked-out tanks.

It was fortunate indeed for No. 2 Troop that we were ordered by George not to go further forward through the next bank to attack the fortified buildings at La Jarrière. An account by a French farmer, M. Bertrand, from Le Perrier, describes La Jarrière as literally stuffed with mines and that a dozen hectares around it remained a wasteland for a long time because of the danger from mines. He tells movingly of a number of tragedies that occurred to the families from the area when they returned to their homes a week or so later stunned by the desolation to them. Jean Brissot, *The Charge of the Bull*.

The shelling was still heavy. It did not worry us in the tanks; however, the A.P. shots were finding their marks. I had been hit, but luckily the shot only skimmed the near front of the tank and did not come through, otherwise I seemed to be leading a charmed life, as we could not have been a better target. I kept my troop moving up and down firing both our Browning m.g.s and 75 H.E. as hard as we could at the hedges and hill in front. If we had not kept shifting about all the time we should have been "brewing up". Each time we finished a belt, I backed my tank out a bit into better cover, reloaded and came up again. Brough and Caulfield were doing the same. We poured m.g. and shells into La Jarrière. One shell successfully settled with a Spandau in a hedge near La Jarrière. One of my shells hit a tree just in front, went off and again concussed me slightly.

My crew were doing splendidly. Inside the air was thick with fumes and the floor piled high with empty shell cases and boxes; I was kept busy throwing these out as hard as I could while the Operator, Corporal Wilson, was slaving away getting the rounds out of the various magazines and Corporal Finch, the Co-driver, was handing rounds through the turret mesh from the front bin; soon it was exhausted. Corporal Newton and Bailey W., the Driver and Gunner, did their jobs without a word, as they always had done in training, very well indeed. I spotted at last the pencilled flash of an anti-tank gun firing on the hill opposite 2500 yards away so pulled my tanks back and set about doing an H.E. shoot on it. Endless training in bracketing in Yorkshire produced the right result and after a dozen rounds of 'gunfire' the gun did not open up again. It was the only anti-tank gun I actually saw fire, but there must have been many on that hill.

It was about 12 o'clock. Anthony had been wounded when a mortar bomb actually landed on the edge of the cupola of his turret, burst and killed his gunner below. Val tried to move round to the right flank, had got into a comfortable position but had himself been hit by shrapnel in the head and gone back. He had attempted to get down the little sunken lane on the extreme right, we found yesterday, and had been wounded by splinters flying off inside the tank from an 88 hit, I was later told.

The infantry on the right had lost two-thirds of their men, while the left-hand company had lost all its officers and were still in the lane. George went down it in his tank and tried to help them move on, but without any officers and despite great gallantry against all the m.g. fire from La Jarrière on their left, they could not push on more than a few yards. On the right Willy Harvey-Kelly, the only officer left, was holding on, but had too few men left.

Things were now quietening down a bit. I was not doing much good where I was and ammo was running short. Bill ordered me off the forward slope about four o'clock, so I pulled back to an orchard on my left. I had reversed back when I found some frantic little men shouting and waving at me. Eventually I discovered their trouble, I had reversed on to the muzzle of their anti-tank gun hidden in a hedge. Naturally the poor men were indignant. By now 242 and the Perrier ridge must have been cleared by the Welsh Guards after a slow and costly battle, and the 5th Coldstream were fighting their way into Chênedollé. On our right the Grenadiers were able to reach the Vassy road at Viessoix with a troop of tanks and some infantry without quite so much trouble. They were holding on tenuously.

My tank had been hit again by an H.E. and several near misses and I was dazed and feeling not too good. I got out of my tank and, having left everything to Brough, walked around as I did not think much more could happen. I found the infantry Company Commander, Feathers, was still very anxious about an attack coming down from 242, so I put my troop into the orchard facing left. X Company had been held back from the battle on the ridge.

I was looking for George or Bill to see what was going on. No. 3 Squadron had been brought up behind the village when we had run into trouble and were sitting there. Tony Priestly, I saw, who commanded No. 3. I climbed on his tank and told him what had happened. I went into the orchard where the Mick Battalion H.Q. was and there found Bill's tank.

Sergeant Holmes, his Operator, said he was at an 'O' Group. He told me Nigel had been killed. This was a great shock as I was almost certain I had seen him running back.

It was Corporal Bastone, Nigel's gunner, I must have seen, for he escaped miraculously from the turret unhurt. When I climbed aboard Bill's tank, I found Guardsman Looker, his gunner, chalking up a tally of the poor squadron's casualties on the gunshield. As far as I could make out we had only seven or eight tanks left out of the entire nineteen. Apart from Bill, Hugo, George and the Sergeant Major's tanks from Squadron H.Q., my three and Sergeant Shipley's, there appeared none left in action. No one can tell why my three were not destroyed on that slope. To survive it was essential to keep moving. I can only hope that the stuff we poured into the strongpoint of La Jarrière from above managed to draw off a little of the enemy fire from our gallant friends.

Bastone was exceedingly lucky at Sourdevalle. On the first evening he was unhurt when as Gunner in George Dawnay's tank they were hit on the gun by a Panther or an 88. Because Sergeant Banks had been killed that evening Nigel Pratt's crew was one short, and the Sergeant-Major sent Bastone to replace him as Gunner in that tank for the next day. When Nigel's tank was hit by an 88 right through the turret from the left, Bastone alone again escaped from the turret unhurt. The Driver and Co-driver were trapped below and he climbed underneath the tank and released them both unhurt through the escape-hatch. Hence the extraordinary coincidence that occurred over 40 years later.

At the 40th Commemoration of the Liberation of Enschede, Holland, three of those invited by the Town were former Guardsmen Hurworth, Sergeant Bastone, and myself, all present there at the battle for the bridge.

When Bastone told the story of his two escapes at Sourdevalle, it turned out Hurworth was the driver of Nigel's tank who was one of those released by him. Until then they never knew whom the other was.

Some of No. 3 Squadron's tanks had moved up to the ridge and I looked unsuccessfully for Ian's tank to tell him about Nigel. They were great friends. I found John Sutton in his tank and, afterwards, he said he was very surprised to see me wandering about quite oblivious of the shells landing all around. I remember going to the R.A.P. to find out who was there and finding it a tragic scene, dozens of people lying in a long shallow ditch sloping down to the road. The doctor and his assistant were working frantically. Nigel Bingham, Intelligence Officer, was organizing the ambulances. Across the road was a long line of still figures laid out on the grass.

I ran into Bill at last. Seeing my state he put me straight in a scout-car and sent me back. I was taken to the Battalion R.A.P. at the bottom of the hill and Johnny Thompson gave me some very refreshing tea and a wash. Johnny Gull asked me what had happened to the knocked-out tanks and where they lay, but I don't think I could tell him much. Back to 'F.2.' echelon, where John Baddeley gave me water to wash, an enormous meal, and I went fast asleep. I was woken up later that evening and sent to 'B' echelon, about five miles back. There I found Henry Allsopp who was 'L.O.B.' and Kershaw who gave me some clean clothes, a wash and an excellent dinner. I went straight to bed and slept till well after ten next morning.

Soon after I left, the squadron, devoid of any troop leaders with only eight tanks, and the infantry having lost over a hundred men, it was decided to withdraw. Under smoke from the gunners the tanks and infantry came back. No. 3 took over the hill for the rest of the day and the Household Cavalry later from the Micks. In the next day or so it was decided to pull the division out.

The Germans were now trying to withdraw from the pocket and the battle rolled away eastwards. It was high time too, as it had been some of the fiercest fighting of the campaign. All the battalions in the division were exhausted and weak with losses.

Our own attack at Sourdevalle in appearance was a complete waste and achieved nothing, except perhaps to keep the enemy off someone else and from withdrawing from the pocket. Why we attacked without artillery or with Hill 242 untaken was a matter for the higher command to decide, but to us it seemed the greatest error. It was a terrible and tragic morning, and at the end had turned into a real medieval battle-field with dead strewn everywhere, amidst burning tanks, empty shell cases, abandoned rifles, equipment and field dressings; and refuse of modern war.

I shall never forget Friday August 11th, 1944.

Later Comment

Of the battle Colonel Joe wrote, "We attacked 'two-up' and immediately our two leading companies came under devastating fire and suffered seventy per cent casualties. . . . The German guns and tanks on the far slope could not miss the Coldstream tanks as soon as they appeared over the crest, and promptly destroyed them. The companies pressed on . . . advancing steadily through the fire and nothing could be done to support them because the bulk of the brigade's fire power had been retained for the attack on Chênedollé. . . . All the officers but one were killed, including the gallant Anthony Eardley-Wilmot, who had obtained the Military Cross at Cagny, and Lord Edward Fitzmaurice. The only officer to survive was Desmond Reid, who was badly wounded by a mortar bomb. Company Sergeant-Major Larkin's body was found on top of a German Spandau post. The Guardsmen fought like fiends, but to no avail. Luckily I had not committed the two reserve companies, and I decided to call the battle off."

Was this and the lives it cost really to no avail? We could not be told the main purpose of these attacks were not simply to gain ground. In effect the divisions of 8 Corps had played a significant part in the great tactical encirclement of the German 7th Army. Since the American breakout at Avranches and the enemy's ill-judged counter-attack at Mortain on August 9th, this major movement was rapidly taking shape. Long afterwards Monty's biographer, Nigel Hamilton, reveals this in a most interesting letter written that day by the C. in C. to the C.I.G.S., Field Marshal Sir Alan Brooke.

"9.8.44.

The Enemy attack at Mortain was just what we wanted. It was held without difficulty. I put the 2nd. T.A.F. (Tactical Air Force) on to it, as well as the 9th Air Force, and all the pilots all had a great day. They claimed 120 'flamers', but I doubt that.

"On the left the Canadian attack is aimed at Falaise. I have ordered them to take that place securely, and from it to operate southwards towards Argentan and westwards towards Condé.

"8 Corps, the right wing of Second Army, is moving on Tinchebray today, but I do not expect this advance to progress far. Its main task is to hold the enemy to his ground.

"The right wing of 12 (U.S.) Army Group, 15 U.S. Corps, is at Le Mans, where it will secure a bridgehead. I have ordered it then to operate northwards to Alençon; this is a very important thrust.

"I am aiming at closing in behind the Germans. The Canadians should be able to fight their way to Falaise, but they will not have the easy time they fancied, but they should get there; at present their forward movement is not making rapid progress. The Germans will fight hard for Falaise I think. I don't think the Americans will have any difficulty in getting to Alençon, as there is nothing there to oppose them.

"If we can get to Falaise, and can also hold Alençon strongly, we should then be able to close the gap in between – and that would be very excellent.

"But the Germans will fight hard; it is good defence country and we must not expect things to go too rapidly. . . ."

As in 'Goodwood', and now on the northern shoulder of the envelopment closing round the Falaise Pocket, the British Infantry and armour *were holding the enemy S.S. Panzer Divisions to their ground*, a crucial factor in the overwhelming Allied victory in Normandy, about to reach the climax.

Saturday, 12 August. We now start another pause between campaigns. We were in a pleasant orchard with a nice farmer. Henry and I were living in a tent. Billy Denbigh was commanding the Echelon. I woke up feeling much better, though with a good deal of headache.

I was beginning to remember what had happened and only then I realized that Nigel was dead. This upset me. Nigel was a great friend. I had known him well since he joined the battalion, especially the days

93

at Brighton, the short leave we took at the Spread Eagle, Midhurst, and over in France. Always quiet, sensible and reassuring, with a great sense of humour, we could express our feelings to one another which was a great help in war. He was very brave over here and I admired him for it, as I knew how frightened I was at times. His tank was destroyed when an 88 from Chênedollé went right through the turret. To me, and I know Ian, there could be no one else quite to fill his place. Killed in action is the epitaph most worthy of him. I have a strong feeling he had some foreboding before the battle.

In action where one sees so many of one's friends being killed and wounded, it seems to become a natural thing and one treats it with calm indifference, knowing I suppose one is so close to it oneself. But for those at home a long way away, the shock is always much worse. As time went on, especially after Nigel had been killed, I began to fear death much less, if at all. The fear of mutilation, of living one's life crippled and helpless, was to all of us the worst.

The next three days we spent in that orchard at Le Graverie, not far from Le Beny Bocage. They were peaceful and pleasant. Breakfast in bed, get up at half past ten, coffee at eleven! Entertain officers for lunch and sleep all afternoon followed by a tremendous dinner.

The Commander came over to see me one day to find out what had happened at Sourdevalle. He was extremely agreeable and told me I must rest for as long as I could. Michael Fox from 'A' echelon nearby came several times a day and cheered us up, though he had just lost a great friend of his, Luke Lillingston, in the Leicester Yeomanry, who was Bill Harrington's stepfather. I found Michael and Henry most charming these few days. We had a great dinner party one night, ending up with the farmer giving us some Calvados, 'gut-rot' so strong that a small drop sent everyone 'off net'.

I went to Brigade to dine with Dermot and John Yerburgh. A non-abstemious dinner, as Brigadier Norman Gwatkin was entertaining freely with champagne. Some Americans came and bombed the Grenadiers next door. This caused rather a stir and much anger, with shouts for yellow smoke.

We were surprised one morning when we were visited by a crowd of officers from the battalion. Later we learnt that the Commander had burnt his tongue at breakfast so everyone had fled the wrath. It was warm and pleasant in that orchard and we were sorry to leave. The farmer killed the fatted cock for us and we had a great feast.

The pocket the German 7th Army had been caught in was being rapidly sealed off. With only a narrow gap remaining between Falaise and Argentan, through which the enemy could withdraw, the Canadians were pressing down from the north to join up with the Americans. Swarms of heavy bombers had passed over us going in this direction, though several hundred tons in one Fortress raid had fallen on the Canadian lines ten miles from their target.

On the 17th I was sent to 8th Corps Rest-Camp at St Aubin-sur-Mer north of Caen. I did not want to return to the squadron yet as I was told it had changed so much. Val and Anthony were in hospital at Bayeux, the former being sent back to England soon. The two days at St Aubin were a great change. I wrote letters, bathed and slept. I started writing this. Oliver Heywood arrived and we had a leisurely day on the beach.

I had a letter from Peter Heneage, a school friend, who said he had been wounded in the leg and was now in England, but as it was not bad I expect he was pleased to be back. At the Rest-Camp I was told that Harry Graham-Vivian had also been wounded quite badly, I'm afraid. I learnt that Kevin Maguire who shared my room at Sandhurst had been killed in his tank during the last battle. I felt very sorry. So too, alas, had Hugh Dormer, a remarkable individual with a D.S.O. already after his name as a Subaltern, as well as other good friends in the 2nd Armoured Irish Guards with whom we had been so much.* I learnt all this from John Gorman who I had a tent with, the Mick who settled scores with the Tiger at Caen by his famous order 'Charge and Ram'.

Saturday, 19 August. In the afternoon I left St Aubin to go back to the battalion, still resting at Le Grand Bonfait in the Vire area. It was a long drive in a three-tonner with the R.S.M. as well, through Caen and Villers-Bocage, both a pile of rubble. We arrived at 32 Brigade H.Q. to find nothing waiting for us, typical 1st Battalion never to provide transport when wanted. We managed to get them on the field telephone and at last a truck came. While waiting at Point 176 the R.S.M. and I walked over and found David Martyn's grave which was close by.

Late that evening I got back and slept under the mess tarpaulin.

---

* We had shared the Officers' Mess at Warminster Barracks in 1942 with the 2nd Irish and 1st Grenadiers and had got to know some of them well.

Sunday, 20 August. For me this was a depressing day. The squadron was no longer the same. Bill and George were still there, Hugo had left and was ill in hospital at Bayeux, and I was the only Troop Leader left. The men were mostly new and changed. The old No. 2 had died on the ridge at Sourdevalle.

I spent the morning reorganizing my troop. Three young officers had come and one of them had taken my troop over while I was away and created havoc. On top of this one of my sergeants was waiting a Court Martial for being found drunk on Calvados the night after Sourdevalle. Everybody seemed determined to have him broken to a Guardsman, especially the Commanding Officer. I was equally determined he should not be.

I kept my own and Brough's crew the same. Caulfield I put into my new 17-pounder 'Cougar IV', and the other tank 'Caribou' I gave to Sergeant Newton. Previously he had never commanded a tank, only driven it. Newly promoted after his fine job driving me in the battle, I thought he would do it very well.

Emmerson was a great loss, an extremely good tank commander, always using his initiative but was inclined to rush headlong in at times. Both he and his crew were irreplaceable as lesser material was coming up as reinforcements. Sergeant Arnold had died in hospital on August 11th, I was told, another sad loss.* Emmerson was an extremely nice man and always good company. His communist ideas led us to have untold arguments which I always enjoyed. But he could be depended upon to take a great interest in any job he had to do and I was lucky to have him.

I had my four tanks organized now. It really was a good crowd and had fallen little, if any, in standard. In this I was lucky. All the other troops in the squadron had been messed about completely. There was still very much a No. 2 Troop spirit, which pleased me a lot.

Dinner with Ian and John Sutton in No. 3 and saw Reggie

---

* All wounded were evacuated quickly to the General Hospital outside Bayeux. During the ceremonies to commemorate the landings in Normandy on the fortieth anniversary, before the wreath-laying by H.M. The Queen and the President of France in the British Military Cemetery, Bayeux, I found the graves of many Guardsmen who had died following this battle. Among them was that of my former gunner, Lance Sergeant S. Arnold, aged 23.

Longueville there too, who was now in the 4th Battalion. I was pleased to find some friends again. This evening I had a long talk to Bill and he seemed upset too about the squadron. Sourdevalle must have been very disappointing for him.

Monday, 21 August. George and I went up to Sourdevalle in a scout-car and walked over the battlefield. 'Sod-valley' they called it. Still a very ugly sight. In one field there were no less than ninety graves. Nigel's tank had been recovered some days later and taken back, and he was buried at St Charles de Percy.

The area at the bottom was mined, so we could not look for the Panther or the 88 I had knocked out. Bill had seen the Panther and said he thought it was mine. On to the enemy hill opposite, and we could see we never stood a chance. He must have had a perfect view of all our movements, an anti-tank gunner's dream.

I drove back through the other battlefields of Vassy and Estry. All bore signs where the division had fought fiercely and at great cost.

We had an amusing dinner party this evening, Dickie Gooch, "the officer with no neck" Nigel used to call him, George, Nico Collin and Ian. Murray St Clair and Henry came along later. We laughed a lot.

It fell to me as Gunnery officer to take all the ammo trucks back to Bayeux this evening to change it over. An all-night job, but the Commander said I wasn't to go; to me most satisfactory, to John Sutton, sent instead, it was not.

Tuesday, 22 August. Wet and miserable day. Stayed in all the time under my shelter, which Wicking and Kershaw had constructed, and read. In fact both George and I were lying on our beds when the Major-General commanding Brigade of Guards, General Budget Loyd, with retinue of Brigadiers and Generals behind, appeared round the corner. Nightmares! We were badly caught out, but managed to creep round behind without being seen. George I am afraid hid. I was spotted by Colonel Ririd and beckoned up to the General to explain the battle at Sourdevalle, followed by grunts that only such great men produce.

General Allan Adair who was behind said that things were really going well and that General 'Boy' Browning had told him there were still four Airborne divisions ready to drop, probably on the Pas-de-Calais area to wipe out the flying bombs.

By now what had happened was this. The Americans had completely over-run Brittany except for Brest and a few pockets. They had swept round, and with the Canadians, Poles and French, had closed the pocket between Argentan and Falaise. Nearly fifty thousand Germans had been bottled up and taken prisoner, and many more dead. The R.A.F. had done tremendous slaughter there. The Germans were falling back over the Seine, but as they had no real bridges none of their equipment was across.

The Americans and ourselves had bridgeheads already across the Seine, north and south of Paris. The South of France had been invaded by the Americans and French and all was going well. Marseilles and Toulon were in our hands. Risings of the Maquis were rumoured all over France.

The Division and the 11th Armoured had been left out of mopping up the pocket in order to have a badly needed rest and refit.

But the real great news, though we had been expecting it for several days, was that Paris was free. Liberated by her own people. The Americans had been halted outside Versailles and the French people themselves, followed by the French Armoured division, had risen and driven out the invader. A great day for France, all day long the Marseillaise was played on the wireless. This was 25 August.

Ian and I planned to go for a tour in Brittany today, but had to put it off till tomorrow. Michael Hamilton came to dinner with me, a pleasant change from the others in No. 2.

Our sergeant was due to be court-martialled tomorrow and so I set about trying to get him off and persuade Bill, who was not entirely for him being court-martialled either, but had to be loyal to the Commander, to give evidence and to try and get him off. It was a ridiculous charge really. There were few people who wouldn't have had a lot to drink after coming out of a battle like that, but he was caught in the open in a bad way. At this stage of the war good tank commanders were few and far between.

I had done all I could and was glad I should be miles away when it happened.

Wednesday, 23 August. Ian and I set sail early to go to Mont St Michel. Disappointed at first when we could only find an old Ford 15 cwt truck to go in, it turned out to be a great machine and went like the wind. We went through Vire and raced along in the American sector out of the awful Bocage country, wider spaces, less wooded, and above all less scarred by war. Through Avranches, scene of the great breakthrough, we went south to Mont St Michel. The truck sped along at a tremendous rate, nearly sixty-eight at one moment. We picked up some American officers and girls on the way to the Mount and stopped at the entrance to the causeway and took a look. Much bigger of course than St Michael's Mount at home, it is a fine sight. The Yanks were thrilled and insisted on taking a picture. Complete tourists we were determined to be and we were.

We walked into the walls, up the narrow street, now empty of flashy tourists in colourful gay clothes, and climbed to the Abbey on top. Met Henry and John Rodney there. A lovely hot morning, it was a really pleasant view from the top of the walls as we looked down at the calm sea beneath.

We had lunch in a small restaurant below, now full of American 'tourists' arriving. We ordered an omelette each, but it was so good we ordered another, accompanied by rather mediocre Vin Blanc. I must say the French black bread we were given is very unpleasant, all they have had poor people for years. A wonderful little old man, his face lined with character, made us laugh a lot as he cut slice upon slice of bread very slowly and deliberately.

As the car went so well and the roads were totally empty, we decided to push on to Rennes, some forty miles south. Ian refused to drive, so I left him to map read. We drove, no, raced, on south over some pleasant country and everywhere the people seemed pleased to see us. They handed out eggs and bottles of cider all the way. One village had a streamer across the road saying "Thank you", which I thought was rather nice

In Rennes we parked in the Grand Place, petrified of losing the truck. We could not immobilize it and the Maquis would have pinched it like a shot. We walked around the shops and the main street, a great change to be civilized for once and took an iced beer in an estaminet. Then we ordered dinner in the Faisan D'or, but, as we had an hour to wait, drove out of the town to a village where there was a great Château that once belonged to the Marquis de Châteaugiron. We marched in to find a talkative but pleasant Frenchman who showed us round. A dull inside, it had been used by the Germans as a barracks, and he showed us the cells where they locked French civilians for small offences. Our French was again heavily taxed especially in explaining the Coldstream Guards were not the Police. We parted with great handshaking and drove back to Rennes for dinner. On the way we were stopped by the Maquis to whom we gave some petrol. We were the first English they had seen since 1940 and they were delighted, more handshaking, wine, and 'Vive' everyone, followed.

After a rather expensive though reasonable dinner we left the Golden Pheasant to drive the odd eighty or ninety miles. It was a lovely evening and I enjoyed that drive a lot. We went very fast to arrive as it began to get dark about half past nine. It was the greatest fun that day, and Ian was excellent company. I only hope we can do it again someday soon, perhaps in Germany; who knows?

Thursday, 24 August. By now we had been in the area long enough, the flies were getting thick and people were beginning to feel ill, a lot of us had the usual complaint. Besides we were some two hundred miles behind the front line. We moved this afternoon to a field at La Bazoque, north-east of Flers under the shadow of the hill Mont Cerisi. A dusty route and we twisted and turned all over the place. He must have been a brilliant Staff Officer who worked that out.

Friday, 25 August. Nothing much today, except I got my tanks well maintained and cleaned up. My troop were settling down quite well. Our defaulter had been reprimanded only after our efforts, so all was well. Two officers went off to the Falaise Gap to find some equipment and came back with a German staff car, a frightful car but they were pleased by it. The destruction must have been terrific and they were impressed by what they saw.

Next day, as part of a wide-scale clean-up operation, I spent a morning with the troop searching for any enemy equipment in an area where there obviously wasn't any. We had a long exhausting walk with no results. I did come across a Château and on going inside found it was fully furnished and lived in. On enquiring I learnt until a few days ago a German General lived in it. A British 'espion' had lived there too all the time and had also left only a few days ago. No wonder it looked so well cared for inside, even the lawns were mown.

Later Comment

Over thirty years later I found this house again completely by accident, when we were following a 'route touristique' near Condé sur Noireau. We came upon the house standing among beautiful trees beside a stream after crossing a small iron bridge where I had stood on with my men looking at this lovely spot called Cahan all those years ago.

On the way back through Condé I saw several women with heads shaved for being collaborators. A good way of branding them and they looked miserable.

Sunday, 27 August. In the afternoon the new tanks had to be 'shot in'. As Gunnery Officer I had to officiate at the back of Mont Cerisi, but when a 17-pounder went off close by, my head began to sing and ache again. However, I kept quiet about it. I haven't yet recovered from last time. The hill, embraced by a dense wood curved down one side, belonged with the Château to an Englishman who used to shoot there. Ian met the gamekeeper when fishing the stream.

I found the expected orders for a move being given when I came back. We collected maps and found out what was to happen.

The present front line was more or less the Seine where we had two or three bridgeheads. South of Paris the Americans were reported over the Marne. We were now to start an advance from the Seine with the Americans on our right directed towards Belgium. But as we were still miles behind, the division was to move up to the Seine tomorrow by tank transporter.

Bill came back in the evening and had been to the Falaise Gap. He said the destruction was terrific, he had seen "thousands of destroyed trucks, some five hundred guns and fifty tanks, but only a few dead Germans". His, I know, was a conservative statement too.

I went and had a drink with Ian and John in No. 3 this evening. Earlier Oliver Heywood told me he was to become Adjutant as George Dawnay had been long enough. Oliver will do it very well. Bill was now going off with Colonel Ririd to stay two days at Mont St Michel, as the Commander badly needed a rest. George would take the squadron on the move to the Seine.

This was now the start of the wild rush to Holland. Some people described it as the greatest advance in our history, but whatever it was I shall never see anything like it again.

Monday, 28 August. The battalion moved out this morning to Flers where it embarked on tank transporters to go to the Seine. George was acting Squadron Leader and with Hugo ill I had to go forward to recce the next squadron area. Thankful that I shouldn't have to travel by transporter, I set off in the scout-car following Henry Allsopp, acting Second in Command of the battalion. Through Flers we drove, then east to Argentan to the meeting point at Crulai just south of L'Aigle. All the way the road was thick with transport going east, everybody was rushing east and we were a long way behind. We were saying that the poor old Guards Armoured Division would never catch up until the peace march into Berlin.

Argentan was badly knocked about, though I've seen worse, but the road was strewn all the way with hundreds of burnt-out German vehicles caught by the R.A.F. in the Argentan Gap. An unbelievable sight as Bill had told me yesterday. The smell of putrefaction was horrible, but German prisoners were, I'm glad to say, made to clear it up. The French had stolen all the German horses from their transport and were riding them away. German policy of relying on horse transport for their rear supplies the whole war may have been an economical success earlier on during their great victories, but in defeat where mobility was the keyword they became a pitiful sight, too often to end only in merciless execution.

We had lunch at the meeting point. Henry scrounged a welcome egg each and we sat there for a peaceful afternoon. Later we recced an area for the squadrons, then retired to a school near Verneuil to sleep. This was the Ecole de Roche, France's only attempt to copy an English public school; a luxurious school with swimming baths and squash courts but the Germans had used the back as a prisoner of war camp for British prisoners after Dieppe. The R.A.F. had bombed the camp heavily and I'm afraid had killed a number of the prisoners. The few remaining staff of the school which had kept going until 'D' day were charming and took us in. Being schoolmasters they could talk English and talked a lot, very interestingly about life during the occupation. By way of keeping the Germans out they displayed a notice at the gate, "achtung, dangerous bomb."

Dickie Gooch now arrived. He had taken over command of the battalion from Colonel Ririd who was not at all well. We learnt that the battalion were to remain on their transporters all night and would halt on the road ready to go on next day. They were not expected until four o'clock and I had to find them and give a message to George, in command of the column. Henry, Miles Bodley and I slept in the school.

102

Miles persuaded me reluctantly to have a very cold shower, he was horribly spartan. However, it was the last bath for three weeks.

Tuesday, 29 August. Up at four and searched the countryside for miles down the road in pouring rain for the transporters. The R.A.S.C. Captain in charge of the transporter company insisted on parking all the transporters down the wrong road which resulted in taking about three hours turning them round next morning. I did my best to persuade him not to. All he could say was it was a great honour to carry the 1st Battalion as he remembered carrying it in buses in 1940 at Yeovil, a feat I did not a bit want to hear at that hour, however kindly meant.

I found George and gave my message. He looked wretched sleeping on the Operator's seat of his tank. They must all have had a very uncomfortable night. Raced back in the rain, took my boots off and slept until my driver produced some breakfast. The room had by that time been turned into the Intelligence Office and was covered in maps.

The Battalion was to move on towards the Seine, disembark from the transporters after about seventy miles, cross that evening and harbour the other side. Off in the scout-cars to find a harbour once again to a village, Boisset-Les-Prèvanches, to meet the brigade harbourers. Raining hard, so Henry, Miles and I set up our cookers for lunch in the station waiting room. It became rather a party as all the other guides turned up. The Stationmaster, splendid in a brass pillbox cap, arrived and looked very businesslike with an enormous watch. What his present job was no one could tell. No trains had run or were likely to run for weeks, and there was only one engine in the station evidently caught by canon fire from aircraft.

We all climbed into the R.S.M.'s scout-car with Jeff Darell and drove off to the Seine. A long and slow drive as all traffic was pouring over the two bridges. At one point there was a Brigadier standing in the middle of the road holding up everything either way. Simply furious; for some reason nobody else had a right to be on the road except his Brigade, so we made a detour round.

It was a great moment when we eventually crossed the Seine at Vernon, the beginning of the great advance to Holland. I had a feeling of pride and achievement as we rattled over that pontoon bridge into North-Eastern France. Just as we reached the other side a Brigadier came up to us and said, "Are you the advance party of Guards Armoured? Thank God you've come at last." I was impressed by the high banks and clear stream of the river, rather like the Thames at Cliveden and as wide. The R.E. had done well to make three bridges across.

We found our area a few miles on near a village called Harricourt, the front line that morning. But now that 11th Armoured had pushed on nearly to Beauvais we were still some way behind. I walked about and found a wood for the squadron to park the night and returned to Henry and Miles for supper. All our food pooled, we produced a terrific supper complete with eggs. The R.S.M.'s scout-car had accumulated more food than the Q.M.'s truck I think, and I was so full I didn't want to eat again for ages.

We sat and waited for the tanks to come. The Grens arrived about nine p.m. It then started to rain and we moved up to a crossroads and sat in the rain waiting. A bloody night, the squadron did not arrive until nearly six in the morning, so we talked and swam about all night. I got our last tank in about dawn, spread my blanket down again and went to sleep. The tanks had left their transporters and done the last twenty-six miles on their tracks.

Wednesday, 30 August. After an hour's sleep I was woken to collect maps and codes from Nigel Bingham, our Intelligence Officer, and angry when I squelched round in the mud to find Nigel was not ready for another hour. I was in poor form. My inside was terrible, I think through overeating during the last few days. I met Michael Hamilton, washed and shaved and as fresh as a new pin, which made me feel worse. Snatched a small breakfast and started handing out the maps to the three troop leaders. We had enough maps to reach Moscow, but in two days we had run over them all. Brough had been looking after my troop, so I knew everything was quite all right when I transferred my kit back into 'Cheetah' from the scout-car.

About midday the Battalion, leading the Brigade, moved out to advance to south of Beauvais. 30 Corps consisting of ourselves, the 11th Armoured and 43 and 50 Infantry Divisions, was going to make the breakthrough, with the American 1st Army on our right. Our Corps Commander is to be General Horrocks. At the moment the 11th were ahead at Gisors, halfway to Beauvais. They were to be on the left, we on the right centre-line. The Division was now at last in regimental groups, 1st and 5th C.G., 1st and 2nd G.G., 2nd and 3rd I.G. and 1st and 2nd W.G. We ought to have been grouped like this from the early days as it worked so well.

The first day the Coldstream Group led. As far as Gisors the road had been liberated by the 11th so it was just a drive with the armour leading, led by Basil Sparrow's recce tanks. The route followed a river line to Dangu then to Gisors where the Battalion turned east to Chaumont-en-Vexin; lovely country to drive through with rolling hills on either side of the valley and covered with green woods with an occasional château dominating the scene in Versailles style. The nicest part of France we had seen yet. All the way along we were met by the cheering, overjoyed French. I shall not attempt to describe the welcome until later on but it was all the same at every village and house. Through Gisors, where we were met by an enormous crowd and on we went to Chaumont, the first town the Battalion liberated. There was no opposition so we just drove straight through. Flags and banners were already strung out and we were pelted with fruit and flowers.

Here we ran into some American armour who crossed our road and were advancing just on our right. They looked good and were quick at deploying. An amusing little incident happened just now. Colonel Dickie said he heard a shot come over him and ordered No. 1 Squadron to deploy round a wood. Henry Alsopp also came up and said he had heard a shot whizz overhead. Oliver confessed to me afterwards that it was he who let off a couple of shots while loading his Browning inside the Commander's tank. Although there were a number of enemy frequently being reported, no real shots were fired.

Basil Sparrow, commanding our Recce Troop, came up on the air to say he had just been onto the next village of Beaumont-les-Nonains by civilian telephone who said that 200 Boches were pulling out. It was the last thing one would have thought one could do, and it showed how cooperative the French were.

I was sent with my Troop to 'hook left' round a village with the attractive name of Le Mesnil Theribus. I much enjoyed that little patrol in and out of houses and farmyards, dismounted at every corner, revolver at the port, to see if any anti-tank guns were lurking about, and disappointed not to run into anybody.

We laagered that evening just south of Auneuil near Jouy-le-Grange after covering thirty-six miles off the speedometer. An enormous laager, all the attached gunners and R.E.s came in to seek our protection for the night.

Bill had turned up driving from Mont St Michel in two days, and was

105

now Second in Command of the Battalion. George Dawnay became our Squadron Leader and Jeff Darell had come over to be Second in Command to us.

Thursday, 31 August. It was to be a short night and little sleep. Reveille about 2.30, ready to move about 3.00. A great mistake though, for we pulled down to the gateway and waited until dawn before the Grenadier and Mick Groups and the last vehicle of brigade had passed us, since we were in reserve today.

The day's objective was to cross the Somme south of Amiens, towards Albert, while the 11th were to take Amiens. We had to bypass Auneuil as it was still held, and so led on to Beauvais where the welcome was as always tumultuous. We raced along through Beauvais to Breteuil towards the Somme. It was a wonderful day. I was lucky to be leading the Battalion and set a pretty good pace. At one moment Colonel Dickie complained the pace was too slow so I told my driver to go all out. We charged madly down all the hills at a tremendous speed, but 'Cheetah' was only running on four 'banks' of the engine so crawled up hill. This was a saving breather and allowed the tanks behind to catch up.

Later Comment

Compared with British-built tanks or with the Panther, Shermans were relative sluggards. The Sherman V we had, with its Chrysler engine made up of five banks of six cylinders each bolted together, was officially capable of 23 m.p.h. maximum speed on the level road. Cromwells could go twice that speed, and a Panther was said to go 30 m.p.h. One can assume that in this sort of advance in moderate hills our average pace was not great.

At every house or cottage and crossroads was a small band of women and children to cheer and greet us. All along were Maquis armed with any sort of gun and shotgun rounding up the odd Germans about. Outside Beauvais we passed our first flying bomb site, impossible to make out what was what. Still we raced on, regardless of bogie-wheels and tracks. One of my tanks sheared off all the nuts on one side of the sprocket but I decided to keep it going, much to the anger of Johnny Gull. In front the Grenadiers had practically no opposition until the Somme, except shooting up an occasional convoy. The Recce Welsh and 'Galloping Grocers' were well out in front shooting up Germans struggling vainly to escape.

It was another day of lovely country. The Cathedral looked very fine catching the sun as we came down the hill into the town. The last time was in 1938 when we passed through Beauvais in the Ford coming back from Paris.* Towards the Somme we were back in the battlefields of the last war. Few trees were standing and the houses all new. We passed through Villers Bretonneux, a famous name for the Australians. One saw the great cemeteries to remind one that what we were doing now in one afternoon cost a quarter of a million lives and nearly three years last time. If only they could have had the armour of today, their enormous sacrifice and our troubles would have been infinitely less severe and the world so different.

What happened on the river was confusing but the Grenadiers and Irish had crossed with a little skirmishing and the Grenadiers lost two tanks. At first we raced up and down trying to find a bridge to take our weight and eventually crossed at the villages of Fouilloy and Corbie. I was proud to be the first tank in the battalion to cross the Somme, especially as it had the code name 'Falmouth'. The Maquis were rounding up hundreds of prisoners amongst the hysterical crowd. They were merciless and I saw them deal effectively with one German who was being tiresome.

We laagered that night on the high ground just north of the Somme. Soon we cooked an enormous and much needed meal and set about maintaining the bogies and tracks. We had to change the sprocket on 'Caribou'. Earlier in the day I had great pleasure in coming up on the air to Johnny Gull and demanding one complete new sprocket.

A wonderful day and we had advanced nearly sixty miles. I walked over to Oliver and Michael, and I am glad they felt the emotion of the day as much as I did. But I was getting extremely tired and realized I was making Brough do more and more. A better night, although I spent part of it helping change the sprocket. We slept till about five.

The 11th Armoured had liberated Amiens itself and captured Eberbach, the German 7th Army General. He said that it had been the plan to stop us on the Somme, but everything by then was so disorganized that every German was making his way out of France as quickly as possible.

---

* How sad that this view of such a wonderful building has been ruthlessly obscured by concrete high-rise blocks of ugliness as one enters this way today.

Friday, 1 September. I had just finished a very good egg for breakfast when George called for an 'O' group. He had the exciting news that today the 1st and 5th Coldstream were going to take Arras. Unfortunately it was the squadron's turn to be in reserve. Basil was to lead followed by No. 3, then No. 1, Battalion H.Q. and ourselves, followed by 5th Coldstream. A lovely clear morning, there was excitement in the air. At eight o'clock we moved out and took the road for Arras. I had to leave 'Caribou' behind as they had not yet finished putting on the sprocket nuts, but hoped they would catch up soon.

At the start opposition was negligible, the sides of the road were strewn with burning transport and dead horses, shot up by the Recce Welsh or 'Grocers' the evening before. A number of Germans and an odd horse-drawn convoy were still about and these were reported in all directions, but unfortunately they avoided our road. At Dernancourt we turned north up to Hèdauville. The Grenadiers were to take Albert on our right but when they arrived the town was still too strongly held by enemy for them to enter themselves, so they contained it until the infantry division following us arrived.

By now we were moving pretty fast and, as there was no opposition when we reached Hèdauville, Colonel Dickie took the direct road to Arras. Every village we rushed through was the same, the liberated free people were showing their appreciation in the only way they could. Happiest of all were a small party of British prisoners set free by the side of the road. All along were small groups of the Maquis with their toll of German prisoners, some of whom were shot outright. On the air Colonel Dickie came up to say he wanted everyone to acknowledge the villagers' welcome. "I want all tank commanders to receive the French as well as they receive us. It is a great day for them and a great day for us," he said.

Rumours were constantly flying around and at one moment thirty Panthers were reported approaching Arras. More burning German transport was passed, and even a one-man submarine they were trying to get away by land was reported. About midday, a few miles from the town, the leading tanks began to be fired on sporadically by Germans in the fields. But Colonel Dickie would allow no slowing down in front in case, as he said, "our stable-boy friends get there first from another direction". Colonel Roddy Hill, 5th Battalion, asked what the position was, only to be told he would expect him at the barrier at the main station, doubtless over bottles of champagne.

About one-thirty Basil's leading tanks with a little sporadic shooting entered the outskirts of Arras. Significantly he reported that the streets were deserted except for a few odd Germans, who were running into the houses. The plan was for him to make straight through the town for the river bridge. Ian and John were lucky enough to be the two next troops, and were to go for the railway station. No. 1 Squadron were to go for the main street, and we for the main central square. Basil ran into a German convoy and anti-tank gun, but shot it up and did very well through the town to the bridge which was intact. By now we all had entered the town and the few Germans who were shooting or throwing odd grenades were being rounded up and shot by the Maquis. I had a good burst of m.g. at a German hiding in a railway truck. We had entered along the N.319 from Amiens, crossed over the bridge over the railway just west of the station, joined the Boulevard de Strasbourg nearby where Basil had shot up the convoy winning him the MC, and almost immediately turned left into the Rue Gambetta.

As soon as we were well into the town in the Rue Gambetta every door and house was thrown open and out from every street alleyway the liberated people of Arras flooded and swarmed around the tanks, "like a gale but from all sides at once". They completely abandoned themselves, rejoicing, shouting and cheering. Old men and young girls dancing down the street climbed onto my tank kissing and embracing me, shouting "Vive les Anglais" and "No more Gestapo". To steal Oliver's remark from the battalion War Diary it was not just cheering like that at a procession of an eminent person or royalty, but the overwhelming joy of sudden relief. The bells pealed and Arras was free.

Eventually I found myself in the main square and put my troop in a position at the far end. We had come up a small rise and suddenly turned into this magnificent square, with the elaborate gothic Hotel de Ville towering immediately to the left, known as Le Place des Héros. There were still a few odd shots going off, a grenade had been thrown just in front of me. We had difficulty in finding our way into the centre as the maps were impossible; in consequence tanks were going in all directions. There were several anti-tank guns about the town and Bill went off on his own and destroyed one. Ian told me afterwards he was shot at by one and destroyed it, while the Maquis stuck the French flag down the smoking barrel. Tragedy marred the entry for Derek Eastman whose company of the 5th Battalion were mopping up. Still deeply upset he told me months later he found a child mortally wounded in this incident, sheltering in a nearby house, and he had sought to comfort the distraught family. The beastliness of such powerful weapons too often meant soldiers could not avoid the innocent suffering. It added immensely to our general loathing of war.

The main square in Arras is very fine and undamaged. I sat there for some time. Our tanks were decorated with flowers and even carnations. Children stuck French flags in, and we were filled with bottles of champagne and beer. The square was now a dense mass of people completely lost of control. It was an emotional sight to see so many people so happy, and we really felt not as conquerors but liberators. All the time the patriots were rounding up the Germans and collaborators, giving us information, searching the houses, marching away prisoners. They showed no mercy and revenge was in the eyes of all of them. The Germans were petrified and many did not leave the town alive. Assuredly les Enfants de la France had risen to destroy the hated invader.

Later Comment

Jocelyn Pereira, the 5th Battalion Intelligence Officer, has written of Arras that day: "It was a psychological victory, for, though the Germans were not properly armed or equipped to make much of a defence, there were well over a thousand in the town and they could have imposed a considerable delay on the operation if they had chosen to fight, but a rapid and calculated show of force proved the right technique for the situation and we had little trouble. In fact we soon had so many prisoners that they were an embarrassment to us" – *A Distant Drum*.

It was late in the afternoon when we moved out of the town and took up a position on a ridge just beyond. Hundreds of prisoners were coming in in all directions and the remains of horse-drawn convoys lying all over the roads. I went too close to a burning house and the camouflage netting over my tank caught fire so we halted, and as we had lost a bogey rubber too, we stopped there by a small farm. A mass of Germans I saw in the distance, so I sent Brough off with the rest of the troop to round them up. The Battalion had formed into a position in a wide arc with the 5th Battalion dug-in to protect us. Having

110

collected several hundred prisoners and gathered all their arms which he put in a truck and sent down to Arras, Brough returned smiling broadly. He handed the prisoners over to the Maquis, so I can imagine they had a pleasant time. 'Caribou' appeared and had apparently caught us up, but Sergeant Newton had gone off on his own with the Maquis, "shot up hundreds of Germans in the woods" and they had enjoyed themselves too. So we cooked dinner and drank champagne.

However, the celebration was rather disturbed. Two Spitfires came and shot us up – a sudden devastating noise and bullets spattering down the road, as we dived under the tanks. They machine-gunned two of our vital petrol trucks, brought up so devotedly to refuel us, but which now brewed up splendidly on a nearby crest. Yellow smoke was let off frantically and they flew off.

I went over to Battalion H.Q. to have my eyes cleaned by Johnny Thompson, and saw Oliver. We discussed the day, fittingly the fifth anniversary of the outbreak of war. This had been a great Coldstream day. Arras was a town full of Coldstream memories both in 1940 and the last war, while none of us will forget its liberation in 1944. More than that, we had outstripped everyone else, including the Americans, and had overrun six flying-bomb sites which must have meant a hell of a lot to the people in London. The talk of Battalion was how Aylmer Tryon, the General's A.D.C., in Division H.Q. close by had dismounted solemnly from his tank, and where the words "Vive Le R.A.F." had been chalked on the side by the crowds he had added, "less two Spitfires".

The battalion moved into a laager, but we worked until one a.m. changing some track links out on the road. We had done another forty miles today. The Irish Guards had gone on this evening to take Douai, another twelve miles on.

Saturday, 2 September. We moved out that morning to Douai, passed Vimy Ridge and harboured at midday on the aerodrome at Vitry. Here we spent the day maintaining and resting while supplies were brought up along the enormous length of communications. Everything still had to come from the Bayeux-Caen area. The aerodrome was mined for demolition when we arrived, but a civilian who laid them showed the R.E. where they were. They were soon lifted.

It rained most of the day. The tracks of my tank were worn and I foresaw another night's work putting new links on them. I was very

111

nearly blown up, too, when a 75 H.E. shell was let off by mistake and went off a few yards away from me. Luckily no one was harmed, but it taught us a serious lesson at the time. We had other important business. My four tanks were laden with wines and champagne. I put Brough in charge of collecting the bottles that stacked the turret floors and this evening I entertained Ian and John Sutton in my bivouac with some of the champagne from Arras. Wisely Brough only allowed me two bottles, but I regret to say John soon got the most alcoholic, the conversation genial and mulled, and before worse could happen, protesting hard, I escorted them both back to their tanks. It amused my crew a lot.

By dark my track was only half done, so I had a roster for the rest of the troop to work in one-hour shifts overnight.

Late that evening the orders came through that the Guards Armoured Division were to free Brussels, between eighty and one hundred miles away. The whole squadron was collected and told in a hangar. It was the most ambitious plan.

Weather permitting, the Airborne Army was to drop at dawn to free the remaining V.I. sites. BRUSSELS! – the excitement!

When I came out Brough had the whole troop except drivers working on my tracks. By eleven thirty we had changed about ten more plates and the track was on again. There was no need for me to stay, but stupidly I did, having had hardly any sleep during the last week, and reveille was to be soon after four.

Sunday, 3 September The day started with an eye-straining half hour on the floor of the hangar marking maps of the route. No less than six one-inch maps were to be crossed and the centreline went along by-roads most of the way. This was designed to bypass crossroads and likely pockets of resistance. I had only a rotten little candle to see by, and it kept falling over, and the maps disappearing.

The division was to advance on two centrelines, on the left the Grens, followed by ourselves, and on the right the Welsh and Irish. The right centreline, straighter and shorter along the main road, but more likely to meet opposition. It was to be a race between the two columns to get to Brussels first. There were no less than ten report lines named after British battleships. A long and tedious drive across the pavé roads of Belgium lay ahead, the country all built-over, industrial and black.

We left Douai at dawn and followed Battalion H.Q. I was leading the squadron, flying my troop flag on the aerial. The outskirts of Lens and Lille were passed and we crossed the Belgian frontier at Bachy about midday. Here extraordinarily enough the 2nd Battalion Coldstream were in fact billeted in 1940. George moreover was greeted by the two same people in whose house he had lived, who were standing by the road. They were all three dancing round each other with delight.

In front the Grenadiers were held up by opposition at Pont à Marcq while we waited at Mons-en-Pavéle. A 1st and 2nd G.G. force attacked it, losing forty casualties, but the rest of us bypassed and pushed on. This put us behind in the race. On through Tournai, which some American armour had already reached from the south, we moved on towards the city. The usual tumultuous reception wherever we went. I think this was even more so here than in France. A running commentary was given us from brigade; now the Irish were being bombed by our own aircraft, Typhoons, so this held them up and allowed us to catch up level.

In the early afternoon the column halted to refill with petrol. This arrived immediately and in half an hour we moved on. 'Cobra' had lost a bogey wheel rubber, so I rang for the fitters, and we changed it in twenty minutes during the halt, very creditable indeed considering in the old days it took us two hours. I was determined to get all my tanks to Brussels. The sight of the squadron fitters arriving on this occasion was splendid. Their great White half-track scout car swinging down the column at a roaring pace, the fitters sitting out on top, beaming smiles all round, leaping off before the vehicle jerked to a stop as if it was a fire-engine, this was their great day too.

At Lessines we had another long hold up. The Grens ran into a horse-drawn column and had a wonderful shoot up. It was quite a time before we could get past the wreckage. Already the Belgians were out carving up the horses for meat. Several houses here were being wrecked by them, windows smashed and swastikas being painted by the front doors, showing they thought the owners were collaborators.

In the evening the pace increased. We were going full speed towards the Capital, but it became dark when we were still about ten miles away. The last report line, 'King George', had been passed, and we pulled into the main road to Brussels from the west. The tanks were all spread out now, losing sight of each other, but the last few miles into the centre of the town we did at full gallop.

113

When the leading troops arrived it was found that the Germans had left that afternoon and the free Belges were in control rounding up the remainder. The Germans had set fire to the Gestapo records at the Palais de Justice when they left and the glow lit up the sky. The Welsh Guards were first in. The Grenadiers were halted for a short time for permission to enter. A certain amount of light skirmishing took place and the Irish had a fight round the Palais de Justice, but there must have been many Germans still left hiding.

The lights went on in the city and all windows and doors were flung open. To describe the welcome would only be to repeat what had happened all the way across France and Belgium. Here it was magnified to cheering thousands. My tank halted behind the one in front in the centre of the town at the Bourse. Immediately I was smothered with kisses, flowers and wine. The smaller scout-cars completely disappeared from view. All the old songs were coming out again, Tipperary was being shouted out. Soon we were dragged away from our tanks into houses. Forcibly, with two or three girls round my neck, I was taken into a house and given a royal feast. George was there already guzzling. We drank glass after glass, bottle after bottle appeared and we had to be self-controlled not to be laid out.

In time there was a shout outside, "The tanks are moving on", and so there was a scramble of crews coming from the houses. We all bundled in again accompanied by our hosts and dozens of Belgians standing on the back. Eventually we managed to move on. There were tanks going in all directions, Grens, Micks, Welsh and ourselves racing round corners, skidding against the curbstones. It was the nearest thing to a bump-supper night at Cambridge with Belgians clinging to the tops of the tanks shouting and singing.

After following the Doctor's scout-car we ended up in an open square to harbour the night, George sending me to guide what I could find of the Squadron into its place. I managed it. Guards were posted and then, completely whacked, I covered myself with a blanket and was asleep at once. Ninety-six miles in a day is a long way in a tank.

On another such occasion, only it was before a great victory many years ago, "there was a sound of revelry by night" to be heard in the streets of Brussels.

Monday, 4 September. Stayed on the square all morning while the populace came to see us eating breakfast and washing, rather like

114

animals at the zoo. Parties were marching down the street waving flags and singing English songs. I was asked several times to post letters to England for their friends and some families. One poor man said he had only just got out of a Gestapo prison after being put there in 1940 for hiding British soldiers. He had heard nothing of his wife in London since then.

After lunch we moved to a better place in the Boulevard at Koekelberg near the north of the city. It was a triumphant drive round Brussels. The Commander led the procession flying his colour on the aerial mast and we drove slowly round sitting on the top of the turrets. All my four tanks had reached Brussels and I led them round flying our troop flag on the aerial with a Belgian and French flag on either side of the turret. Down the colourful avenues, every window had its allied flag and the girls were clothed in their national colours. Flowers and streamers were thrown up at us. The people could still hardly believe we were here, it had all happened so quickly. How they must have hated the Germans.

Division H.Q. entered Brussels today led by General Allan in his tank. He must have been a proud man. It was a wonderful climax for us after all the earlier slogging at Caen and Vire, and the great drive to Belgium. We had covered nearly two hundred and fifty miles from the Seine in under a week, and it had been one of the most spectacular advances in history. A great day for the Brigade of Guards to have been allowed to free Brussels; many of them had passed back through there in 1940. The only regret was for those of us whom inevitably we left behind, never again to leave the land of Normandy.

Colonel Dickie addressed the battalion this evening for the first time as Commanding Officer, but I thought was rather disappointing. Arras was the first town to be taken by a Coldstream battalion, he said, since the 3rd Battalion took Jerusalem in 1938. The news was good, the Grenadiers had already pushed on to take Louvain, and the 11th Armoured had captured Antwerp intact.

It was a free night to the British, but most were too exhausted to do anything much, while No. 3 Squadron had been out all last night convoying the 'soft' vehicles into Brussels and were all completely done in. For those who could, the chief of the Underground movement held a tremendous party at the Koekelberg Brewery, but I soon retired to a very comfortable bed in what had been a German billet.

Tuesday, 5 September. This morning I had a great disappointment when I was sent for by Colonel Dickie who told me I must be "L.O.B." (left out of battle), and go back to the Echelons for a rest for two or three weeks, as I was tired. He was embarrassingly complimentary, particularly about Sourdevalle and since, and understood I was rather upset at having to hand over my troop after having brought it so far. Peter Loyd was to take over my troop and during the morning I handed over and took my leave of them. Brough understood my feelings and said he was sorry I should be going when we were so close to Germany. I thanked him for what he had done and left him smiling as always – for the last time. I must admit I realized afterwards I was exhausted and Colonel Dickie was quite right. In a way I wasn't sorry to leave the squadron, as it had completely changed in the last few weeks.

Everybody was recovering from the night before, and I went into a cafe with Henry and John Sutton to have a glass of iced beer. Then an extraordinary thing happened. The rumour went round that the Germans had capitulated and "*La guerre est fini*". In a few minutes it had spread over the whole of Brussels and the Belgians went completely mad, dancing about shouting. "*Il est fini*, the war is over". We did our best to tell them it was only a rumour, but they all believed it. At the one o'clock news they soon realized it was untrue; it was probably started by some 5th Columnist.

After lunch the Battalion moved further out of the town to the Sports Palace to harbour. It was a great relief to get away from the crowds who by now had become tedious.

Bill took Henry, Tony Weigall the Padre and me to a German ordnance store nearby to collect what we could. At the Douanerie we found the most enormous cellars packed full of crate upon crate of champagne, tinned food and wine. Most satisfactorily, all the bottles had printed across the label, "*Réservé à la Wehrmacht*". We had begun unloading ammunition onto the pavement to make space in the trucks when Dick Schreiber arrived from brigade. He told us to stop at once. I have never seen Bill so angry. He refused and we continued to unload the boxes. Soon two three-tonner loads were filled and we sent for more transport. Most of the division had by now found the place and it was full of officers carting out loads of champagne. At one moment I saw three excited Lieutenant-Colonels from division shoving an enormous trolley of the 'Widow Cliquot' along the vaults, a ludicrous

116

sight. Needless to say the divisional M.P.s were put on the gates to stop any outsiders getting in. We had enough wine to last for months. From now on champagne was flowing like water in the armoured division.

Many years later when Bill Kilmany, as he later became, and I talked of this adventure at the Douanerie, and he was reminded how brigade tried to stop us unloading shells onto the pavement, he stuck his chin out and once again his fury returned – "Hmm, I was angry," he went on quietly reflecting.

One of the many bottles we 'liberated' that day remains as a lamp on my desk, a much-prized reminder of the Wehrmacht's huge loss and our gain.

Oliver and I had found a quiet room in the stadium conciergerie to sleep in, though it was rather uncomfortable on a concrete floor. Unfortunately my servant, Brown, had broken down on the way to Arras and was missing with all my kit.

Wednesday, 6 September. Today the armour moved on towards the Albert Canal. All flags and chalk marks had been removed and the serious business was to start again. I stood on the square in front of the stadium and watched them drive off, a sad moment to see my troop driving off towards Germany with someone else in command.

For two days the spearhead of 21st Army Group, 30 Corps, had halted in and around Brussels, Louvain and Antwerp. It needed a pause for supplies of petrol to catch up so as to continue our advance towards Germany before the enemy recovered. Such is all we knew, but of the crucial significance of this delay none of us could be aware. A great argument had been going on at the highest level during this period over the strategy to finish off the war this year – it has taken many years since for this to come filtering through to those of the public who still take an interest. One can only wish and wonder now what a different world it could have been, and for so many who might have survived, had the armoured divisions of Monty's 2nd Army and of Patton's 3rd Army not been halted, but allowed to race straight on side by side, morale and experience at their peak supplied from the air at the expense of all others, regardless of risk or the hurt feelings of allies and the public at home and in the U.S., to seize crossings over the Rhine and plunge direct into the vitals of the Ruhr before the resources of the enemy solidified once again. Hours counted. General "Jorrocks" wrote

117

in his *Corps Commander*, "I have since felt that at this point those responsible for the higher direction of the war in the west had faltered. From now on things began to go wrong." A sad repetition.

I left Brussels in 'A' Echelon in company with Michael Fox in a captured German General's staff car driven by T.Q.M.S. Thornton. Being L.O.B. with no job the next fortnight was to be, I thought, extremely boring, so will cease to describe everything in such detail. A long drive ended up not far from Diest at a gloomy place called Schoot near Tessenderloo. There we harboured and spent the first part of the night drawing petrol for the battalion at the R.A.S.C. supply point.

The night brought home to me the vulnerability of our 'soft' echelons in this sort of mobile war and the life of the men in them. Michael quickly organized us into all-round defence with twenty or thirty trucks in a field strung out along a thick hedge, our drivers, spare crews, fitters and storemen armed with rifles and an occasional P.I.A.T. Slit trenches were eagerly dug, since the experience of that fierce bombing raid on the Echelon north of Caen had shaken these Guardsmen. Michael's own jeep had been almost buried then by a near miss and the nerves of his servant, Beresford, were obviously still shattered. So when firing broke out at the end of the line of vehicles and I went to see what was up, I found two jumpy men had been shooting wildly into the darkness. They thought they had seen some movement and had no response to their challenge. An anxious night, and we were stood-to for some time. Any stray enemy armoured-car patrol could have wrought havoc.

Thursday, 7 September. Colonel Dickie insisted, after hearing about this from Michael in the morning, I should go back to the Divisional Admin Area for a rest in the Transit Camp. So I set off to go there, reported to be on the far side of Brussels. A fruitless drive there and back, for I found it not five miles from where I started at Schaffen outside Diest.

The armour had reached the Albert Canal, ten miles on, constructed as a massive defensive line along the north-eastern side of Belgium, and there was a fight going on to cross. A good bit of work by the Welsh Guards and the 5th Coldstream had succeeded after a hard fight in crossing the canal at Beringen.

Saturday, 9 September. I drove over to 'B' Echelon in the morning and

118

found Michael and Billy Denbigh. It was then I heard the battalion had had rather a sticky time last night. Miles Bodley, Malcolm Lock and Murray St Clair from No. 1 had all been wounded, Miles very seriously, the others only slightly. About half a dozen tanks had been destroyed and No. 2 had lost three.

Unhorsed crews were coming back now. Williams, the Driver of 'Cobra', came up to tell me his tank had been hit and Sergeant Brough killed. The Squadron had to push on north from the Albert Canal crossing at Beringen. Apparently they were told they must take the village of Heppen that night. It was getting dark, already two tanks had been knocked out and brewed up by a Panther in Heppen. Williams, a likeable, quietly spoken Northumberland miner poured out the story to me under real stress. No. 2 Troop was sent to get into the village. Brough's tank which was leading was hit just as he pulled onto the road into the village. "The tank brewed up at once". Williams managed to climb out untouched. Brough was very badly hit but somehow managed to get out and shout at Williams to stop the others. Wood, the Operator, was wounded, but the other two, Yardley and Cox, never got out at all. Brough had not been found yet.

Later George told me he crawled a few yards away from the tank and was found the day after lying in the ditch. He had lost a leg and the other one was badly smashed, so it is incredible how he managed to climb out at all. The tank had been hit by an 88 m.m., which went right through the name 'Cobra' just in front of the Co-driver, Cox, from a Jagd-Panther. The enemy tank was only fifty yards away up the road when it fired so they had little chance. This was the first of its kind we had encountered, the most potent weapon of all, an 88 m.m. mounted on a Panther hull. It was a real monster and itself was destroyed a day or two later at Hechtel.*

I am in no position to criticize this and other things in the squadron that evening, but I was besieged with a mass of ill-feeling from the unhorsed crews and elsewhere. I wouldn't commit myself at all, as I know only too well how confused and difficult things can be, but I had a feeling there was something wrong somewhere. When I next saw him

---

* An example of this horrible weapon is on display today in the Imperial War Museum. I believe it is the actual vehicle that did so much damage that night and was later destroyed by the Welsh Guards.

119

I tackled Bill about this. He understood exactly what I meant and confirmed what I felt.

Some time afterwards George told me that a message from our infantry had gone wrong. They had successfully cleared Beverloo and were advancing up the main road from the south to clear Heppen before nightfall. No. 1 Company had reached the first objective, the railway station, halfway into this long village, but could not dislodge the enemy from it. In support of them No. 1 Squadron came under heavy fire from tanks and S.P. Guns. They had lost three tanks and several others were bogged.

No. 2 Squadron with No. 4 Company were then sent round to the west of the village across the railway lines to complete the last stage of the attack. The light was failing and on emerging from a wood they were accurately engaged by an S.P. gun from the back of the village and became out of touch with the infantry. They were told by Battalion H.Q. to get on with it and enter the centre of Heppen from the west, since the crossroads there had now been reached by the 5th Battalion. In fact the message was wrong, for the infantry were still several hundred yards further south and had only reached a small crossroads by the railway crossing. No. 2 Troop began to advance, but as Brough turned into the road from the west his tank immediately burst into flames. By then it was dark, with burning houses and vehicles dangerously silhouetting the remaining tanks, so the squadron was ordered to extricate itself and had done so with some difficulty. It must have been a horrid evening.

To me it meant the loss of a great personal friend. I made Brough my troop Sergeant two years ago against a deal of opposition; he was then aged twenty-two. During that time he had become someone I could rely on for almost anything if I had wanted to. Many people had a different opinion especially the Sergeant Major, as he had several faults, but militarily he was a first-class tank commander and could read a map as well as anyone I know. He was keen to do anything, however, pointless it may have seemed at the time. I remember well the argument we had once where we were in the early Salisbury Plain days, the good fun we had out troop training in Norfolk and how I lost my temper and shouted at him on a disastrous exercise in Yorkshire that ended up in shouts of laughter. It was part of his exceptional character that I never heard him swear once. With ample sense of humour he always smiled whatever happened, and as a friend I could always tell him what I felt.

120

1. No. 2 Troop, No. 2 Squadron, Salisbury Plain, Autumn 1942. *Left to right, back:* Guardsmen Liddle, Jepson, Whittle, Sergeant Brough. *Middle:* Lance-Sergeant Caulfield, Corporal Arnold. *Front:* Guardsman Williams. "Cheetah 11", a Crusader Mark 111 armed with a 6-pounder gun. The Troop flag on the aerial survived until April 1945.

2. "Spithead and the Island fading on the horizon... then there was nothing but two long lines of landing craft pitching and rolling". (p. 15).

3. 2 Squadron H.Q. Salisbury Plain, 1942. *Top:* Guardsman Watchman, Sergeant
   Rogers. *On Gun:* Squadron Sergeant-Major Robertson, Guardsman Carr.
   Sitting below, left to right: Sergeant Holmes, Guardsman Robertson, Captain
   Hugo Chisenhale-Marsh, Guardsman Looker. *On ground:* Captain Tony Watkins.
   Standing: Major Michael Fox.

4. Convoy headed by a Cromwell followed by a Sherman leaves the beaches for the
   de-waterproofing area.

5. "I heard the sickening whizz and crack of an A.P. shot and saw a neat round hole appear in the wall behind" (p.42). These holes could still be seen in 1955 through the wall behind where my tank stood that evening near the right of this picture.

6. The "Moaning Minnie". An abandoned six-barrelled rocket launcher still loaded with 75-pounder bombs. This mortar fired each separately over about 10 seconds which "shrieked into the air". Noisy and frightening though not very accurate.

7. Cagny Church after the bombardment of 18 July. Two A.R.V.s – Armoured Recovery Vehicles – in the foreground, perhaps assisting the Sherman in a bomb crater.

8. Cagny Church restored, 1995.

9. "A mass of stuff was pouring south, the whole of 8 Corps was rushing after the 11th Armoured who were doing very well" (p.51). 2 August, 11th Armoured reach the village we then called St Charles de Percy, (really La Ferronière), on the road to Vire. The first tank is a 17-pounder Sherman, but the next two are M 10s, self-propelled anti-tank guns not strictly tanks, with 17-pounders mounted.

10. 4 August, No. 2 Squadron move up to the line in the evening to St Charles de Percy area. "In a deeply wooded valley just south of Le Tourneur we halted while the 4th Grenadiers in their Churchills came back to harbour" (p. 57). We are on the Caen to Vire road at the bridge over the Souleuvre at Cathéolles. Sergeant Caulfield's tank, 2B, is in foreground, R.B.'s tank, 2, and Sergeant Brough's 2A., ahead. Note the stowage bin missing off the back of my tank.

11. The same point on the Caen to Vire road, D577, in August 1955, where No. 2 Troop was photographed at Cathéolles in the wooded valley on the way up to St Charles de Percy.

12. "On the right Nigel's troop had all been knocked out" (p. 88). The field where this happened. The lane which George Dawnay went down to help the Micks runs behind the near hedge. No 2 Troop was in the field beyond the lane and we were all trying to advance parallel to the lane from left to right. Hill 242 is clearly visible in the background where the Panthers on our flank were positioned.

13. Sourdevalle. Photographed from our objective, the Vire-Vassy road, in August 1955. "With an open cornfield we had to advance down to the stream, and then rising ground on which the Germans were entrenched."

14. Nigel Pratt.

15. Crossing the Seine at Vernon.

16. The Place des Héros, Arras, which No. 2 Squadron liberated.

17. Major-General Allan Adair, G.O.C. Guards Armoured Division. It was at Arras he had won his Military Cross in the First World War.

18. The Commanding Officer and the Adjutant: Lieutenant-Colonel Dickie Gooch *(right)* and Captain Oliver Heywood.

19. The Nijmegen bridge. Looking over "the Island" and the road towards Elst and Arnhem. Immediately beyond on the left is Lent; Bemmel is centre-right three miles away.

20. No. 2 Troop, after "the Island", October 1944, outside billets in Hatert, Nijmegen. *Top Row:* Guardsman Walker, L/Sergeant Palmer. *Middle Row:* Guardsmen Gruchy, Thompson, Edwards, M. *Front Row:* Guardsmen Meadows, Daniel W., Sergeant Shipley, Corporal Driscoll, Corporal Siddons, L/Sergeant Fawcett, R.B.

21. Ian Liddell's bridge across the River Ems north of Lingen where he cut the wires and led the attack.

22.Guardsman N. Brown.

23. Ian Jardine.

24. Near Goch: waiting to join battle to clear the Germans from the west bank of the Rhine. Dermot Musker, Jimmy Priestley, R. B.

25. Approaching the Twente Canal at Enschede on 1 April. No. 2 Squadron in action ahead against Germans in house on far right. R. B. and No. 2 Troop on far right of photograph. "My troop was deployed to deal with this and I moved across to use my seventy-fives and Brownings" (p.203).

26. Following on from the previous photograph, the 5th Coldstream with No. 3
Squadron mop up and take a number of prisoners while No. 2 Squadron speed
on towards the bridge.

27. "Rocket production working well". Fitting a single rocket – code name "Tulip"
– to one of my tanks. Each warhead weighed 60 lbs. Shortly after we bolted a
second rocket beneath to double up the warheads and improve the trajectory.

28. "The battalion drawn up in three close lines just south of Calcar, objective, Hamburg". John Sedgwick engaged in "a long stint of map-folding".

29. Beside the barn at De Veldgeuver Farm near the approach to the Lonneker bridge at Enschede. This picture was taken in September 1945. The graves are those of my Tank Crew, Guardsmen L. Hanson, F.J. Wright and N.T. Bradbury.

30. This photograph was taken in 1994 from the same place as illustration No.13. *Left to right:* D. Lapworth (Irish Guards), T. Twite, D. Haydock, T. Fawcett, J. Modlen, B. Finch, W. Daniel, J. Short, K. Hurworth, R. Boscawen (all No 2 Squadron, 1st Coldstream Guards).

31. The author and Sergeant T. Fawcett by the entrance to Houtakkex Farm at Bemmel in May 1995 – with ochard behind.

32. No. 2 Troop in Enschede for the 50th Anniversary of their liberation, 6 April, 1995. *Left to right:* K. Hurworth, D. Haydock, W. Daniel, T. Fawcett, R. Bastone, R. Boscawen.

33. At our home in Somerset in the 1970s, my wife with General Horrocks.

In action he was a brave man and in action he had a brave man's reward.

Sunday, 10 September. Visited Michael and Billy at 'B' Echelon again and attacked some champagne, more abundant than water at the moment. All day unhorsed crews from the Brigade came back to the Transit Camp, mostly Welsh and Irish. There had been a stiff battle on the Albert Canal and at Hechtel beyond. Among them I saw the crew of my own tank 'Cheetah'. They told me that the tank had been bogged on the night at Heppen and had to be abandoned which was sad. It meant by now my old troop had pretty well come to an end, those who survived being sent back and split up. Very disappointing it should finish like that, especially as we had never had a chance of a successful battle, but only the unsatisfactory slogging business early on. That it was a good troop I never had any doubt. Not one man was there who was not of a high standard.

This 'Cheetah' was the first Sherman I had back in Norfolk last year, and had done well on 2,000 miles without a new engine. A good tank as far as a Sherman goes, and it had accounted for one Panther.

I visited the Field Dressing Station this afternoon to see any of our wounded, but they had all been cleared back to Hospital. So I went for a long walk instead and climbed over a windmill which was working. This was rather fascinating, a real old-fashioned mill with enormous wooden cog-wheels. Somehow this took my mind out of the dispiriting present.

By a brilliant stroke of the 2nd and 3rd Irish and the Household Cavalry, the division had cut the Escaut Canal and captured the bridge across. Henceforth known as 'Joe's Bridge', it was the key to the next major obstacle across our front, the Meuse-Escaut, about fifteen miles north of the Albert Canal and only a mile or two short of the Dutch frontier. This was very good news and pleased the higher command a lot. In fact, they said it had shortened the war by making a bridgehead for the next operation.

On Tuesday, 12th, I moved over the Albert Canal and the camp was pitched just beyond Beringen. Next morning we moved on to a clearing in a large pinewood two or three miles north of Hechtel, beside the main road that led up to Joe's Bridge and on into Holland.

Humphrey Gascoigne, a Grenadier in charge of the Transit Camp, and I went to Brussels in the afternoon to see if we could find some captured German vehicles for our use. We were unsuccessful and returned after a long drive as Brussels was now seventy-five miles back. Every few yards the roadside was strewn with burnt-out Hun vehicles caught by the R.A.F. There were dozens and dozens. On the way back we stopped at a cafe and drank some excellent iced beer, while the barmaid insisted on playing that ill-fated corny old tune from 1940 over and over again at full blast on an ancient gramophone: "We're going to hang out the washing on the Siegfried Line, if the Siegfried Line's still there". I suppose she thought it might encourage us.

Thursday, 14 September. By now I was fully rested and getting bored with having nothing to do, so I went up to the battalion who had been resting for a few days just up the road. I saw Oliver first and he said they were still short of tanks, there was nothing for me to do, and it was much better to stay 'L.O.B.' for a bit longer. Later I tackled Bill and he insisted on the same. This was very boring and I said so, and went back determined to get the best out of it. Michael Hamilton I saw up there too, but everyone seemed rather tired and suffering from colds. A crowd of reinforcements arrived at the camp this evening including David Kennard and Greville Chester, both Coldstreamers, so we tackled more than the usual amount of champagne.

Later Comment

The two canal lines, and the Pirbright-type country between them, had given all units in the division a most gruelling time. The Coldstream Group had lost one hundred and twenty-one casualties including thirty-one killed amongst them Billy Hartington and three other officers, and Miles Bodley, grievously wounded in the Beverloo-Heppen battle. The 1st Battalion had eleven tanks destroyed and others out of action. Both at Bourg-Leopold, formerly the Aldershot of the Belgian Army, and at Hechtel the Germans had blocked the main roads through the area. In the confused and costly battle for Hechtel lasting four days the Welsh Guards Group finally overcame the fanatical resistance by paratroopers and cadets from a training battalion on 11th September. Thus the Germans had demonstrated again how quickly they could recover from a hopeless situation and put together the stiffest resistance from a ragbag of formations when under decisive leadership; in this event General Kurt Student, the veteran paratroop commander and victor in Crete.

Next day I escorted two German officers back to a P.O.W. cage, miserable specimens who all the time looked as if they thought they were going to be shot. Nobody wanted them and I had great trouble in

122

finding anyone to take them off my hands. Most people laughed and said, "Why not throw them back?" Eventually Corps A.Q.M.G. himself was the only person willing. I saw Dermot this afternoon. He has become a captain at brigade. I am very glad as he has had a poor deal.

Saturday, 16 September. Back to 'B' Echelon in Hechtel to see Michael and tackle some champagne before lunch. Somehow I had acquired a German Volkswagen off the R.E., an amphibious one, a funny little open boat on wheels, painted black, with a propeller behind, a rotten car really, but it was just what I needed now.

All this time supplies, guns and men had been pouring up to the Escaut Canal ready for the breakout from the bridgehead. The plan is to take place tomorrow and the Guards Armoured Division are to lead. This evening I drove up to the battalion, harboured on a sandy heath, to the right of the main road about a mile or so behind the canal, near Overpelt. They were getting ready for tomorrow's attack. I had dinner with No. 2 Squadron, John Baddeley appears to be there now, acting second-in-command, but there was rather a strained atmosphere. Nothing like the old carefree days in No. 2. Afterwards I met Ian and spent some time talking to him of everything except the war and then drove home depressed at being left out of it.

Later Comment

Orders for operation 'Market Garden', the major advance into Holland, had been given to the battalion during the day. 30 Corps was to advance some sixty miles along a single axis linking up with the three major river crossings that formed the delta of the Rhine. The objective of the Guards Armoured Division was to establish itself around Nunspeet beside the Zuider Zee and so cut off from the land the remainder of the German army in the west of Holland. The Irish Guards group were to lead 5th Brigade in the breakout with a cabrank of Typhoons blasting a corridor non-stop on either side of the road towards Eindhoven, followed by 32nd Brigade in which the Coldstream Group were. It was the most ambitious and exciting plan. That is about all they knew, and nothing of course could be written down at the time.

Sunday, 17 September. The day broke dull and overcast, a morning much like any other without any extra noise than usual until after midday, when the attack opened. A moderately heavy barrage went down and then came the drone of aircraft, a heavy solid drone, which lasted all afternoon. It was uncanny to think that during that short time a whole army had been landed in Holland. At the same time the G.A.D., led by the Irish, advanced over the Escaut to meet them.

Later in the afternoon I went to Heppen in the Volkswagen to find where Brough was buried. I found his tank by the side of the road where it had been hit, but could not find his grave. After a good deal of incoherent signs and noises with some local natives, I gave it up. I had a look round and saw where the Jagd-Panther had fired from. It was only fifty yards away. This was the first Jagd-Panther we had encountered, and it was now to be seen knocked out by the Welsh Guards about to cross the main road west of Hechtel. One of the most formidable of all German vehicles, it had a long 88 m.m. S.P. gun mounted on a heavily armoured Panther chassis. Hugh Griffiths managed to get it from behind and evidently pumped a number of A.P. shot into its backside.

Back for tea at considerable speed as the extraordinary machine certainly shifted, though it made an alarming clatter and did not have any brakes. Afterwards I went up to 'A' Echelon to see whether Billy Denbigh had any news of the attack. He had none since the battalion had not yet moved, so we attacked the 'Widow' instead. Everywhere one goes champagne is produced, one almost washes in it these days.

Monday, 18 September. I drove up to the battalion at lunchtime and saw them moving out over the Escaut Canal. On the way back the Volkswagen's front axle suddenly gave out and after a grinding crunch it skidded to a standstill. Slept all afternoon while hundreds more gliders and Dakotas flew over.

The next five days I had little to do and were very frustrating. Practically no news about the battle filtered back to us and all we saw were the slow-moving soft transport of the airborne divisions and 30 Corps going up towards Joe's Bridge.

On Tuesday morning Michael Fox sent for me in his jeep and we went off back to Main H.Q. 2nd Army at Louvain, where he had gone to look for a job. We arrived and looked around. Just what one expected a last war Army H.Q. to be, a château surrounded by a mass of tents with every kind of luxury. We saw the situation map and I was surprised to see how thin our troops were on the ground. Only a handful of divisions stretched from Holland to the Channel Ports. The airborne landings had taken place at Arnhem, Nijmegen and Grave, and up the centreline.

124

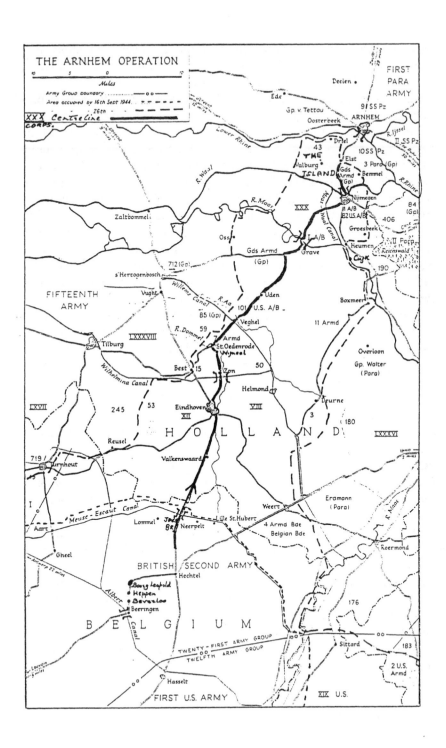

THE ARNHEM OPERATION

Miles

Army Group boundary ....━━━━○○
Area occupied by 16th Sept 1944. ━━ ━ ━
XXX Centreline
CORPS.   26th

FIRST
PARA
ARMY

Deelen
Ede
Gp. v. Tettau
Oosterbeek
91 SS Pz
ARNHEM

R. IJssel
II. SS Pz

Lower Rhine
Driel
43   Elst   10 SS Pz   3 Para (Gp)
THE   Gds   Bemmel
Valburg   Armd
ISLAND   (Gp)
R. Waal   R. Rhine

R. Maas   Nijmegen   84
Zaltbommel   XXX   11 A/B   (Gp)
82 U.S. A/B   406

Oss   Groesbeek   II Para
1 A/B   Heumen   Reichswald
712 (Gp)   Gds Armd   Grave   190
s'Hertogenbosch   (Gp)   CJK

FIFTEENTH   Vught   R. Aa   Uden   Boxmeer
ARMY   Willems Canal   85 (Gp)
LXXXVIII   59   101 U.S. A/B   11 Armd
Tilburg   R. Dommel   Veghel
Armd
St. Oedenrode   Overloon
Wijnel   Gp. Walter
Best   15   Zon   50   (Para)
Wilhelmina Canal   Helmond   Deurne
LXVII   245   53   Eindhoven   3
XII   VIII   180
H O L L A N D   LXXXVI
Reusel   Venlo

719   Valkenswaard
Turnhout
I   Weert   Eramann
Meuse-Escaut Canal   (Para)   R. Maas
Aart   Lommel   Joe   Lille St. Hubert
BR   Neerpelt   4 Armd Bde   Roermond
Gheel   Belgian Bde

BRITISH SECOND ARMY
Hechtel
Bourg Leopold
Heppen   176
Beverloo
Beeringen
B E L G I U M   Sittard   183
TWENTY-FIRST ARMY GROUP
TWELFTH ARMY GROUP   2 U.S.
Armd
Hasselt
FIRST U.S. ARMY   XIX U.S.

We had to wait for the Military Secretary, so drove outside and cooked an excellent lunch with eggs and champagne. After lunch we went to Herent, a small straggling village west of the River Dyle, about a mile to the north of Louvain, and Michael showed me where the 1st Battalion had fired its first shots of the war on the canal in 1940. He found the house in Herent where Battalion H.Q. was, and the dug-outs and slit trenches were still there in the garden. Lord Frederick Cambridge, commanding No. 2 Company, had been killed by a shell when they withdrew from this canal line, one of the first casualties of the war we had. Michael found where they had buried him in the corner of the garden, but his grave had since been moved to the village church-yard. The line of the Dyle was the furthest forward position the B.E.F. had taken up after their rapid advance into Belgium when the German blitzkrieg opened on May 10th 1940.

Shortly after, during the withdrawal to the beaches, Michael had become Company Commander of No. 2 and had remained so through-out the changeover to armour, until he left us about a year ago. He told me that, when Colonel Ririd had given up in Normandy, he had been offered command of the 1st Battalion. But he had refused, because he said he had not commanded armour for too long and now felt unquali-fied to do so. This I believe was regrettable, both for the battalion and for himself. Michael was an experienced and efficient officer, he had been A.D.C. to both General Wavell before the war and to General Alanbrooke, as Commander 2nd Corps, during the phoney war of 1939. Well liked by all ranks, I have absolutely no doubt where Michael would have been in the battle. Perhaps, too, if he had he might have curbed slightly his liking for good Port, that occupational hazard of many notable Coldstream Officers.

After looking at the cemetery at Herent Church, we returned to Army and Michael saw the M.S. He was to be appointed a G.2. at Army. A most amusing day and especially interesting to see how 2nd Army H.Q. works these days.

Next day Michael and I went back to Heppen to look for where Brough was buried. We were still unable to find it though we saw Billy Hartington's grave there. In the evening I borrowed a shot gun which had come from a French farmer who had buried it for the last five years. With Michael's driver, Harris, I walked over a moor near the Escaut canal. We saw a number of blackcock, some partridges and duck. They were very wild but I bagged a mallard and a partridge though it was too dark to find the last. Quite an amusing evening and my first bird this season.

As far as the war went, the G.A.D. had reached Nijmegen and on the 20th, by a brilliant feat, the Grenadiers had captured the Nijmegen bridge across the Rhine. The Arnhem pocket held by the 1st Airborne Division had not been relieved yet and was hard pressed. No news of the Coldstream Group.

All day fleets of Dakotas had been going over bringing supplies to the airborne troops.

Another day I went out with Michael again to a coalmine at Beringen and had a bath. A dirty bath, but it was hot, and the only lying-down bath I had had since the Rodney, a great luxury. The R.E.M.E. workshops were there and I saw my old tank 'Cheetah' being refitted with a new engine, so it wasn't done for yet. Michael insisted on one final look for Brough's grave, but in vain, though we did find those of his crew, Yardley and Cox, in a small public garden at Beringen.

Tony Watkins, Watty, arrived up at the camp on Saturday evening as a reinforcement. He was in good form despite three weeks' awful journey up from Normandy. It was a great relief to find someone I knew and we polished off a lot of champagne this evening. We've had more free champagne this week than we are ever likely to see again in a lifetime.

Sunday, 24 September. Today I crossed into Holland. We left the Escaut area to go up to the division who were somewhere around Nijmegen in the Rear-Division convoy. Watty and I were travelling in the front of a couple of three-tonners. It was the slowest drive I've ever done. We crossed over the Escaut at Joe's Bridge and went on up to Eindhoven.

Nine brewed-up Irish Guards' tanks lay within a hundred yards near the Dutch frontier so they must have had some trouble. I heard later that these tanks were nearly all in the second squadron of the column and were caught by a Mark IV tank with a 50 m.m. gun hidden in a house on the flank. The Micks said that the Typhoon support was magnificent. They were diving down and rocketting beside the tanks themselves, a new squadron taking the air every few minutes. I've always thought that this was the way to use them.

We went through the edge of Eindhoven and passed Philips Radio factory. The town had been badly bombed by the Germans in a spite raid last night. Despite this one could soon see the much higher living standard amongst the Dutch, as their houses were all well built, clean and attractive looking.

We reached Nijnsel that evening, a small village ten miles north of Eindhoven between Son and St Oedenrode in the dropping zone of the U.S. 101 Airborne Division, to find the Germans had cut the centre-line, the only road, a mile in front and had brewed up a hundred of our vehicles. So there we had to stay. Completely unprotected, not far from some three hundred S.S. paras, the road ahead suddenly appeared deserted. Tony Watkins, Henty Smith, Welsh Guards, and I set about making a defensive position in a small house. Henty I had not seen since he left school years ago. We shut the unfortunate inhabitants in the cellar and with the few Guardsmen available set about to man each window. They had rifles with little ammo, and I only had my revolver with six rounds. There was one 17-pounder anti-tank gun in the column we brought up, but it too had no ammo. There was little else we could do and we spent an anxious and uncomfortable, if not frightening, night awaiting the Germans, added to which it was pouring with rain. We were mortared and shelled, but never actually attacked. Two splendid Padres in a mobile Church of Scotland truck just outside invited Tony and me in but several times we had to jump out of it and throw ourselves into a soaking ditch.

During the night a lone jeep suddenly appeared at our position and the sentry on the road and I stopped it going any further. To our utmost astonishment the voice from the blackness said "Corps Commander". He was told the enemy had cut the road ahead so the driver turned about immediately and went back. He managed to get round the Germans in an armoured carrier and on up to the forward troops.

Later Comment
General Horrocks had been back earlier in the afternoon of the 24th to a confer-ence with the Army Commander, General Dempsey, near St. Oedenrode. In his account of this they had taken the decision then that if an attack by the 43rd Division across the Neder Rijn could not be mounted to relieve the perimeter west of Arnhem, they must withdraw the remnants of the 1st Airborne Division.

It was a relief when morning came and the American parachutists put in an attack. The attack, however, failed and the road was still cut. They did not seem to know what was happening, but the enemy were reported to have a brigade across the road by now. Supplies were reported running out further forward and ammo was badly needed. But the division had captured an enormous army food dump at Oss, over a million tins of food, so they certainly couldn't starve.

Meanwhile a few Sherman tanks of the Division's Forward Delivery Squadron had passed rapidly through us to put in a brave but disastrous attack with the Americans. The assorted enemy force from one of General Student's para divisions that had come across from the west was much stronger than expected and these tanks ran up immediately against some 88.s in the woods beyond the next village. Not normally trained to fight as a unit, while some of the crews probably would not have been in action before, their attack ended in the tragic loss of several men and vehicles.

Unknown to us at the time, for the past two days the Grenadier and Coldstream Groups had been attacking south towards us a few miles further up the centreline. They had been ordered south from the Nijmegen area to reopen the centreline at Veghel which had been cut there by a force from the eastern flank. The Coldstream Group had cleared the area to the east at Volkel and Boekel about five miles to the north-east of us, not without some casualties, I'm afraid. But no sooner had 30 Corps' only road, the famous Club Route, been opened there than the Germans had cut it again from the west near us, as we had found.

In the evening the 7th Armoured Division, who had been fighting their way slowly up on the left flank of 30 Corps, arrived and put in an attack on the gap. By midday next (the 26th) it was cleared and we moved on. Tony and Henty insisted on trying to watch the battle as they had only just come out from England. I did my best to persuade them they would see nothing and only get 'stonked', but we had to walk right up to the leading armoured battalion before they were satisfied. The little square in Nijnsel was a chaotic sight, full of vehicles of all kinds who had just escaped the gap. I saw Tony Leetham there from 5th Brigade H.Q., very indignant indeed as his jeep trailer's tyres had been punctured by mortar splinters. Further back we found Michael Fox, an occasion for more champers behind his jeep.

When we moved on through the gap the U.S. airborne were still literally dug-in along the ditches on either side of the road prepared for

129

further counter-attacks. The tangled wreckage of our supply vehicles was a sad spectacle, with one of our knocked out Delivery Squadron tanks upside down resting on the top of its turret in a field.

We crossed the Meuse or Maas at Grave and finally pitched camp at a wood near this river at Overasselt, where we spent a peaceful day. David Ryder, Irish Guards, had been sent back to the Transit Camp to rest, slightly 'bomb happy'. It was he and his platoon I had attempted to support at Sourdevalle. In the recent battle he had done well and had been recommended for an M.C., but had had an awful time.

The news came this evening, the 27th, that Arnhem had been evacuated and out of the 6,000 men landed only 1,200 had been brought back safe across the northern Rhine. It had been a very hard fight by the 1st Airborne Division against overwhelming odds, but they had held out for nearly nine days. They must have had a terrible time and it must go down as one of the hardest battles of the war. The bold plan had fallen at the last fence. Not in vain though. They had enabled 2nd Army to hold the Nijmegen bridge across the Waal or Lower Rhine. During the evening we had listened to one of the most moving broadcasts I have ever heard by Stanley Maxted, a Canadian War Correspondent, who was among those few who came back over the Rhine. After nine days fighting with 1st Airborne in Arnhem his description of the withdrawal of these gallant men brought us near to tears. In single file, holding on to the man in front, boots wrapped in blankets, he told us they had walked silently through the enemy lines under steady machine-gun and artillery fire to the little assault boats which ferried them back across the swift current of the Rhine.

Later Comment

In the Transit Camp I knew very little indeed about what had been happening in this long and complicated battle stretching from the Belgian frontier to the Arnhem bridge. Few would have known much more than what was happening to their own immediate unit, I expect. Indeed, little information at all had reached 2nd Army about the situation of the 1st Airborne Division for the first four days. So much has been written about Operation 'Market Garden' since, it is difficult to realize that at the time most of us had only the vaguest outline of the bigger picture. We certainly did not know that when 1st Airborne landed there were two Panzer Divisions, our old enemies from the Bocage, the 9th and 10th S.S., located in the woods north-east of Arnhem. Now these two, after the withdrawal of 1st Airborne, were able to turn full attention to eliminating

30 Corps' bridgehead over the River Waal beyond Nijmegen. The battle was far from finished.

Thursday, 28 September. By now I had become fed up at sitting doing nothing and was determined to go and see Colonel Dickie. So in the morning I went up to the battalion with Tony Watkins in a jeep, about six miles away. He was going to No. 2 Squadron again to be second in command. Battalion H.Q., with the 5th Battalion, were situated in a brick factory at Gaal just south of the Grave bridge. The Coldstream Group had moved north again from Volkel, relieved by 50 Div. who had been fighting their way up the eastern flank of the corridor, and the Group were now covering the Maas bridge at Grave against another possible attack from the west. No. 2 Squadron was guarding the food store at Oss.

There we found Colonel Dickie, Oliver and Ian drinking champagne. Ian had now become the Commander's tank troop leader, a nice comfortable job. The Commander said straightaway he would send me back to No. 2. I was really very glad, and although I had hoped not to return to No. 2, anything was better than nothing and Tony's arrival made a vast improvement. So after a glass of champers I returned in high spirits to the Transit Camp across the Maas.

It is an enormous bridge and it was extremely lucky that we should have captured it intact, only slightly damaged by bombing.

I said goodbye after tea and drove to 'A' Echelon with my kit in Humphrey Gascoigne's Humber. Arrived at the battalion and spent the night in a wood with Henry Allsopp and Sydney Middleditch in a tent. Henry gave out a rum ration to the men that night, and contrary to the K.R. that, if any rum is left over, the jar must be smashed to the ground by an officer, we finished off the remains amply aided by Sydney; there's something to be said for being a Quartermaster. A new young officer was there, Alan Horn, who had just arrived in the battalion.

We were extremely sorry to hear that Miles Bodley had died of wounds. This was especially sad as his brother had been killed only a month ago. He had a great many friends who would miss him.

Friday, 29 September. Moved up to Battalion H.Q. in their brick factory, I was to remain there until the Squadron came back from Oss. I found room in a tent with Oliver and John Rodney. H.Q. mess is full of some charming people now and I would have much liked to have been in it. Ian and I went for a walk round after tea to try and find a shotgun as I had some cartridges and there were a number of partridges about, but we lacked the third essential article. There were none to be had.

Ian showed me the spot behind the brick factory where a Spitfire had crashed only a few yards from him when he was going round the Guard. It had almost disappeared into the ground as it came down in a steep nose-dive like a thunderclap. A very apologetic pilot came round later. He had borrowed the plane from somebody else and had some explaining to do.

On the 30th I spent a leisurely morning writing letters in the mess. Later I was sent to relieve Gerald Style, 5th Battalion, who was sitting in the Post Office at Schaijk liaising between the civil and military telephones to the squadrons at Oss. So I settled down in a comfortable office with an armchair for a pleasant two days, I hoped.

Not a bit of it. Immediately the message came through that the whole battalion group had to move that afternoon to sit behind the Americans south of Nijmegen, who were expecting another counter-attack from the Reichswald Forest.

Later Comment

In the earlier part of the battle the 1st Coldstream was supporting the U.S. 82nd Airborne Division, under General Gavin, who were thinly spread along the Bergendal feature, a long low woody ridge that ran down the eastern flank between Grave and Nijmegen. Despite a number of major counter-attacks this remarkable division held firm on this vital flank.

Reluctantly we all packed up and moved over to a wood called Brewy near Hatert (behind Bergendal) just before dark. I had no vehicle, so I travelled on the top of Dick Howitt's scout car, as cold a drive as I shall ever remember, but I was allowed to knock back some rum out of the two-gallon glass jar at the end. We went the wrong way and eventually arrived to find that at Battalion H.Q. four shells, probably our own, had landed on them killing one man and wounding several, including Johnny Gull slightly in the arm. He was being carried away protesting furiously. So it was lucky for us we arrived late. As a result I was persuaded by Henry to sleep in the slit trench out in the open. I dug out an old trench and got down to sleep, but about one it poured with rain

132

and I woke up drenched, blankets and all. It was the most miserable night and I was still soaked and dreadfully cold next day.

Sunday, 1 October. Spent the morning trying to get dry by various means, hanging my clothes in the cooker tent. The battalion was together now and I went back to No. 2 Squadron after lunch at Battalion H.Q., an amusing lunch mainly at John Rodney's expense. I finally returned to No. 2 Troop again after tea, though since all the troops had become so mixed up I had no particular feelings about this one. I took this over with Sergeant Shipley as Troop Sergeant and Sergeant Fawcett as the other Tank Commander, but there were only two of my original men in it, Channon and Meadows.

Shipley was one of Val Hermon's old troop and a cool reliable Yorkshireman from Driffield, Fawcett an old friend from Salisbury Plain days, another Durham miner, older than most of us. I liked them both. We are now reduced to three tanks per troop.

It was rather a silent and subdued dinner in No. 2 mess that evening I thought, and I had mixed feelings at being back. A noisy and wet night as there was shelling quite close; I slept in the officers' mess tent, perched precariously on a car backseat.

The Island

Monday 2, October. During the morning we moved out a mile or two to continue the rest the battalion were meant to be having. A mile back the order came to stay where we were and await orders to move north. One of those indefinite infuriating orders, "Stand by to move at one hour's notice". At four o'clock we moved north through Nijmegen across the Waal and took over from the 2nd Irish, backing up 231st Infantry Brigade of 50th Division who were holding the Nijmegen bridgehead on what we knew as 'The Island'.

The Germans had been counter-attacking heavily and the Micks had had a sticky time. Freed from the threat to Arnhem, the Germans were losing no time in seeking to lance this abscess over the Nijmegen bridge.

Nijmegen is a nice clean-looking town and I should have liked to have spent a day there. However, we went straight through to the bridge. This was being shelled when I crossed. A truck was hit in front of my tank as I reached the entrance. The bridge, built in 1936, is vast. It is known as the Grenadier bridge after their brilliant exploit capturing it.

133

It was remarkably little damaged, fortunately. When the four Gren tanks under Sergeant Robinson charged over in half evening light followed by Peter Carrington's tank, the Germans were hanging from the girders of the huge span firing down upon them. Demolition squads too were actually under the bridge with the charges but they were soon ousted by our sappers. Tony Jones in his scout-car was immediately behind the tanks and performed a fantastic feat to make the bridge safe, for which he gained his M.C. One of the minor spans had been damaged since by a suicide party of Germans who floated an explosive down, strapped this to a pier and exploded it. However, the gap had soon been 'Baileyed'. A mile below they did successfully blow down a span in the railway bridge, then stupidly tried to swim back upstream again, but they were soon exhausted and captured by the Dutch.

On the other side of the bridge we stopped, filled up and cooked some supper. Just before dark George Dawnay came back with his orders. The battalion was to sit behind the Hampshires and Dorsets who were in 50th T.T. Division and were holding the line north of Bemmel. Bemmel is another name I shall never forget. Only a few miles of flat ground separated us here from the bridge at Arnhem, but it might have been a continent away now.

We moved up with No. 2 Troop in the lead. At one corner I had to leave Bradbury my new Co-driver as a guide to the rest to be picked up by the last tank. It was to be some time before he met up with us again.

The Squadron was put in the line with the 1st Hampshires in two orchards, two troops in each. It was getting dark so I placed my troop in the front orchard to stay the night all together, and went to find the infantry.

We were to have an exciting time in this orchard. A rectangle about three hundred yards long and one hundred in depth, it was filled with large well-spaced trees laden with apples. To the front was a wide open space, with another large orchard on the right of it and a smaller one on the left. A few ruined houses in the space five hundred yards away were supposed to be in enemy hands.

At the back of our orchard ran a track with a deep ditch behind it, too big for a tank to cross, but at the right-hand end was a small bridge of old oil drums over which we crossed. Just beyond this bridge to the right in the corner of our orchard stood a farmhouse and barn attached, called Houtakker, I later discovered.

134

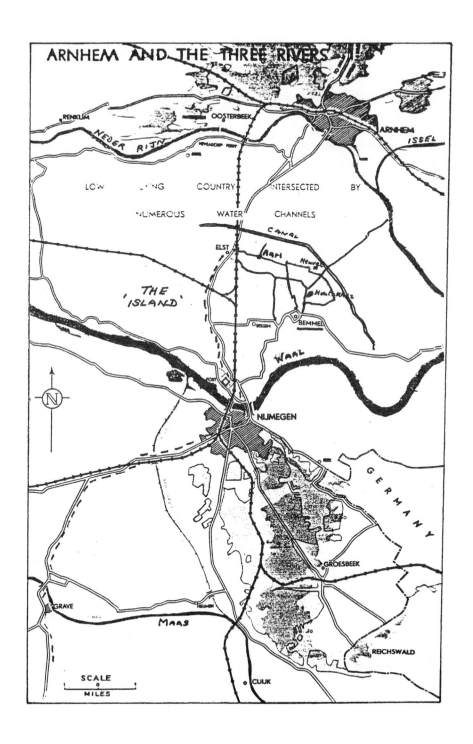

ARNHEM AND THE THREE RIVERS

RENKUM

OOSTERBEEK

NEDER RIJN

ISSEL

ARNHEM

MEIADORP FERRY

LOW   ING   COUNTRY   INTERSECTED   BY

NUMEROUS   WATER   CHANNELS

CANAL

ELST

Aam

Heuve

HeultWAG

THE
'ISLAND'

BESSIM

BEMMEL

WAAL

FORT

N

NIJMEGEN

BEEK

G E R M A N Y

GROESBEEK

GRAVE

HEUMEN

MAAS

REICHSWALD

SCALE
0   1
MILES

CULIK

Behind ours was another orchard about the same size and at the back ran the road south to Bemmel. Sandy Neville's troop, No. 3, were in reserve by this road. Across the road behind him was the infantry Battalion H.Q. in a cottage and Squadron H.Q. tanks. The other two troops were in another orchard further up the road. I found some infantry of the Hampshires in the farmhouse. They were a section of carriers with, they told me, two 6-pounder anti-tank guns on the front edge of the orchard protected by about six Bren guns, and that was all. Otherwise, like all infantry in the line they knew nothing much. It was bright moonlight, full moon, the Harvest moon I think, when I walked back to their Battalion H.Q. to find out the situation. Their Commanding Officer told me that in an orchard on the right and slightly forward of mine was a company, and another of the Dorsets on the left. I was at the apex of a sort of V of open ground held by the enemy. We were on the corner, I learnt later, where the line turned back to the west towards Elst, almost a right-angled turn, from where we sat. The 1st Dorsets and the 2nd Devons with No. 3 Squadron were holding the line over our left shoulder, with an old friend and former Coldstreamer, Colonel John Carew-Pole, in command of the latter.

I found Watty standing in the orchard and he walked back to see where my troop was. By now the mortaring had started and several times we lay flat. George had come to see me too, and the idea was that I should sit by the little bridge all night and move up to the front of the orchard before dawn. We all walked up to recce a position at the far front end and found a place for two tanks just to the left of the anti-tank guns.

While there we were badly caught by some heavy mortaring and lay flat to the ground as it landed all around, George remarking in the middle of it how good the apples were. I tried one and it made all the difference. It was a delicious apple and I handed one to Watty. Luckily we escaped untouched but it was the beginning of a ceaseless bombardment.

We spent the night close together in the tanks with precious little sleep, each doing an hour's guard on the bridge. I then sat in the Co-driver's seat as he had not returned yet. All night we were shelled and mortared. At one moment a heavy concentration landed on top of us. It was disagreeable, but I was glad to say sitting in my tank I did not mind the shelling, though some were very close. The tank was hit once or twice and I soon got a headache from the noise. We had one casualty, Guardsman Tibble, Fawcett's co-driver, from a splinter in the shoulder. We put him in the farmhouse cellar for the night, but he wasn't serious.

About five o'clock we stood-to and I walked up rather anxiously to the front of the orchard with the Tank Commanders to show them their positions. Then we moved the tanks up and sat there the whole day. A day rather as one might have expected in the last war, the enemy we could see walking about, having his breakfast a few hundred yards away. We were pretty idle too and he must have seen us walking and cooking. Bland, my Driver, who was cooking in a slit trench behind the tank, put out his hand to pick up some bread and it was immediately welcomed by a bullet whistling past. Mortared and shelled sporadically, every few minutes we were sniped at by a Spandau. In return we gave a few bursts of Browning back when we saw them move. To my surprise we were not shot at by an 88, since we were fairly exposed.

I can't say I minded the day really, though it was none too pleasant when every now and then down came a heavy stonk. I succeeded in polishing off a large part of the *Times* crossword between watches and once or twice I walked over to the farm and sat there. But remembering Sourdevalle we kept a very alert watch and everyone in their right places so we would not be caught out by a Panther attack. We nearly were then, and also I had a plan worked out if attacked.

Later Comment

Regrettably Guardsman Tibble never returned to us; his wound was more serious than we thought. We had in fact to take a great deal of care to avoid casualties. Guardsman Daniel then driving Sergeant Shipley's Tank tells the story in after years how he got out of his tank and lit the stove to brew up some tea. Scarcely had he done so when I came up the orchard and told him if he did that again I would shoot him, and he adds, "I almost believed he would have done."

I expected to be here that night. Rumours were there was going to be a small attack next day to drive back the Hun to a better line, as he was still shelling the Nijmegen bridge. However, Watty came over in the evening saying be ready to move back before dark. I thought this rather odd at the time. Meanwhile the Infantry Battalion H.Q. and Squadron H.Q. had moved back to some houses north-east of Bemmel out of the shelling and had switched off the air. I waited till dark came for a message and then moved my tanks to the back of the orchard again, since it was not much fun sitting out alone unprotected by infantry at night. Earlier on it had been raining, but now it turned out to be a lovely moonlight night again. I saw four mallard flighting in low over the orchard to feed. I longed for a gun as they were beautifully in shot. Many times I waited for such a chance on a September evening at Penkivel in Cornwall.

No message came through, so I went back to find Sandy to see if he had had any. He hadn't. We searched around the farm across the road for someone where Battalion H.Q. had been but it was deserted. We were narrowly missed by some mortaring for our pains that landed a few feet from me, and I flattened myself in a muddy rut in the road. A carrier in the middle of the road had just had a direct hit inside and was in a pretty good mess but no one was on board. I would have to go back to find George and looked about for some transport as it was two miles by road. Two D.R.s by chance came walking up the road to pick up two guides, so I decided to go back with one of them. We walked quickly back what seemed miles, to the bikes they had left, as mortars were landing sporadically, and had an anxious ride through Bemmel which was being hit by some pretty heavy long-range shells. Several times we had to stop and get off where the road was cratered. Each time the rider stalled his engine. I was thankful I was patient. I noticed the little lighted sign of an R.A.P. on the way and this proved very useful later on.

George, Watty and Nigel Bingham I found all sleeping in a snug warm cellar and I felt envious. The message I had received was unfounded and we were to remain, as I thought, in the orchard. After profound apologies from Watty I returned in the scout-car. The driver was rather windy and succeeded in running into an ambulance and later on into a truck head-on, not to speak of a cat or two; however, no damage was done. I left the scout-car at the entrance to the orchard, turned him round, and he went speeding off into the darkness. How many did he hit on the way back, I wondered.

It was a lonely, eerie walk back across the orchard and sinisterly silent. I found my tanks, pulled them back close into the farmyard, set a guard in each and myself stayed in the farm with two of my guardsmen. The rest slept in the tanks. The infantry had found a large cellar underneath and to be near the infantry commander I slept on some straw in a corner

138

of the cattle stalls, a loft full of hay above, so I hoped not too much would come through.

The night started with the usual unknown bursts of fire and mortaring that we had had all day. I soon went to sleep.

About ten thirty I was awakened by a terrific barrage. The Hun had started belting the orchard suddenly with everything he had. I jumped up and looked out to see shells landing everywhere. There were not only mortars and ordinary sized shells but heavy shells making a crater some five or six feet wide, 210 m.m., I should think. I saw the sparks of a mortar land about five feet from me in the farmyard, so went into the farm to get everyone back into the tanks and stand-to. Just then a windy infantry sentry came running in shouting, "There are enemy all round us". I had everyone out in the tanks now, but stayed myself to see what the infantry commander wanted to do. The house was hit two or three times with a tremendous crash of glass and bricks, and the infantry had all gone to ground in that fatal cellar. More of them came running back out of the orchard murmuring about the limit of human endurance. So I thought it was time to leave, made a dash for my tank and managed to jump in unhurt.

By now the barrage had been going on for about ten minutes and I could watch it creeping up and down the orchard. It was very concentrated and showed great credit to the Boche gunners. There was considerable Spandau fire too. Not only were the tanks being hit by H.E. but the dust and smoke was such that almost nothing at all could be seen. Our eyes and throats stung from that acrid smell of H.E. So I decided to pull back out of the orchard.

I called up the tanks on the air. With relief Shipley answered straight away, the other tank's wireless was hit and out of action, and we moved across the little bridge back to where Sandy's tanks were. A good deal of confusion followed as some of his crew were sleeping under their tanks and were caught outside. The mortaring wasn't too bad here and we sat and waited. After a while the mortaring died down a bit and I started to move back into the front orchard expecting an attack to come in. I could not get Sandy to move an inch, for during this I learnt he was wounded badly in the leg by shrapnel. Luckily I remembered the R.A.P., so directed his crew there with him on the back of a tank.

I moved cautiously across the bridge and groped our way up the orchard, my tank going in reverse I remember, turret traversed towards

139

the enemy as I had not had time to turn round. There was a great deal of small arms firing going on and it was plain that the enemy had infiltrated into the orchard behind the barrage. We edged our way down towards the end and I expected to meet two or three Panthers sitting there. We were being fired at by Spandaus all round and the tracer came whistling past.

So we halted and let the orchard have everything we had. It was very reassuring to hear our own guns firing at last. We raked the orchard with Browning for nearly a quarter of an hour, spraying in all directions, especially the flashes of the enemy m.g.s. which appeared very close. Four or five Brownings lit up the orchard with their tracers, but we could see nothing clearly defined except the dark shadows of trees in the moonlight. It was only too apparent we were right amongst a heavy attack by German infantry. Our own had disappeared and I suspect were all hiding in that cellar. The barrage had been too much for them.

Apart from the high-speed crackle of the Spandaus I had been surprised to hear the slower beat of the Bren firing at us and so I was rather anxious about their two anti-tank guns they had abandoned. The Boche could easily have turned them round on us. However, the Hun had had enough of our Browning and had withdrawn. I don't suppose he expected tanks. How long we kept up our fire, I cannot say for sure, but I know I was much relieved to find we had held on to our position. By the size of the barrage he probably had about a company attacking behind it, so our time hadn't been wasted. If they had cut the road behind us it would have been a difficult situation to clear up next morning. Later we discovered our infantry had cleared out, leaving their guns behind, a bad let-down. It was a tricky position to be left in, as tanks are little use at night without local infantry protection. Anyone can sneak up unseen on them.

All this time I had been trying to contact anyone on the air, as they had all switched off, which was bad. I was very glad to hear John Sutton's voice call "Tare two" at last. He was in another orchard further west, and had been attacked, but his infantry were still there. I came up and told him my position, and talked to him. Eventually we got someone on the air, I think Nico Collin, who managed to get the gunners to put down a concentration on the enemy lines in front of our orchard.

The rest of the night went slowly, but, apart from shelling, there were no more attacks. Sergeant Fawcett came and reported that his Operator was missing from the beginning, so we presumed he had been wounded in the farm. Fawcett and Corporal Snaith, his gunner, without Tibble too, had had to fight his tank with only three men, and that must have been hard work.

Wednesday, 4 October. At first light I went along to the farmhouse to find the infantry. They were there in the barn, evidently they had had enough of the mortaring and pulled out. It was bad, but hard to blame them, for they had had an awful time, and a few days' rest since 'D' day when they led the assault on Le Hamel.

I was angry to find Fawcett's operator, a Corporal, lying asleep in the straw. He had no real excuse. It could have been a case of cowardice in the face of the enemy, and I could see he was very frightened; this was the first case I had come across, and I was glad he hadn't been in my old troop. Sergeant Fawcett had sent him over on foot to my tank to tell me his wireless was out of action during a lull early in the night. He was shivering then, I thought from cold, so I poured some whisky into a mug for him, which he took, and disappeared off the back of my tank. I told him he had endangered his crew and ordered Sergeant Fawcett to put him in open arrest.

The infantry were now moving out ready to put in a small attack at twelve o'clock. A brigade attack was going in to drive the enemy back to a canal, so as to hold a better line, by the Hampshires, and the Durhams on their right a little later. They asked me to cover the open ground in front of us with supporting fire during the attack. With both troops to look after now, I stayed the morning in the orchard keeping a lookout and had some breakfast and a shave between the mortaring. Later on I showed the Tank Commanders the positions where to fire from. George turned up and I explained the situation. He told me the other two troops were going to support from the orchard further to the right. In this landscape of deep ditches and canals, tanks were unable to move far, if at all, once they left a road.

Later Comment

By the morning we were grimy from cordite smoke, muddy, tired and cold. I was wearing a long Guardsman's issue greatcoat clipped up at the neck, I remember, which I had not felt like taking off since we moved into the line. The scene in the orchard, when drawn broke, was a sordid one indeed, scattered death and bits of debris. According to one officer's description of the battle in the *History of the Guards Armoured Division,* "the artillery and mortar-fire was as intense on this occasion as it was in the days of the Caen battles, some very heavy guns were used, a few craters being large enough to hold a carrier." I can readily endorse this. We were not many miles from the Ruhr and the enemy's ammunition seemed unlimited.

Yet our morale remained at the top. The Guardsmen had fought their tanks, through hours of total darkness inside, in a highly proficient manner. None of us wanted to talk much, but we shared that wonderful feeling of relief, coming out of a battle, only those who have been in action really know; we had held the line and we had come through, despite all the enemy could fling at us.

By a turn of fate my own tank at Bemmel was the last survivor of the four with which No. 2 Troop had gone to war across the Channel, Caribou; the same one that had served me so well on that terrible day at Sourdevalle, and had advanced with the Troop from the Seine to Brussels and onwards to the Rhine. Shortly after the battle, worn out and old through such honourable service, Caribou was withdrawn from the front line for good.

At five to twelve I moved the tanks up to their positions and at twelve o'clock we let them have it. It was a brilliant little attack that, the best I have ever seen. The infantry were literally shot into their objective. It all fitted in rather like a jig-saw puzzle. The 25-pounders, the least effective part, laid down fire on the enemy mortars, the open ground in front was raked by Bren and rifle fire from two supporting companies on either flank, and ourselves in the middle, while the other two troops were plastering the ground with H.E. in front of our advancing infantry. Over our heads came the roar of heavy Vickers machine guns firing indirect on the enemy rear. The first objective was soon taken and I had to stop firing as our own troops had already overrun the position. The attack moved on and by two o'clock they had reached their final objective, the next canal, a mile ahead. Not without loss unfortunately, they had suffered some sixty casualties due to mortaring. Their Brigadier, Alex Stanier, however, was extremely pleased with the help we were able to give them.*

* The Brigadier was heard by Sergeant Fawcett to say "If we had only had the support like this before, there would have been no need to disband tomorrow". 231 Brigade had been in action since 'D' Day and had taken tremendous casualties. It was easy to see they had had enough.

I visited Houtakker farm at Bemmel with Tommy Fawcett in May, 1990. It was difficult to find, but once located it is still very recognizable to me. Although the buildings

We stayed on in the orchard in case of a counter-attack and got heavily shelled again by long-range guns. Clouds of earth kept going up just in front and a tree was lifted completely into the air and disintegrated. John Baddeley, also supporting from the orchard, came up and talked to me, driving his tank alongside mine. He moved away. A few minutes later while doing a recce out of his tank, he had a nasty wound in his chest from some shrapnel, but I think he will be all right.

A rather surprising thing happened when an infantry man jumped into a slit trench at the beginning, not ten yards from where I had been standing and walking about earlier in the day. He found a very live German there complete with Spandau who must have come in during last night's attack. He had had a perfect opportunity to pick us off. Sergeant Fawcett very swiftly had him marching to the rear, hands stretched high: 'his feet didn't touch'!

Having sat in that orchard for two days' continual bombardment, I decided to have a little of my own back so cocked my gun up to extreme elevation. We laid the gun carefully and fired about twenty shells into Germany. I only hope they did some damage.

After a time the attack died down and the remainder of the squadron was withdrawn out of it to a harbour area in reserve. The shelling had come on heavily again and, as I was doing no further good there, I pulled out across the little bridge to the road behind. Several wounded were staggering back through the orchard and I sent my men to help them back to the R.A.P. At last, about four-thirty, I was ordered to withdraw my tanks through Bemmel to some houses north-east of it. We were held up on the way by someone knocking over a telegraph pole blocking the road, and while clearing it I met Bill Gray, coming the opposite way in his tank. He was surprised to see me walking about, as someone had told him I had been wounded. However, I was quickly able to discredit that story. A jeep went by just then with a badly wounded officer on it, so Bill had to move on and I lost the chance to hear more.

I found the rest of the squadron and pulled the tanks in. After having been in them almost continuously for forty-eight hours, we were glad

---

are all new and much more extensive, a small orchard near the road remains. We were very warmly received by the Lensen family who still own the farm. Mrs Lensen whose husband owned the farm in 1944 was fetched by her granddaughter from a house nearby and joined in a great welcome. Tommy Fawcett could still remember remarkably well much that occurred in those orchards 46 years ago.

to leave. We found ourselves a house and I managed to get all my troop in it under cover. The sudden relief from the strain of the last few days had an amazing effect on all. Everyone was extremely lighthearted and cheerful, especially as they knew they had done well. After a meal with Watty, when we related to one another our recent experiences, I went to sleep down in a cellar. Shells were still landing in Bemmel a few hundred yards away.

We have now settled down again for a rest and I am able to write this in the comfort, or rather luxury, of a Dutch house just south of Nijmegen. It is in fact a council house, but to English standards is of much higher standard than that. To sit in a soft chair and write under an electric light in a warm homely room is a paradise to us now.

Thursday, 5 October. Slept for a good twelve hours and it was well after eight when I was roused and encouraged my troop to have some breakfast.

We cleared up our little house and got quite comfortable. We had fixed up a lamp from a tank, and in the evening had lighting in our room. Allen Horn, an Ensign who had just arrived to replace Sandy Neville and I sat there. John Sedgwick had also joined No. 2 Squadron recently and taken command of No. 3 Troop. I wrote letter after letter. I hadn't written for ages, so took the opportunity to write to all my friends. I had a letter today from Harry Graham-Vivian who told me he had been wounded by a Panther at Point 238 with the 5th Battalion in the Normandy Bocage. He seemed to be cheerful and recovering all right. I am glad, as I was told he was pretty bad. I heard from Jock Hardwicke, one of my Cambridge friends from Trinity days, for the first time for years. He seems to be enjoying himself, in a submarine, H.M.S. *Subtle*, in the Far East of all places. Nannie wrote too; she sounds very well, but war-weary like us all.

The day was punctuated by piercing squeals, as the Guardsmen set about killing pigs that were wandering about. As a result we had a splendid pork chop for dinner, and with Fawcett and Shipley to help, spent an amusing evening and settled with a bottle of whisky. They both did well in the orchard, and altogether everyone seemed pleased with our little effort there.

The next day we spent doing much the same, undisturbed except by the shells landing in Bemmel.

One of our bombers disintegrated in the air overhead and the crew baled out. They were struggling frantically as those below watched, powerless to help, to get their parachutes to float into our own lines. It must have been a terrifying moment for them. I hope, and wonder, if they landed safely.

I had a letter from Father, little news really, but he was pleased to have had my letter describing our advance across France and Belgium.

In the evening we were to be relieved by the Americans, and without any regrets prepared to leave 'The Island'. We moved back to Battalion H.Q. after dark, just north of the Nijmegen bridge, ready to cross. But our relief never turned up, so we had to remain the night. My tank drew up alongside Ian's. He too had heard I had been wounded, and was duly distressed, I'm glad to say!

Saturday, 7 October. We stayed in that field till midday, when at last the order came to move. I walked over to No. 3 and saw John Sutton who seemed no worse for his excitements at Bemmel. I told him how glad I was to hear his voice on the air that night. Colonel Dickie came up to me and seemed very pleased about Bemmel too. Ian, John and I walked around the area during the morning and visited a nice house which Battalion H.Q. had been using. It had been owned by a 'Quisling', married to an American. Nicely furnished, it had the visiting cards of many eminent Germans, including one of General von Arnim. Bill was there, looking round to see what he could find.

We moved back across the Rhine by pontoon bridge beside the big arch, through Nijmegen, to exactly the same spot we had left the afternoon before going up. The officers' mess had already been set up in a house and we settled down to have a few days' rest. Part of the battalion was bombed on the way across and Jeff Darell's tank almost hit by a 500-pounder, but extraordinarily enough was none the worse.

Sunday, 8 October. A very peaceful two days sitting there. I went to church in an orchard in the morning and later set off to have a bath in Nijmegen. The next day I attended Commanding Officer's Orders to give evidence against the Corporal who had defaulted rather seriously. He got off lightly, being reduced, George saying, "I don't want him as a Corporal any more".

I went for a walk round some fields nearby with Ian and we put up several coveys of partridges. If only we had had a gun.

Next morning was wet; reluctantly we had to move out across the canal to be in reserve behind some Americans, their 82nd Airborne

Division, who expected they might be attacked from the Reichswald Forest. We had managed to find ourselves exceedingly comfortable billets in the outskirts of Nijmegen, near Hatert. Winter is fast approaching. It has not actually turned cold, but I fear it soon will, anyhow the rain seems to have increased. Worst of all it begins to get dark at six-thirty, not much fun under canvas.

Tuesday, 10 October. Poured with rain. All the squadron are under cover in houses at Hatert and the Dutch welcome us in a remarkable way. The officers' mess is set up in one nice house, and we have two good rooms, much to the envy of Battalion H.Q. who were not so well off. The houses round here are extraordinarily well built. They are council houses but have every amenity except a bath. The electric light still works, though occasionally we are plunged into darkness with shouts for candles, followed by a vote of thanks to Watty's grandmother who had sent them out to him. Rumour is that the electricity comes from occupied Holland, although the Germans do not realize.

The Dutch appear very amicable. They couldn't be anything else, I don't think, but we learnt that some of them here were collaborators, or had sons in the S.S., and the 'Underground' frequently came round and arrested spies. The tragedy of being so close to Germany, during their long period of neutrality in the First World War, meant many children were born of German soldiers stationed along the frontier. These had been conscripted into the German army or the Dutch S.S., and we were becoming aware for the first time of the hatred and misery such circumstances twice over had brought to many hundreds of innocent families.

We were told we would be static for a considerable period, like three weeks, which if one could believe it was a great relief. However, peacetime conditions having set in for a bit, peacetime activities must of necessity take place.

My chief need was for a shotgun, which would have meant an endless amount of pleasure, as there were lots of partridges about. Ian and I set about looking one afternoon and got right into the centre of the Underground Movement in Nijmegen. After passing through the hands of several youthful officers, we found ourselves in their armoury, where they had every sort and kind of lethal weapon, but no shotguns.

Friday, 13 October. An unpromising day, but in fact it turned out to be a pleasant one. It started with a lecture from the Corps Commander,

General Horrocks. We all bundled into Anthony Gell's comfortable captured General's car and drove off. Anthony had come back to us in full 'Flash' Gell form, and certainly was none the worse. This was a big morale raiser, especially to me. None of us had read where the lecture was, however, and as Corps Commanders are in the habit of residing at Corps H.Q., we went there to see, but there were no signs and after finding Derek Wigan, we were put on the right road to the barracks at Grave.

It was a very interesting lecture. The General first started by congratulating the G.A.D. on their performance, and told us the complete story of the airborne landings, the advance through Holland to Nijmegen and the failure at Arnhem. The Irish Guards showed up well early on at the Escaut and Eindhoven, and the Grenadiers also on the Nijmegen bridge. Unfortunately, he enraged the Coldstream contingent by saying the Irish Guards were the only battalion who could have made the breakout. Some of our officers never forgave him for saying this.

He spoke little of Arnhem, as if he regarded it as a greatly overwritten-up operation, but was full of praise for the Dorsets battalion who had never been mentioned at all in any of the papers. They had in fact got 2000 of the Airborne Division out across the Lek from Arnhem at the cost of their whole battalion.

The task of supplying 30 Corps along one available road, over nearly sixty miles, to a large extent unprotected, often under fire, and frequently cut, had caused him some unpleasant moments. I think he told us it had only been fully open for forty-eight hours during the whole battle, while the Coldstream and Grenadier Groups had to be turned round from the north to remove these serious threats to our lines of communication. The men in the never-ending stream of supply vehicles had carried out this most hazardous job in a most creditable manner.

In a way it was probably a lucky thing, he said, that Arnhem had failed in the end, as the Germans had far more troops up there than had been anticipated. Had we been able to push further towards the sea, we might have been badly cut off behind. Part of the reason for Arnhem was that we had not enough aeroplanes to drop all the 1st Airborne Division at once – it took three days – and because they had landed several miles from the town due to the German flak.

Hitler had ordered all the German reserves to drive us off the

147

so-called 'Island' between Nijmegen and Arnhem at all costs, so no wonder we had such a warm reception at Bemmel.

Not only had we succeeded in liberating a considerable part of Holland and had inflicted some 20,000 casualties on the enemy, 10,000 of which were prisoners, but the Corps were the only troops to have actually crossed the Rhine and held a real bridge across it. It wasn't possible to supply an army across the Rhine by a pontoon bridge in winter.

He ended up by saying that the next operation would take us right into Germany itself, with 30 Corps at the head. "One more 'killing match' will finish the war, but don't count on being home by Christmas." However, nothing could happen before Antwerp, the only reasonably intact port we had, was cleared.

Later Comment

It was necessary for the Corps Commander to place this emphasis on what had been achieved, and to play down the inability to reach Arnhem. He had made it clear enough though, in his final words, that the chance of ending the war in 1944 had been lost for good. Few then could have foreseen the enormity of the cost in lives and freedom these additional months of war would bring.

Concealed totally from us, of course, was the meaning behind his poignant words, the Germans had far more troops at Arnhem than anticipated. It was thirty years later when I had come to know General 'Jorrocks' well, as a constituent of mine in Somerset, he said to me often, "I cannot understand why Monty never told me those two Armoured Divisions were in the woods behind Arnhem. Monty knew."

The massive pressures on the Allied Higher Command to bring the war to an end in 1944, emanating from London and Washington, that led us to biting off more than we could chew at Arnhem, have been frequently told. This sad postscript is from one great battle commander, General 'Jorrocks', in a letter to me on 18 June, 1978.

"Arnhem was a tragedy because it should never have been fought at all. When my XXX Corps reached Brussels we were ordered to halt because of shortage of supplies, as these were coming all the way from the beach-head and the drivers were getting exhausted. At this time there was nothing between us and the Rhine – my Orders were to establish a bridge-head across this famous river – apart from one division of ancient Dutchmen who had been guarding the coast and had never seen a shot fired in anger. We called them 'The Stomach Division' because many of them had ulcers. In addition, there was one pretty useless brigade of Dutch S.S. We could

148

have brushed this opposition aside and seized our bridgehead over the Rhine without any difficulty at all – but no, we were halted for lack of supplies. Yet in the United Kingdom was sitting Brereton's huge Airborne Army, doing nothing. If the Powers that Be had given me one of their divisions for supply purposes, and another to Patton on the right flank, the war would have been over in 1944, thus saving many lives and also preventing the poor Dutch having to suffer one last winter of agony.

"In my opinion, this was one of the worst strategic blunders of the whole war." Brian Horrocks.

He and Nancy became real personal friends and we often saw them. Many times I heard him discuss this battle and say sadly how Monty never told him about the two Panzer Divisions – not because it might have endangered 'ultra', he believed but because it might just have stopped this very last chance to end the war in '44 from going ahead.

After an idle afternoon I spent the evening at a Commander's conference. I have now become that unenviable person, the battalion Gunnery Officer, in succession to John Baddeley. We went on for hours discussing a fearsome training programme for the next few weeks, drill parades, TEWTS, and other such tiresome things, all as a result of the Corps Commander's closing remarks in the morning.

My servant, Brown, who turned up some time ago, has just been back to France with John Sedgwick. They succeeded in finding all my kit and John's where Brown left it in a house in Arras when his truck broke down there last month.

It was Ian's twenty-first birthday, so we had a party for dinner at Battalion H.Q. with a considerable amount of champagne and apricot brandy. More than full, I staggered home after an enjoyable evening.

Saturday, 14 October. We had our first Commanding Officer's Drill Parade abroad, much to the delight and amusement of the local population. We marched and saluted in approved style. Fortunately I am no longer considered a young officer for the purposes of being chased by elated Drill Sergeants.

An idle afternoon with little to do except have a bath in the public showers in Nijmegen. Michael Hamilton came to dinner this evening. He is in No. 1 Squadron now. Afterwards I went to a film with him and John Rodney at 32 Brigade H.Q. Not a good film, but quite a pleasant evening.

149

Sunday, 15 October. Brussels leave is the great thing that is buoying everyone up and the roster is well on its way. I'm looking forward very much to spending forty-eight hours' leave there. I told Ian I would try and go with him. After a lengthy walk with Oliver this morning, we eventually reached an odd church where the battalion was having Church Parade, progressed solemnly through the service with a surprisingly good sermon. At last Ian and I were able to go out shooting partridges. He produced an extraordinary 16-bore single barrel gun with a five-cartridge magazine. We took it in turn to fire wildly at birds but never contacted, and we recce'd several good partridge places near Grave, an amusing afternoon's exercise, if nothing else.

The next two days were spent frantically maintaining. The Commander had decreed inspections in all directions starting with tanks down to the latrines. To justify my position slightly, I inspected all the guns at great length throughout the Squadron, prompted by the great Sergeant Palmer, our Gun-fitter. I found myself organizing a Trade Test for gunners, which everyone had different ideas about. We were inflicted with P.T. in the early morning and another drill parade.

This evening I was told I could go on leave to Brussels tomorrow, so felt cheered. I found Ian and we decided to push off as early as possible next day.

Wednesday, 18 October. After a frantic hour in the morning, and succeeding to persuade Joe Lee to run my Gunnery Test Ian and I set off for Brussels in the jeep. We were stacked full behind, we had two passengers, and were transporting our own drink in the way of champagne and whisky. These proved later to be a tremendous asset. Brussels was about 175 miles away and as far as Eindhoven progress was slow and exasperating. The whole of the 7th Armoured Division were going back down the road to help the Canadians open Antwerp.

Ian and I drove in turns, he completely regardless of the nerves of any other occupants of the car; fortunately by now my nerves seemed almost non-existent. At one moment he appeared to have an extraordinary affinity for a 25-pounder S.P. gun.

After Eindhoven the road cleared and we made good speed. I took the wheel for the last lap from Diest and certainly could not be accused of dawdling. We arrived in Brussels fortunately before dark and found ourselves a room at the division's Eye Club. John Sutton's and Billy Denbigh's jeep arrived only a few minutes after us, even though they started much later. Brown came with us and immediately found a home to stay at. Our Guardsmen always seem to have an incredible way of getting taken in like this.

After starting the evening with a bottle of champagne we set out on a most hazardous drive to put the jeep away safe. They were being stolen as quick as you could turn round. We whizzed in and out of trams in the blackout, hand permanently on the horn. After dinner with a further bottle of champagne, we both set off to sample Brussels' much heralded night life, only to be extremely disappointed. Returned home after wasting a considerable amount of money on buying drinks for and alternately dancing with hardly passable Belgian girls. However, I spent the most comfortable night since England, in sheets.

Thursday, 19 October. I woke to the unfamiliar ting-ting and rattle rattle of the trams and the bustle of traffic below. The town was alive and so different from the empty, shuttered streets we knew near the front line. Looking out of the window across the roofs of Brussels in the distance were the remains of the blackened Palais de Justice, destroyed by the Germans as we entered. It stood as a monument to German brutality. We spent an unsuccessful morning shopping and getting money from the cashier. It was raining hard, but in the afternoon it cleared, so we drove round to a gunsmith, Monsieur Mahillon, in the Rue Royale with the optimistic idea of acquiring a shotgun. As I entered the shop I thought it extremely unlikely that we should.

We gazed at the gun racks rather knowingly, passed a pair belonging to the Comte de Paris, and found a case containing 'four-ten' shotguns at 1800 francs apiece. Neither of us possessed this amount, but on the appearance of Monsieur Mahillon himself, he agreed in a short time to barter for a bottle of whisky and Ian's German automatic. Excitedly we drove to our rooms to fetch this kind and were at the shop in no time. With a little more persuasion we managed to buy a pair of these 'four-tens' for a bottle of whisky and champagne, Ian's Lüger and 800 francs apiece, following by exchanging one round of sten gun ammo for one cartridge. We left Monsieur Mahillon's shop triumphant. This completely made our day. These were two nice little guns and our aim was to go out shooting at the first possible opportunity.

151

Having no money left we returned to the Eye Club and went to an English film with John Sutton in the evening, then a delicious hot bath followed by another comfortable night.

We set off at an almost gentlemanly hour next morning back to Nijmegen, made good progress and returned at lunchtime. These two days were the greatest fun and almost the best time spent since England.

Saturday, 21 October to Monday, 6 November. The next fortnight was more like peacetime than war. An exceedingly happy fortnight, in my case dominated by two factors, firstly, operation 'Pepperpot' and secondly Ian's and my days' shooting. The first extremely hard work and interesting, the second meant more fun.

Next morning after Brussels I was summoned before the Commander in the Orderly Room and told the plan.

The battalion was to take part in operation 'Pepperpot' with the 43rd Division who were to attack into the Reichswald Forest. Our role was to sit back and shoot the 75s as an artillery regiment at 8000 yards behind the enemy lines, while the 17-pounders and Honeys were to shoot their Brownings. This was part of the plan for a set-piece infantry attack on a section of the Siegfried Line. Every square yard of ground in front was to be raked by some fire or other during the six hours preceeding the attack. It was a thing no other armoured battalion had thought of doing, so far as we knew. The difficulties were considerable, but as Gunnery Officer I came into my own. The targets given us, we were given complete freedom as to how to engage them.

Shooting our 75s from this range was definitely a gunners' problem, so I set off immediately to see the gunner battery of the Leicester Yeomanry usually attached to us. The Battery Commander, Bob Clark, a most charming man, was only too pleased to help us.

After a long discussion on Saturday afternoon, – much to my irritation as I was longing to go out and shoot our new four-tens with Ian – we decided roughly where and how to do it. I found a reasonable place to fire from, a clearing in the wood below the crest of the ridge held by the American Para Division and took the Commander there next day. The thing was agreed on.

The next week was spent in chasing round the various A.G.R.A.s, the H.Q.s of the large gunner formations, and 43rd Div. H.Q. I had one splendid morning driving sedately round with Colonel Dickie in his staff car to various H.Q. At each we had a large gin or whisky, Colonel Dickie

152

pulling their legs hard. By the time I got back to lunch I could hardly stand.

The Ammo. problem was considerable. We had to order 40,000 rounds of 75 H.E. for the shoot to last six hours. Visions of horror at a remote ordnance factory 'somewhere in England' required to churn out a new production line of shells. The order anyhow was a considerable shock to the RASC and as this went on I foresaw sooner or later it would be cancelled.

An afternoon spent with Bob Clark calibrating three of our guns with his 25-pounders. I sat in an O.P. with him looking over the German lines towards the Reichswald Forest and batted away at a church on the German frontier. We hit it eventually and a house inside Germany at 8000 yards, which was good for a 75. Bob was extremely painstaking and helpful, though we got stonked at one moment.

We had to solve many technical problems: how to site the tanks, dig-in the ammunition, control and fire, and cool the guns – and get the plan approved by Colonel Dickie. I got to know him well during this week and found him most charming and always out to be helpful. However, on Sunday morning, like many things one does in the Army, the whole operation was called off. I am not sorry, for it might have been murder for the infantry, though it was great fun working out.

Later Comment
Could we have sustained three rounds a minute from some forty tanks for hours on end, and with accurate enemy counter-fire? Often I have wondered since how it would have worked. We thought it would then. The unspoken mood and theme at this stage of the war, among staff and everyone else, was to find any means of keeping casualties to the absolute minimum, which no doubt brought such a scheme as this into being.

In the battalion things were going on peacefully, Drill parades and P.T. followed by maintenance and all the normal nonsense. We were well dug-in and comfortable in our mess, and all the Guardsmen much at home in their billets.

In No. 2 we did ourselves well on Kershaw's cooking. Dermot had now come back to us, as Second Captain, from brigade. We had two nice rooms in the house, one was the dining room, the other we all slept in. George, of course, was as intolerable as usual to live with, especially in the morning, he bounded out of bed, flung all windows wide open and turned every one else out.

On November 3rd John Sutton held his twenty-first birthday party. One of the most enjoyable evenings, the most charming people there, a mass of drink, sounds of much singing and well-oiled frivolity.

Little news from home, everything seemed fairly peaceful. George has now returned to the 3rd Battalion and Edward appears to be invading Greece, possibly liberating Athens, but no news from him. Mary has been on leave so naturally no letter from her.

A most charming letter from Sergeant Brough's sister, May, one of the nicest I ever had. She asked if his mother might be allowed to keep the old No. 2 Troop Board with the names of the tanks and a Coldstream Star, and I am more than pleased she had it and was keeping it. I shall always keep that letter, exactly what I would have expected from his family.

Later Comment

His sister, Miss May Brough, wrote to me in May 1980 from near Doncaster, "We still have the Troop board with your name on. My parents were so proud of it, we continue to count it amongst our treasured possessions. My brother and sisters join me in wishing you all the best of health and happiness for the future."

War seldom keeps absent, and we heard that Reggie Longueville had just been killed, I'm afraid, with the 4th Coldstream. He was shot down while out of his tank after it had been hit, near Venraij. A former Troop Leader in our squadron, he was remembered with affection by every guardsman who knew him.

A Dutch schoolmaster, Herr Schilling, used to come every evening to teach Watty German in return for tea. He was quite interesting and told us that the Mosquito raid on the Hague last year, reported to have destroyed a Gestapo building, actually destroyed all the duplicate identity cards of the Dutch. This enabled any amount of forged ones to be obtained, and so made life much easier for them.

As for our shooting activities, Ian and I enjoyed ourselves immensely with our four-tens. Nearly every evening we set off in a jeep after partridges, and one or two afternoons with other guns. Our best bag was thirteen partridges. Ian shot a snipe one evening and missed a wood-

154

cock, – unforgiveable. We both shot a snipe which fell into the Rhine, but were unable to find either. I was lucky to have a friend who had much the same ideas as I had in what otherwise would have been an intensely boring period.

One evening towards the end we ran into a Dutchman, who told us of some woods on the 'Island' where there were some pheasants. Next evening we set off there and found the woods at Loenen, not far from the front line. Fortunately as we left the jeep we saw the keeper. He turned out to be a charming man and walked us through the woods with his blind dog. We shot five pheasants that evening and saw quite a number, a most successful 'armed reconnaissance'.

As soon as possible we determined to come again, but the most disappointing thing of course happened the day after we had discovered our shoot on the 'Island'. Orders to move came through.

We had one more chance. On November 9th we came over with Dermot and Bob Clark and had a very good day. The keeper and a retinue of dogs greeted us. Straightaway he went to a bell hanging in a small white wooden turret and pulled the rope vigorously. Several beaters appeared. We shot thirteen pheasants, five hares and an owl, and I was hit in the forehead by a pellet from the old keeper to add to the joys. It was great fun.

Several V-2 rockets had been arriving round about and in England. Ian and I saw one going up one afternoon – a vapour trail going straight up beyond the German horizon.

Later comment

These vertical vapour trails, drifting gently sideways over the flat horizon, – I had first seen one out shooting partridges – were a serious pointer to the future. In a matter of five or six minutes they could be landing with a terrifying suddenness on London. We were of course not told of the damage they caused, or the effect on morale, but the newspapers had given us quite a bit of information about those V-2s, and they certainly were impressive. We were far too preoccupied then with the present to think much about, least of all to understand, how rockets would come to dominate the post-war world, let alone space.

During this time the Canadians and other units of 2nd Army had been engaged in clearing Antwerp. This mainly consisted of clearing the

Island of Walcheren and the Scheldt. It had been a bloody battle. By now this was done and the port of Antwerp should be open by November 15th. On the south side of our salient we had been attacking to clear up Holland this side of the Maas, but recently the Germans had attacked the Americans at Venlo and pushed them back three miles. In case this attack developed, we were at two hours' notice to move south.

The 6th Guards Tank Brigade were engaged in this and had captured Overloon and Venraij. Later, to the west of the salient, the 4th Battalion, Coldstream, had liberated Tilburg, their first large town.

Further to the south the Americans had been bogged down round Aachen and little was happening. Various rumours about the Americans were going around, but it was evident the one reason for their sticking in September was shortage of petrol. It was also rumoured that General Patton went to Aachen contrary to Monty's wishes, as he no longer commands the Americans. This resulted in half our supplies and strength being diverted to them and was partly the reason for the failure at Arnhem. The Arnhem push was rumoured to have been Winston's own plan, and, if successful, might have ended the war. On the other hand, if we had all gone to Aachen with the Americans, it might have been equally successful. We shall never know until, perhaps, many years after the war, and then we will have little interest in it.

Later Comment

With the knowledge of hindsight from many historians, including General Horrocks' writing, these rumours, with the exception of that about Churchill, were remarkably accurate.

Wednesday, 8 November. The Commander called all officers to a conference in a school and explained our move. The conference was horribly reminiscent of that old barn near Bayeux, where the rasping voice of Colonel Ririd had told us of our first action. It seemed like four years, not four months, since then. How incredibly things had turned out. I had thought then we might be spending the winter near Paris. How different my outlook and state of mind was now. In the early days we were like excited schoolboys beginning a new adventure, as so we were. Now I was calmly indifferent to everything and entirely lived for the moment. Looking round the room, I felt very lucky, or unlucky who knows, as Ian, John Sutton, Malcolm Lock and myself were the only remaining Troop Leaders who started at the beginning and were at that first conference.

Like all moves, we had known and expected it for several days, even though it was top secret. The plan was for 2nd Army to take over more of the American line while they attacked towards Cologne. The division was to move south to hold the line north of Aachen, just north of Geilenkirchen, near Sittard. We were to move in the early hours of Sunday all the way by dark to our position near Sittard, so it promised to be a very unpleasant journey. It was getting cold, at one moment even snow started falling. However, luck came my way. On Friday morning Ian came to say his turn to go to Brussels had come again; could I possibly come too? I was unable to go, but we went to see Oliver, and he managed to find a solution. We arranged to go on Saturday.

Saturday, 11 November. Soon after breakfast Ian and I again took to the road, via Hertogenbosch and Tilburg, both cleared since our last visit, and ate our lunch of excellent cold pheasant sandwiches by a dirty Belgian canal. We arrived at the 'Eye' Club in Brussels soon after one. John Rodney met us there. He seems to have one of the best jobs possible, as he now runs the 'Eye' Club, reasonably, seeing how his home is in Brussels.

Sunday, 12 November. Rose earlier than one might have expected for a Sunday morning after a night on leave in Brussels, better left un-described, though none the less enjoyable. At breakfast Ian suggested we should do the 'TEWT' at Waterloo that morning. But this idea was 'Kaput' as we spent an infuriating morning trying to get the jeep to start, being towed round by a Canadian truck.

Back at the 'Eye' Club for lunch, we found Simon Birch and John Sutton had arrived. Later we all had a great dinner party with champagne and our pheasants in the 'Eye' Club, served with pomp and splendour, much to the envy of other members. The Belgians were more than generous in entertaining the British on leave and Ian and I spent a pleasant evening with the Baron Jose de Vinq with his sister and another girl. We were put to shame, as he was a brilliant dancer.

Monday, 13 November. A morning shopping in Brussels, and we paid

157

a visit to our friend Monsieur Mahillon and bought more cartridges. He said he enjoyed his bottle of whisky very much. At lunchtime we set off to drive back. The battalion had moved and we were not at all sure exactly where to. Made fairly good speed to Maastricht and crossed the Maas by Bailey bridge there. The old bridge had been very effectively dealt with by the R.A.F. in 1940. From there we decided to go via Aachen, a bad mistake Ian blamed me entirely for. However, for the first time I set foot on the 'cursed soil of the Reich', and celebrated it by drinking some cherry brandy.

We passed through the remains of the Siegfried Line into Aachen, a fine old city but every house was badly damaged, though not so bad as Caen. Unfortunately we spent an hour trying to find our way out and then had a deplorable journey home. It got dark and rained. The road was thick with mud. We searched for an hour or more. At last with great relief we found the signs to the battalion and arrived at Hillensberg, near Sittard on the German frontier. A good meal, and Watty had found me a comfortable bed. For the first time I slept in a German bed.

Tuesday, 14 November. With Hillensberg came winter. The rain and tanks combine to make mud. I went to see the men fetch their breakfasts and picked my way through the mud in my shoes. None of my kit had yet arrived. Hillensberg is a village just inside the German border, and for security all the people had been turned out of their houses and sent to Holland. The battalion had taken over the western end. H.Q. was on top of the hill, while No. 2 was halfway down. One squadron was to be in the line in support of the 5th Battalion for a week in Wehr. Our turn was next week.

The squadron passed the morning cleaning up the tanks. They had not had a good journey from Nijmegen, long and slow, so I was very lucky. They made a great deal of noise coming in, and later a captured intelligence summary said that a change-over had just taken place on their front, and judging by the noise made, 'it must have been a new and inexperienced unit.'

To satisfy the urge to see what lies over the hill, I went off on my first walk in Germany. The owner of the house had left behind his dog, a mixture of a retriever and pointer, and it promised to be a gundog, so I adopted it. An ugly dog to look at, it had 'Prinz' stamped on the collar, and I entrusted him to Wicking to look after. The mess was comfortable, I found a room to myself, and I was able to avoid some of the others. I could read, write, and idle undisturbed.

Wednesday, 15th November. Rain and mud. My kit arrived from the echelon, so I squelched about in rubber boots. Johnny Thompson insisted on inoculating me, as I had found a piece of lead shot in my forehead.

Thursday, 16 November. More rain and more mud. I drove round the battalion in the scout-car, spread out over two miles, to find any problems. Ventured out in the rain with Ian, our guns, and the dog that afternoon. The hound was wild and disobedient – that was the last time it was to come out.

Friday, 17 November. The morning was spent on a recce, that horrible word, with George, up to the front line to find out where to put my troop when we take over from No. 3. The front here was very quiet, so quiet that such remote figures as press correspondents, and even George Doughty, G.3. at division, and a former No. 2 Squadron officer, had ventured to peer over the top. David Kennard met us there, as his company was to be in the line when I was coming up, so it was arranged with George I was to support him. He asked me to come and shoot some duck in the afternoon. With Prinz on the back, I set off in the scout-car. We wandered to and fro in a swamp at Susterseel, and slew five teal and a pheasant; Ian Liddell* and Alan Pemberton were also in the party. My shooting was deplorable, but I could not have enjoyed it more. The 'Hound of the Baskervilles', as David called my dog, worked well to my surprise, and brought back a running pheasant, and laid it down at my feet.

Saturday, 18 November. Another wet and eventless day. No, there was one great event; I shot my first woodcock of the season. This was the only luck we had, but Prinz had a fight with a ginger cat, the angriest cat I have ever seen, and after inflicting wounds on both of us, we managed to drive it off. Returned back to my room, and opened a bottle

---

* Captain Ian Liddell won the VC on 3 April 1945. He led the overwhelmingly successful attack by the Coldstream Group that captured intact the vital bridge across the River Ems at Lingen, inside the German frontier. He first cut the wires to the demolition charges under heavy fire and crossed at the head of his Company, No. 3. Saddest of all he did not live to know he had been awarded the VC, the only one in the Guards Armoured Division. He was killed by a stray bullet three weeks later at Rotenburg.

159

of delicious apricot brandy, and so we become another day nearer the end of the war.

Sunday, 19 November. Early this morning there was a shattering explosion caused by a flying bomb, a V-1, landing just over the hill. Several of our windows were broken and I heard Watty down the passage swear that a shell had landed on his window-sill. Outside, preparations for our move were taking place.

Monday, 20 November. The squadron moved into the line. Two troops were to be up with the forward companies, while the remainder sat back in billets in Wehr half a mile behind. Anthony and I were the first up, so after lunch I moved down the hill from Hillensberg, to be greeted by a few shells caused by some bloody fool, who had brought his tanks over the crest of the hill, and had been seen by the enemy. I put my tanks in position in the wood with David Kennard's Company H.Q., and then set about to dig a reasonably comfortable dug-out.

Here we sat till Friday afternoon. Very quiet, we were not shelled at all except for two duds that landed quite close one night, caused by Johnny Gull making too much noise moving an A.R.V. about at Hillensberg, pulling the Brigadier's car out of a ditch was the rumour we heard, after he had dined well at battalion HQ. A pleasant change to be away from the squadron, though it never stopped raining. Our dug-outs were soon flooded, so I resigned myself to being wet, keeping wet and staying wet. As usual the cheerfulness and wit of the Guardsmen rose inevitably in proportion to the degree of disagreeable state we are in, and my task was an easy one. Ian Liddell took over command at Company H.Q. at night. Long discussions with him and the C.S.M. on every conceivable subject took place throughout the nights. He was going to get married, when he could get leave, the C.S.M. wholly disapproved of him doing so until the war ended, and my support as an ally by the C.S.M. was actively canvassed. All this was diverting.

The enemy were peaceful, but patrolled about our wire by night, and two men got into our wood on Thursday. The 5th Battalion were actively patrolling enemy lines every night too. However, by day they were some 2,000 yards away, so one could walk about quite happily in the open. I even went out with my four-ten one day. Two German

160

patrols had a fight between each other in front of our wire, it made entertaining watching. I had the dog up with me, though it was rather miserable in the rain and disappeared for one night. One evening I saw a woodcock flying high over at dusk.

A heavy raid by Lancasters took place quite close and shook the ground around us for three-quarters of an hour, and two V-2s were seen going straight up like balls of fire.

Friday, 24 November. Great difficulty starting the tanks this morning due to the heavy moisture in the air, and we made a horrible noise towing them to start behind the front platoons. We expected a heavy stonk any minute in consequence.

My troop moved out of the line to our billets in Wehr. I saw to it they all had a good meal and then spent an hour in a most excellent hot bath the thoughtful Brown had contrived for me.

Saturday, 25 November. Another eventless day at Wehr. It was not a village by any stretch, merely a cluster of four or five houses, a railway platform and a shed or two.

I felt depressed all day, I don't know why. I want a change, but that is ridiculous as we are changing all the time. Anyhow I walked through a nearby bog at Wehr with Ian and got two pheasants and some rabbits, as well as getting wet. Drove up to Battalion H.Q. afterwards and had a drink with him.

Really there is not enough to do. One answer would be to say it was high time we were in action again. Above all this, the problem is to decide what to do after the war. The talk turns on this often now. I haven't the background knowledge to decide. The one real answer for sure is I will have to stay on in the army for a time. The war has been such a major part of one's life for so long.

Sunday, 26 November. A fine but cold day, the best for weeks. Walked my dog round in the morning and shot with the 5th Battalion in afternoon near Wehr with not much success. John Sutton came to have a drink with me in the mess. Shelled slightly in the night.

Monday, 27 November. I met a furious Colonel Roddy wanting to know why we had not sent in a 'shell rep' last night. There was no denying we had been shelled for he took me out and pointed to the shell holes, and I duly stopped the rocket for the whole squadron.

Later in the morning I took my tank and did a successful indirect shoot on a house occupied by Germans about 3000 yards away, leaving it knocked down and in flames. This was at the request of our Gunner O.P., since they did not wish to engage their own guns.

Basil Sparrow heard that he has got the M.C. for his part at Arras which pleases us a lot as he always did very well. Later the squadron moved back into reserve from Wehr and Jabeek, across the border in Holland.

Tuesday, 28 November. Cold damp day. I went to a gunnery conference at 5th Brigade under Michael Fitzalan Howard. It was to discuss the problem how to penetrate the front of the Panther. Our experience was that not even the 17-pounder could pierce that, except with special ammunition at short range. Drank champagne afterwards with Peter Loyd.

In the evening the Commanding Officer sent Ian and me on leave again to Brussels, rather inconvenient as I had little money, but one must never miss the opportunity, and so we decided to go off next morning.

A brief word as to how the war is going. On the whole things look better, in fact quite good. The French have reached the Rhine at Strasbourg, Metz has been occupied or passed, and the Americans are nearly into the Saar. Further north the Americans are advancing slowly beyond Aachen towards the Rhine, while 2nd Army has cleared up the 'Maas pocket'. Geilenkirchen on our immediate right has been captured by 43rd Division and 84th U.S. Division lent to 30 Corps, in a hard and muddy battle. On our front nothing much has happened at all. It looks as if we may be here for a week or two more. The war will not be over, it seems pretty certain, till several months of next year have passed.

Thursday, 14 December. I find I have not written anything for over a fortnight, not since I last went to Brussels. We are still at Jabeek and until yesterday nothing exciting has happened, moreover the time was probably better spent on devotedly writing Christmas letters. My last leave was again most enjoyable, but not really cheap. We had an amusing time with a Belgian girl, Jacqueline Demeure, who took us to see Waterloo, where there is a most impressive panorama painting of the battle. On the way back to the battalion we did a round trip by Liège, not Aachen this time. Liège is being badly VI'ed but looked a nice town. We secured two more guns here, mine an ancient and dangerous looking twelve-bore.

The weather had been appalling, raining nearly every day. In this village the mud almost comes over one's knees if one is not careful, and vehicles are bogged frequently. Enemy activity has been slight even though we are only a mile from the line. At night a few patrols come in and occasionally pinch someone caught out alone, but nobody worries much. I fired some 75's one day from an O.P., but the most interesting thing I saw by far was the detection of mines by an R.E. dog platoon. Fascinating to watch; each time the dog smelt a mine it sat down on it and was given a piece of meat. Really we were all getting rather restive with this existence and it was time something happened. I had been to George and asked him for a change somewhere more interesting, but it seems I was wrong and it was not well received.

However, the usual rumours began to fly around, L.O.'s cars were seen running about and conferences called, that portend an attack, and this was the case. Since some ill-disposed person may find this I will leave it till later to describe.

The attack we were going to do on Saturday 16th after several post-ponements was cancelled, partly due to bad weather, but mainly because the Germans had got to know all about the plans through bad security. Aerial photographs revealed they had planted their guns the way we were going to come. We had studied photographs and maps, and the plans were made in unusual detail. Meanwhile a major artillery bombardment from our guns had started, which included some 9.2 inch Howitzers positioned near the village. To my surprise, walking along the road I saw one of these guns through the hedge about to fire. I stood by to watch, putting my hands over my ears, but I was assured by the crew there was no need to do so. The bang would not be so loud. They were right, and as an enormous lump of metal heaved out of the short barrel, the whole gun recoiled rather leisurely, I thought, several yards to come to rest against two large wooden chocks. The distant crump from the airburst fuse was a long time coming. I might have been witnessing a leap backwards in time to a scene of 1918.

We were going to attack the ground opposite us in order to clear up to the River Roer. Probably it was most fortunate for us the attack did not come off, especially for No. 2 Squadron. We were to be in front with my troop in the lead. There were a good many 88s about and the ground very soft.

163

Everyone had been engaged in recent days 'hammering tracks', as we called it, to give us a little more buoyancy in the soft going. This involved hammering dozens of plates, three or four inches wide, onto the outside of the tracks. It was heavy and tedious work with a sledge. We had to take the tanks to a main road behind, break their tracks and lay them out flat.

Instead of an attack we spent a peaceful day at Jabeek, and I went out shooting in the afternoon with Michael Adeane and Nico, while the generals thought again.

Sunday, 17 December. Owing to change of plan the division were to take over the line again from the 7th Armoured. It was the squadron's turn, so we moved into the line at Wehr and took over our old billets, fortunately in reserve this time.

Great changes have taken place among the officers in the squadron. Henry Allsopp had left the battalion to take up a job in Paris of all places, and George has left the squadron to take over H.Q., Watty has gone to No. 1, and Dermot had also left to go back to England owing to his asthma. Jimmy Priestley comes to command the squadron with Basil Sparrow as Second in Command and Timothy Pearson as Second Captain. A complete change, on the whole for the good, as the squadron was slowly slipping back, but it was a pity to lose George and Watty.

Monday and Tuesday, 18 and 19 December. Days of wild rumours and speculation, order and counter-order, deletion and amendment. We were to move back to Louvain to train during the winter for the spring offensive. Then we were staying put. The telephone was ringing perpetually and counter-orders were arriving before the orders they were to have cancelled. The High Command were in a flap, and they had reason to be.

The Germans under Rundstedt, undoubtedly a very able general, had launched a full-scale counter-attack against the Americans south of Aachen with two panzer armies of fifteen divisions each. The first day they had advanced thirty miles in one place. We had little news of any of it, but it seemed possible we should be called in to help stem the attack.

At lunchtime on Tuesday we were greeted by some extraordinary whistling shells that landed outside the mess, but failed to explode. They turned out to be leaflet shells wishing us a merry Christmas and other pitiful propaganda about the offensive. Sittard was bombed this

164

evening. The planes flew low over us, but the Bofors behind our mess seemed quite incapable of hitting anything.

Wednesday, 20 December. Things gradually began to sort themselves out. We packed up ready to move out of the line, while the Queens took over from us. No-one had any idea where we were going to, though it was still possibly to Louvain. Our advance party had already gone there. No more news about the German offensive.

A tiresome day hanging about waiting to move off. We finally set sail after dark about seven o'clock. It was a very long and tedious night drive that did not end till nearly eight next morning without a proper halt. Back we went some fifty or sixty miles towards Louvain, through Diest, and then turned south. It was obvious now that we were going to have to do something because of this German counter-attack. Breakfast was on the road near Tirlemont, where we hurriedly got our tanks ready for action and 'cleared the decks'. We thought it quite possible we might have to go into action that day.

We moved on to a village south of Tirlemont called Neerheylissem, with the 5th Battalion in the next village, Opheylissem. Evidently we were not needed yet, so we went into billets in the village, all the squadron in one barn, for the night. A large meal, and everyone, exhausted, retired to bed. Now and then a flying bomb droned overhead on its way to Antwerp.

Friday, 22 December. A sharp frost and cold day at last, so thank goodness the mud has gone. The sky cleared and soon the sound of aeroplanes told us that the airforce were able to have a real good go at the German breakthrough. The day was spent billeting the squadron and maintaining the tanks. We set up the officers' mess in the Burgomaster's house.

At last we had a clear picture of what was happening, and this was the story as we saw it. Rundstedt, by a masterly piece of manipulation, had during the last two months managed to stabilize the whole line sufficiently to gather together all his S.S. panzer divisions, re-equip and regroup them into two panzer armies. These he had thrown against the Americans where they were not particularly strong. His aim was to reach the Meuse and hold it between Liège and Dinant, to capture the American petrol dumps and then break through and reach Antwerp and Brussels in three days. This last desperate gamble, as he had himself described it, had been blunted by the fierceness and stolidness of the

165

American 7th Army in the north. Nowhere were the Germans within twenty miles of the Meuse. They had not been halted yet; however, the crisis was over. The air was in our favour now, and we had plenty of reserves, including ourselves, behind the Americans. The attack had, it seemed, turned our way, as it gave us a chance to kill more Germans than we could otherwise have done.

Saturday, 23 December. We seem to be going to spend our Christmas here at Neerheylissem, so today was spent preparing for it. Christmas dinners and such frightful things as Officers v. Sergeants football matches were being organized. In the afternoon I went to recce the area for shooting. I found one good wood with several pheasants, belonging to the Comte d'Outremont, and shot two.

Christmas Eve. Preparing for Christmas and making a room ready for the men's dinners. Ian, Matthew Ridley and I went for an excellent shoot in the afternoon near Opheylissem, eight pheasants, one woodcock, and fifteen head all told. We had a brush with two Gardes de Chasse who thought we were poaching, so we left for another wood. Wearing uniform caps, they were furious when I asked them if they were tram workers.

We celebrated with a riotous, bibulous evening, everyone well away, though fortunately I had gone steadily. For at ten o'clock came the call for a Commanding Officer's 'O' Group. Not surprisingly this was considered a joke when the telephone rang and it was announced. Soon afterwards Jimmy returned with orders to move down to Namur at first light next day. It seemed almost incredible, but there it was. The squadron 'O' group was held amongst a number of merry officers and sergeants, Sergeant Major Tomlinson had to be removed quietly to bed first. Some of us went to bed, others unwisely, including Brown, proceeded to saturate themselves in alcohol. The Burgomaster, whom we suspected of being a collaborator, spent the rest of the evening trying to pump out of someone our destination.

Christmas Day, 1944. A very hard white frost. We moved out, as it got light, south towards the Meuse. It was a lovely morning and perfect Christmas weather. Two fat cock pheasants strolled lazily across the road in front of my tank. About five miles north of Namur we halted and drew up in a field to await further orders. Rumour was that the Germans had reached the Meuse somewhere, anyway they were not far off by Dinant.

Two troops were to sit and hold the bridges across the Meuse at Namur in support of the 5th Battalion, mine was to be one, while the rest of the Battalion moved into billets where we were.

All morning the sky was full of white streaks of bombers going over, Flying Fortresses and Liberators streaming across continuously in large numbers.

What a Christmas!

The Commander came back and gave us orders. I was to support David Kennard's Company in holding the road bridge at Namur, and Anthony was to go to the railway bridge. I took my Troop down the steep hill beneath the walls of the great fortress of Namur, guided by Gavin Green, now our Intelligence Officer, through the streets to the bridge. Unfortunately he dropped his map-case on the way, with all the locations of our own troops marked on it. This caused considerable chaos, until it was eventually removed from an expostulating Yank. I went on through the town and crossed over the surging Meuse to take up my position, pleased to be with David's Company. I had been with them before and knew them all. Now began three of the most amusing days I've spent for a long time.

David and Alan Pemberton met me on the bridge, a wooden affair, since the old one had been knocked down in 1940, and in probably every preceeding campaign. Down the centuries Namur had been a natural strategic stronghold, and one recalled it had long been a proud name for the English. The fortress had fallen to them in the siege of 1692 that had earned the Regiment one of its first Battle Honours, and for many years after that event was the name for a Ship of the Line in the British Navy, the flagship of our ancestor, Admiral Boscawen.

It appeared the enemy were still some distance away from here, though they had broken through in places with small bands of Panthers and were reported near Dinant, but it did not seem likely they would reach us. The 11th Armoured were reported in action with them, and the Recce Welsh were swanning around in front of us. Refugees were pouring back out of the Ardennes, and the Belgians seemed on the verge of panicking. A family saga, oft repeated at home, once took place on the bridge at Dinant. Driving across this with the de Cröys in 1938 in their loftily built grand motor car, a curious sneezing sound occurred several times. This we all thought was a

167

refined sort of sneeze emanating from the ample form of Princesse Isabelle de Cröy in the back seat causing squeals of laughter from her daughters, Didi and Lollie, both childhood friends of my family. Suddenly the tall thin Swedish Chauffeur stopped and leapt out to proclaim the danger of an 'explushion'. We all bundled out to see the front tyre subsiding gracefully onto its rim. Without hesitation the Princess swept us into a smart teashop to eat chocolate cakes, the speciality of Dinant.

David Kennard showed me my position at various street corners in the built-up area just across the bridge, known as Jambes, and here I backed my tanks on the pavements. One of them blocked the doorway of a pub. Immediately a suspicious-looking character, smartly dressed with a black hat pulled down over the eyes, accosted me and took me aside. He showed me a pass stamped all over 'Secret Service'. A terrific spy, the real life version from the game 'L'Attaque', I thought, and instructed everyone to keep an eye on him. He insisted on moving my 'char' away from the door – and went in for his usual. A piece of paper such as this with a stamp on it had spelt survival for so long for the people of Belgium.

Greville Chester had his platoon on that side of the bridge. I had met him before at the transit camp at the Escaut when he first came over, also several times at Wehr, and he was soon to become a good friend. We set up our own H.Q. in a comfortable hotel beside one of my tanks, and I billeted my troop in various cafés around.

Then the first extraordinary incident occurred. Three steam trams, 'Emett'-like in their quaintness, on test, came slowly along to cross the bridge from the south. The first one, issuing clouds of steam from every joint, soberly and quietly, as I watched in amazement, came off the rails on the bridge. Complete chaos, nothing could go either way, backwards or forwards. Now a tremendous crowd had collected. Tram officials were shouting and officiating. Too good an opportunity to miss, I got hold of my 'Firefly' and backed it onto the bridge to tow the tram off.

Upon this suggestion I was embraced by a terrific tram official, covered in brass stars. My crew hooked the tow chain on, amidst shouts of "*remorques, doucement, très doucement*", started to tow amidst the cheering crowd. Meanwhile, to add to this chaos, two hundred German prisoners of war were marched past, guarded by a handful of Americans

168

with sawn-off shotguns, and got entangled with the tow rope and the trams. Gone was this tranquil Christmas morn, the Huns played up, tripping over the tow rope, mixing with the crowd, their guards running round furiously, brandishing their weapons. Then the tank heaved. To ringing cheers it slowly towed the tram with a final little jump back onto the rails, to all a great success.

Back at the Hotel I saw more trouble from the window. Down the street an American was being marched up to me by one of the Guardsmen. An official photographer from Cincinnati, he wanted to make a picture of the 'Lootenant' and crew sitting on a tank. So out and posed for him with Sergeant Bastone's crew on the Firefly with the river behind, "Lootenant Boscawen, of Truro, England and crew defending the Meuse against crack Panzers", he would call it, he said.

Later Comment

This picture, to my surprise, turned up as a double spread in a magazine, *History of the Second World War*, some twenty-five years later, the caption erroneous. Later it was a cardboard cut-out used with amusing innappropriacy to advertise Nigel Nicolson's biography of the great Field Marshal Alex, – of Tunis.

Spent a comfortable night; Greville and I did wireless watch from our bedrooms in the Hotel Mosanic by a long lead to my tank below. There were no less than fourteen sentries on the bridge at night, including two 'blower-uppers', and Belgians and Americans galore.

Next morning was spent with the same bustle and excitement. Greville was in great form all day dealing with would-be Meuse crossers. Spy reports were going round continually. The fitters in their scout car were my first visitors, then Ian, now Signals Officer, all out for a joyride, Jimmy, followed by the Commander and Peter Loyd also. In the afternoon Greville and I had a haircut next door and deserted our posts to walk to the top of the Namur fortress on the other bank. Well worth the climb, it was a fine view and much the best place to defend the bridge from. It was Boxing Day, so we went to a local wine shop and bought a bottle of 'Fine old Port' and settled down to this in our Hotel. No more reports had come in about the Germans near Dinant, but the civilians were all in a panic about it. David and Alan had their Company H.Q. on the other side of the bridge in an extraordinary sort of Night

Club, with a steady trickle of clients calling for 'business reasons'. Alan had spent the afternoon chasing a 'Brandenburger' spy who had been asking what the bridge was made of.

Soon after going to sleep I was blown out of bed by a shattering explosion, glass and doors flew in all directions. Greville came rushing in saying a bomb had fallen close by, as if I didn't know it, and went off downstairs. Panic seemed to have broken out in the house below. I slowly pulled on my flying boots and had just gone out of the door when I was greeted by a further blast of glass, as another bomb landed much too close. Greville, caught out in the open by this last one, threw himself under one of my tanks and fortunately escaped. I found my men all right and Greville's too. The bombs had fallen in the next street, one very close in the river, and another down on the railway bridge, twenty-four in all. The Americans continued to fire aimlessly into the air for a long time, and also went round shooting out the lights in the houses opposite, rather a destructive sport. One poor man went to put on his slippers in a house on the bank of the river and switched on the light. An American immediately put an ack-ack shell through the window and the house wasn't quite as nice as it was before, rumour had it at Company HQ. Parachutists were reported to have landed, but never confirmed. On investigation after a light was seen flashing in a house near the bridge we arrested a highly suspicious looking character in a darkened room and took him before a Belgian 'Secret Service Agent' who stripped and searched him. In such a jittery situation for the population, it is not surprising there were so many rumours of spies round that bridge. One certainly had been asking questions about it to a Priest earlier on.

After this I walked back and took a look at the fire caused by the bombs on a house near ours. Standing in the doorway of the house next to the bombed one was a young woman and her young son, laughing there at the fearful mess which her house was now in. She must have been an exceptionally brave woman, quite alone in this deserted spot. I offered to take them back to our hotel, but she insisted on staying the night in her house, her only request being as to how far the Germans were away. I left her calmly smiling in the doorway; no one could ever defeat such courage.

Back at my house the Battalion rang up on the 'air' to ask if we were all right and I was able to say neither ourselves nor our friends were

170

damaged. They told me afterwards they thought that parachutists were coming down by the incessant American firing. Woken a quarter of an hour later by Corporal Siddons, I was told an American was being tiresome in Sergeant Shipley's bunk. I went out there and found a very drunk American officer threatening to fight everyone. A tricky five minutes and I got rid of him in spite of his wish to have a fight with me on the bridge to show there was no ill feeling. The Americans were still letting off occasional bursts of fire so I went up to one and asked them to stop, but was greeted by the reply, "Test fire, Sir". The night had done much to cement that warm friendship with our greatest ally.

Back to an hour's listening watch on the wireless and then handed over to a sleepy Greville and once more to bed.

Wednesday, 27 December. Another day much the same as the last. The people spending the morning brushing away broken glass and clearing up. I found the girl I had met the night before where the bombs had fallen, still unperturbed and clearing up the mess in her house. She eschewed all help, willingly offered by the Guardsmen, a remarkable person and still cheerful, an example to us all.

The Commander came round with Peter Loyd in the morning to see if all was well. "How far are the Germans away?" was the question I have been asked by anxious civilians. The Germans weren't far away, we knew that, and they were only four miles from Dinant about fifteen miles upstream, but now we were very strong here, and no longer any danger of them crossing the Meuse. During the day the 6th Airborne Division of Caen fame took over from us, three battalions where we had one company, and towards evening we packed up and reluctantly moved away. With Greville's platoon packed in the T.C.L. moving behind we left Namur, and after a good clear run clattered into our old billets at Neerheylissem and parked the tanks. The rest of the battalion had arrived earlier on, so we settled down to spend a belated Christmas. It will take a long time to forget Namur.

Thursday, 28 December. A holiday with Christmas dinners, we all attended, while the Commander made a speech in the approved style with the hope for 'Bowler hats or bearskins for next Christmas'. Singing was still heard from the room late in the afternoon. In the evening we had a frightful champagne party in the mess. Dermot and I succeeded in making the Mayor of Esemael, a ridiculous little man, completely inebriated till he fell flat over in a corner of the room amidst roars of

171

applause – last seen suffering a furious scolding from his wife who had him sitting on the lavatory to cool off.

Friday, 29 December. The event of the day was our shoot. Ian and I went out into the Comte d'Outremont's woods and walked around unsuccessfully and saw nothing. Towards the end we met Michael Adeane, then 2-i-C of the 5th Coldstream, and Bob Thompson also shooting with no success. He suggested we had one last go in some rushes. Our luck turned, the rushes were stuffed with pheasants. In half an hour we accounted for eight hen pheasants in view of an infuriated keeper, who went off to fetch the Comte. On the way home, pheasant feathers sticking from every pocket, we ran into a surprised Comte and a difficult few minutes followed, especially as Michael had had him to dinner the night before.

Sunday, 31 December. Cold freezing days with roads like ice rinks. Yesterday was entirely made at breakfast by a green woodpecker perching just outside the window. A state of intensive training for the next three weeks was proclaimed with a conference to start with. Jimmy and I walked round the training area in the afternoon, flat featureless country, littered with two crashed Flying Fortresses. As the Divisional Commander had specially asked for some training period out of the line, it is possible we may be here for the three weeks.

It appeared now that Rundstedt's drive was no longer on the initiative. We were attacking the salient hard. Monty commanded the British and American armies to the north, with Bradley those from the south. British troops had held the advance from reaching the Meuse and the salient was being gradually pinched out.

And so ends 1944. Truly a year of victories and of disappointment. Achievements undreamed of had been surpassed, but still the war was not over, a hope which a few months ago had nearly been realized. It had certainly been the greatest year in my life.

We saw the dying year out true to custom in the Sergeants' mess, and as the last verse of Auld Lang Syne died, we entered 1945 with hope and expectancy, but no undue optimism.

1945

Monday, 1 January. Cold wintry day with intensive training starting in all spheres. I recced the training area for somewhere to fire, though unsuccessfully, and returned almost frozen, settled down to reading *Years of Victory*, a really interesting book, Arthur Bryant's new one, which Mummie sent out for Christmas.

Next day I was sent off to look at an anti-tank range at Lommel near Bourg Leopold. I set off in the Jeep for a slow fifty-mile drive, the roads frozen hard and the Jeep slid about in an alarming way. Through Diest, back across the Albert Canal at Beringen into our old battleground again, it had been cleared up a lot but still odd German equipment such as 88s lying about. Through the gloomy village of Heppen, Bourg Leopold and on to the range at Lommel. There we arranged with Michael Fitzalan Howard, the Brigade Major, how and when we should fire, as we stood shivering. Not a very good range, I'm afraid. As soon as it was over I set off to get warm straight to a pub to eat lunch. Harris, my driver, had been with Michael Fox in that area, and knew the way, so I went to see him up to his office.

He was surprised to see me; now G.2 2nd Army Troops, but bored and unhappy there. In his office I saw all the maps and Order of Battle. The main excitement there was when 200 German Fighters of all sorts, captured Spitfires and everything, attacked on New Year's morning shooting up aerodromes and supply dumps. They chose their moment right and caught the R.A.F. napping. We lost 150 aircraft on the ground. However, in the end we had 188 shot down.

When I arrived back I found the Squadron changed. Anthony Gell is out of No. 2 and instead Ian Jardine has been sent here. He was depressed with life, having to change, but for me it was a good thing. Ian had had his Jeep stolen in Brussels which was causing considerable trouble in all circles.

Snow fell in the night, not unexpected. A tiresome next day preparing for Lommel range and getting the Advance Party organized.

Thursday, 4 January. More snow, but a fine clear day to start off with. I took my troop out training with Ian's, but somehow training seems so ridiculous and futile now one knows what to expect; however, I hope we learnt something.

Jimmy went on leave to England today, the first officer on the roster. Everyone pleased it has started. I hope to go in February.

This evening we had a Coldstream Officers' dinner in the Château of the Comte D'Outremont, with the officers of 5th Battalion. It was a riotous party. The Regimental Band over from England played at full

173

blast all evening and rather spoilt everything by the noise, but perhaps conversation carried on like Communication Drill helped to keep us warm. It was held in a freezing domed hall with two long tables, each officer provided with two bottles of champagne. The entire complement of officers of two battalions, headed by their brigadier, attended. It was really great fun.

It ended in a great tragedy on the way home when Bob Thompson was fatally injured by a truck. I was very sorry to hear he had died a day later. Only a few minutes before I had been laughing and drinking with him, complaining that he was made a Captain when we both joined the Regiment at the same time. He was such a charming person.

Friday, 4 January. I went off in Oliver's Jeep up to Lommel range complete with Brown to stay there during the week's firing and officiate on the range. A busy afternoon with Frank Humphrey, Welsh Guards, an L.O. from brigade, finding billets and setting up cookhouses in a rather dim dirty village called Heide. I billeted myself in a Military Police officers' mess. Joe Lee arrived with his Recce tanks for firing, and after seeing them in, arranging meals and billets and driving up onto the range, went back to my billets to find Brown awaiting with all my kit ready and settled in. What a blessing it is to have a good servant.

Unbelievably there were two more Cornishmen out of the five in the mess, one a Padre from Tintagel with whom I was sharing a room, the other a Policeman from Falmouth rejoicing in the good old Cornish name of John Biddlecombe. We spent an evening discussing Cornwall and Falmouthian crime.

Saturday, 6 January. A cold misty morning after a lot more snow. Left early for the range and laid on targets and ammunition. We did not start firing till about twelve o'clock when the fog cleared, so only a partially successful day.

Harris, my driver, when he was here with Michael, had got himself engaged to a Belgian Girl in the village, raised eyebrows and guffaws all round the mess, as to what he was really about, so I sent him off to stay with her. This evening I went with the others in the mess to an officers' club in Mol nearby.

Later Comment

Many of our senior officers, Brigadiers and above, had been young officers during the last war and had learnt the hardest way what a grim business war is.

Hence the ruling philosophy of these real professionals was that everybody must be as cheerful and lighthearted as possible at all times. So as young officers we took this for granted, but one often found it somewhat of a rarity in other formations. Years later General Jorrocks often told me how struck he was that whenever he visited Guards Armoured it always seemed to be a tremendously good party however difficult the situation. Formal histories can never capture such an atmosphere but it is a lesson that shouldn't be forgotten, I feel.

Several miserable, bitterly cold days with heavy snow falling, no tanks firing or anything, and the roads in a treacherous state. I accompanied Michael Fox instead in his staff car round the Army Roadhead, which was quite interesting to see. The whole of this flat moorland area had become the Army supply dump, 'Bodmin Moor' we used to call it. The petrol dump with four million gallons stacked in small piles of jerry cans, and on through the ammo. roadhead, stacked all along the sides of the roads covering some thirty miles, and we ended up at 2nd Army Rear H.Q. They were no longer so keen since the Ardennes offensive on putting out vast signs as to their whereabouts for fear of parachutists. Part of Michael's job was organizing the defence of all the bridges on the main supply route, and we inspected several wretchedly cold looking pioneers digging away at trenches in the snow. The Pioneer Corps are the most splendid band of little men, always to be seen digging away cheerfully somewhere or shovelling stones into the potholes, whatever the weather; they deserved our wholesale thanks.

Later Comment
The sheer scale of this dump of stores required for 21st Army's next great assault over the Rhine was an eye opener to me. It explained so much of what had been happening. How the rapid advance of 30 Corps from the Seine to Brussels in less than a week last September could not have continued much further, how vital the clearing of the port at Antwerp had become and the long quiet spell that the Armoured Divisions had enforced upon them. The stores just had to be brought in. No doubt too this dump stood very large in the eyes of Rundstedt when he planned the surprise attack in the Ardennes in mid December

Malcolm Lock arrived here from the Battalion to look after the range party, but the expected tanks never arrived. Later on the 9th a jeep

175

arrived telling us to return to the Battalion, as the roads were too bad for the tanks to come up. Malcolm returned this evening with most of the men and I stayed to clear up and go next morning. I had an excellent hot bath at Michael's house.

A long letter from Father from Tregothnan. He had been doing some shooting and had got two woodcock, but it must have been lonely down there this Christmas without any of his family at home for the first time ever.

The British and Americans were attacking hard at the neck of the salient in the Ardennes, and already the German lines of communication were under shellfire. A fierce battle was going on in terrible weather, snow and freezing wind. It was a wonder the G.A.D. had not been thrown in but we are being kept for something worse later, I expect.

Wednesday, 10 January. Drove back to the Battalion in the jeep. A cold and slippery drive and could not do more than twenty mph. Stopped as ordered at the Brigade Reinforcement Holding Unit at Bourg Leopold to find a Battalion truck which had disappeared on its way there. I saw Colonel Jimmy Coates who had sent it to Ostend, so who knows when it will return. Thawed out with some welcome hot soup in a hotel at Diest.

Found nothing of interest on returning, everyone depressed about the war and everything in general. The weather is probably the reason. I went to see Oliver and Bill, who is now in command as the Commander is on leave in England. They had decided to send the tanks up to Lommel, as the other Battalions had done so, and I had to go back there on Thursday.

Sunday, 21 January. The last ten days I have been up and down to the range two more times. On the twelfth had two good days firing 17-pounders. I stayed again at the C.M.P. mess and had one quite amusing evening with Matthew Ridley at Mol. Roads were very slippery and I did a spectacular skid in the jeep on the way back to the Battalion, turning right round in the road in front of an on-coming tank to the alarm of my passengers.

After two days in the battalion I came up here again. Basil Sparrow had returned to the Squadron for a while but is afraid he will have to go away again because of illness. Went with him and the others to a Brigade concert in Tirlemont. At Lommel I went to a demonstration of a

176

remarkable new shell, described later. Three fairly good days firing, but bitterly cold and almost a blizzard one day, so the rum ration was prevalent in operations. A flying bomb flew over the range one day. I saw it going across at a tremendous speed, the first time I have actually seen one by day, though we have heard hundreds. Presumably it was heading for Antwerp.

The news from Russia is good once again. Warsaw has been occupied and they are advancing on a wide front beyond. In the west Rundstedt has carefully withdrawn from the Ardennes salient; a great pity he has lived to fight another day.

Tuesday, 23 January. Went off up again to Lommel to watch the Irish Guards give a demonstration of a squadron artillery shoot. A busy hour was first spent organizing a trade test in the battalion which I put on to John Sutton. Once away we made good progress to Hasselt, though the roads are slippery still. Were held up in a road block for a time, while the army Commander, Dempsey, and Crerar, the Canadian Army Commander, made their way to a conference at Monty's Tac H.Q. I saw Peter Towers Clarke as we were held up behind his car, and also an L.O.B. officer from the 4th Coldstream. He said his Battalion were in the attack near Sittard, not much opposition but they had lost one tank on a mine.

It was a long and cold demonstration, but interesting. Tony Dorman was running it. The new shell we had seen recently, the Gunners are hoping to use soon. The fuse is a radio location set in itself, the 'proximity' fuse. It produced a frighteningly even pattern of airbursts a few feet above the ground and would be most unpleasant to be under.

Drove back myself. I am getting to know this road pretty well and arrived just after dark. Ice all the way, and passed several pile-ups. Went to dinner with John Sutton in Esemael this evening, a good dinner and tackled the champagne. John just back from his leave in England, rather depressed to be back and needed cheering. However, he packed me into the wrong truck to go home, and I did not realize until halfway back.

News from Russia is excellent, only one hundred and fifty miles from Berlin now. Everyone is cheered up about this.

Thursday, 25 January. Set off to go to Brussels on forty-eight hours' leave, accompanied by Richard Boughey from No.3. Drove along an icy road in a 15 cwt truck with its steering gear frozen almost solid. Ian was just finishing his leave unfortunately, but had lunch with him and Richard. Saw an English news film in the afternoon and later Richard and I went to see *Hamlet* done by Ensa with Donald Wolfit. I enjoyed it very much, apart from the intense cold in the theatre, as I had never seen *Hamlet* before. Monty was present in the front row and looked as if he was itching to be invited onto the stage at the end. After a late and lucky dinner we returned to the Eye Club for the night.

Friday, 26 January. Still snowing slightly, but it did not deter me from a gentle morning's shopping or walking round. Had lunch with Richard and Jacqueline Demeure, one of the Belgian girls working in the Services Welfare Centre. It might be described as a gastronomic day, an excellent tea with iced cakes, unheard of delicacies since war began and we had dinner with Jacqueline and the Baroness after seeing an old but amusing film called *I Married a Witch*. Tony Watkins and Michael Hamilton happened to be having dinner in the same little restaurant at the Port Louise, which was quite funny as they weren't supposed to be in Brussels at all. We took Jacqueline off home in the Chaussée de Vleurgat off the Avenue Louise, a long cold walk interspersed with a lift in the back of a Gendarme's car, and stayed talking there for some time. I met one girl there who was going to be dropped by parachute into Germany, but was enquiring whether I thought the war would end within a month; if it did she wouldn't go. Rather unwise to tell anybody. Another long cold walk back to the Eye Club from the Avenue Louise through dark and deserted streets.

Saturday, 27 January. The day was chiefly taken up by a most enormous lunch. Richard Boughey had found the place, '*Comme chez soi*', and took Johnny Thompson, Frank Humphrey and myself along. It was a definite experience. We sat till 3.00 engrossed in eating an excellent meal. I saw old Freddie Clifford at the Eye Club knocking back the drink, just out from England, a wartime Grenadier Major at the Guards Armoured Training Wing at Pirbright, where I have been in his Company.

Most of Divisional H.Q., including the General, was at the Eye Club, all returning from England by plane. One gathered there was something in the wind. Something must happen soon and I have a pretty good idea where it must be.

The news is frightfully good. The Russians are reported within 100 miles of Berlin and have cut off East Prussia.

178

Richard and I set sail back to Tirlemont and Neerheylissem after tea. It was a most enjoyable two days and I enjoyed his company very much.

Sunday, 28 January to Wednesday, 31 January. Still cold and snowy. Suspicions of an impending action are more than confirmed as a week of intensive maintenance on tanks has been ordered. Everything centres round this. Inspections and such familiar cries as 'All officers will wear denims' are prominent. In the morning I went with Ian to a lecture on Regimental History by Colonel Roddy of the 5th Battalion. Interesting. He gave us a poignant description of battle-weary officers in the last war bursting into tears of relief in the line in November 1918 when they heard the Armistice had been signed. In retrospect it seemed incredible to me that those who were now Commanding Officers could describe such events that some of them witnessed as young officers. Was it really so brief an interval of peacetime before this madness began all over again?

The mess had become very tolerable now. We have a good many laughs which is the great thing. I am enjoying reading Arthur Bryant's *Years of Victory*. I dined at the 5th Battalion with Alan Pemberton and David Kennard. David as crazy as usual, and afterwards we set to in a game of roulette – the first time I have played, and ran a partnership with Greville. We managed to remain almost all-square at the end after a most amusing evening.

Thursday, 1 February. I am getting idle about writing this and am generally several days behind, but really since Christmas there has been little difference from day to day. The world news is exciting. The Ruskies are reported on the Oder, 40 miles from Berlin, let's hope they manage to get a bridgehead across. In the west the Americans are slogging away at the Siegfried Line south of Aachen making a little progress though slow.

The Commander went off to a conference at Division today. He returned in great form and proceeded to sink into the brandy after lunch, so the feeling in the air that something is up is confirmed. A short conference of squadron leaders ensued, an operation was spoken of, but no details. Soon we are to be in action again. One's reaction is a feeling of regret in some ways, and yet excitement, and a desire to get on with it. Above all this lies the slight uneasiness, or fear to put it boldly, that every man knows he silently shares with the next. Ian, John Sedgwick and I went on an unsuccessful shoot north of Tirlemont with little more satisfaction than getting the jeep bogged four times necessitating being towed by two horses. Much warmer day and the thaw starting. Jimmy went off to Brussels.

Saturday, 3 February. Today the squadron had a holiday, the terrific maintenance and 'Johnnie Gull inspections' finished. All the men went to Waterloo for the morning. I took them there in trucks and we 'did' the battlefield. We went to Hougoumont Farm held by the Coldstream, complete with bullet marks up the trees and loopholes. I liked seeing it again and it was good how interested our men were. Lunch was had from the Cooker which was a success. George Dawnay also turned up taking his squadron round. I was pressed with souvenirs and buttons by the man who ran the museum, and he took me aside to confide he thought the Coldstream was the best Regiment in the Army. I wondered how many other 'bests' there had been. I found an interesting copy of *The Times* two days after Waterloo with the battle and casualty lists.

After dinners the Squadron drove to Brussels for the rest of the day. It was a lovely day, warm, with the sun shining, snow all gone and the fields were green once more. John Sedgwick and I went to the Eye Club and saw Jimmy there. He had just been ordered back for a conference. I had a much-needed hot bath, and tea at Le Muscadin with John after walking round doing a little shopping. The streets and shops were full of soldiers of all varieties with a holiday air about them, the sun shining down into the streets, it might have been spring. John and I and Tim Smyth-Osbourne, the young Colonel we called him, went to the opera *La Bohème*. Tragic, but some lovely arias, especially 'Your tiny hand', and a pleasant evening with a glass of port between the Acts.

Sunday, 4 February. At breakfast, after a long lie, I received a decided shock when Ian came in and told me I was being sent on leave to England tomorrow. This was a complete surprise, and it was rather difficult to know what to think when the Battalion was about to go into action. I felt an awful rat running out and I felt I wouldn't enjoy my leave as much. However, it was an order; that made it easier.

Church parade was held this morning with a large attendance, rather a nice service with the new padre. On coming back from Church parade the farm next door was ablaze from top to bottom, Belgians panicking

180

and shouting, and carrying out squealing pigs and cattle – part spectacular, part appalling, part pathetic, part ludicrous sight – and nothing that could be done to save it.

A dozy afternoon sleeping in the mess. This has become great fun again. Basil is the mainstay of everything, but I am afraid he is going away, his category downgraded because of asthma, a great pity. Jimmy has been charming to us, except when continually talking 'sprockets'; he was one of the battalion 'D and M' experts. Ian and I, I'm afraid, treat everybody as a joke and tease poor old John Sedgwick about his girlfriends. Each time it makes him furious. However, we have been a happy crowd lately.

Since I was going next day, Jimmy briefed me as to the new attack. There was going to be a big offensive along the west to clear up to the Rhine. Ourselves in 30 Corps were to be with the Canadians, attacking the Reichswald at Nijmegen, moving probably Thursday.

Later Comment

Operation 'Veritable' together with the American Advance north-eastwards from the River Roer was designed to clear all German forces from the western bank of the Rhine opposite the Ruhr. It involved a major attack south-east of Nijmegen across the low ground first that formed part of the Siegfried Line, and through the great state forest, the Reichswald, and the small ancient Rhineland towns of Goch and Cleve. The attack was to open with a tremendous artillery barrage and was initially to be primarily an infantry battle. The rapid thaw after weeks of severe frost would make the ground hard going for vehicles.

5–7 February. Set out early with my bag to Tirlemont to go on leave, only to find it was cancelled or postponed. I spent the morning at Division sorting out the leave party I should have taken, and then returned rather disappointed to the Mess. In the evening we were briefed by the Commanding Officer as to our operation. I was rather impressed by him, he did it well.

Expected to move next day, but the move was put off. I went out shooting, or rather poaching, with Ian, John Sedgwick and Matthew Ridley this evening. We had a most successful campaign in Monsieur Phillip's wood, scoring two birds and then jumping into the Jeep and driving away before the Gardes de Chasse arrived. Unfortunately we broke down as the clutch went, but I managed to drive it home without a clutch.

Last things were packed up this evening for the move.

On the 7th, starting in the morning, the Battalion moved to Oisterwijk, near Tilburg, Holland, a distance of 90 miles. It was an interminable march with nothing to break the monotony of starting and stopping every few yards. We passed through a petrol dump beside the road after dark and someone had run into a pile of jerrycans. The road was swimming in petrol. One expected a devastating fire at any moment, especially with a truck ditched in the middle of it blocking the road. The only thing was to push the truck right into the ditch with my tank and get out of it as quickly as possible. It was an exceedingly nasty moment. Later one tank did catch fire, but I don't know the cause.

We arrived at last well into the next morning and went to sleep straightaway.

Thursday, 8 February. 'D' day of this new offensive on the Reichswald, but it does not take us for several days yet. I spent a long morning getting my 'Firefly' out of a bog at Turnhout. The driver, Corporal Driscoll, had been dazzled last night and gone off the road. After an hour's searching for aid there I secured a colossal Canadian bulldozer. We set to to burn through the tracks with oxyacetylene and towed the trackless tank out with the bulldozer, one ARV, and two Scammels. All of us were well satisfied with a thirsty morning's work, only we had nothing to celebrate it with. On the way back we passed a burnt-out tank of No. 3 Squadron with Richard Boughey climbing over it. I stopped and found it was one of his that had caught fire last night, but no one was hurt fortunately.

I am definitely going on leave tomorrow morning, so got ready and drove to Tilburg to find out. Michael Hamilton is now with the Squadron acting Second in Command, and was at dinner. Brown had set up the mess in the local post office.

Friday, 9 February. Started on my journey home. Drove to Tilburg and picked up the transport to Bourg Leopold. Doing nothing but wait, and sat in a local cinema for an hour. Left by train for Calais, a long and slow journey of fourteen hours; however, I was very comfortable. A Household Cavalry Officer, Younghusband, and I secured the

O.C. Train's private compartment and were able to stretch right out and sleep undisturbed.

Saturday, 10 February. Sailed for England. We were quickly rushed through all formalities and went on board *Princess Maud* and sped across the Channel for Dover. I felt happy leaving France behind, and after a quick crossing, only one and a half hours, it was a great moment as we steamed into Dover. Back at last, thank God, after nearly eight months of war abroad. We were soon on our way in a train to Victoria. How strange everything seemed, the trains, the countryside, the whistle of the engine, the signs in English. It was very exciting. Victoria and a race for a taxi. About four o'clock it turned into Chelsea Square and stopped at No. 14. The door was opened and there was Mummie and Father and Mary, a very happy moment. They congratulated me, and then seeing my surprised look, realized I didn't know, so they told me to my great surprise I had been awarded the M.C. I am not able to express my feelings over that. I assumed it must have been for Bemmel. Father had just heard about it from the Orderly Room. A long evening discussing our varied excitements and adventures, a bottle of champagne, a hot bath, a very comfortable clean bed and nothing to think of in the morning.

Nine days passed too quickly. Mary and I went to Cornwall where we had three lovely days, shooting, riding, and once went out on the river. Mrs Mitchell and Tommy Rowe and all were well, and everything peaceful. The best rest cure anyone could have. Several days in London, shopping, seeing films and theatres. Lunch with Grannie, Pamela and Henry Sherek, and the proud moment in the tailors beforehand at Welsh and Jefferies when Mr Welsh sewed a ribbon on my tunic. Ran into Dermot and Mary Musker at the Guards Club in Brook Street and had a good gossip there. The only note that jarred heavily during my whole leave were the notices outside London restaurants inviting you to book your tables now for victory night. Many bloody battles lay ahead before that would happen, and they couldn't know what a grim and costly struggle to reach the Rhine was now in progress. Finally, down to Eton on Sunday, saw Beasley and George Tait, all full of congratulations and pleased to see me. I went to Evensong in College Chapel.

Monday, 19 February. End of leave. Left Victoria at eleven this evening and went to Dover. Mummie, Father and Mary saw me off at

183

the station, and I felt exactly like going back to school again, but soon embedded myself in a book and forgot about it all.

Tuesday, 20 February. A desperate day. The only bright spot being an egg for breakfast at the Connaught Barracks overlooking Dover. Sailed for France, sea very calm, but foggy. Met with Younghusband again and spent rest of the day at Calais in the dreary Transit Camp full of officers in the last depths of despair, interspersed with a film, *The White Cliffs of Dover*, all about the last war and seeing people off to the Front, – most unsuitable. We boarded the train at last and prepared for a long night journey. Not too uncomfortable, though without lights made it rather tedious. We were hauled out, unnecessarily I thought, at Tourcoing for a cup of tea.

Wednesday, 21 February. Left Bourg Leopold by T.C.V. for Tilburg. I had little idea where the Battalion was or even the Division, or whether they had yet been engaged at the Reichswald. We prepared to spend the night at the Transit Camp at Tilburg, where we came across the outgoing leave party, and we must have presented a gloomy spectacle to them. Film show again this evening to kill more time, and early to bed, billeted in a house with some nice Dutch people.

Had rather a disturbed night from V-bombs which seemed to come over continuously. One very low stopped its engine just overhead which was rather a nasty moment. A clutch of anti-personnel bombs from a Hun jetplane, a 'squirt-job', as we called them, made a rude attempt to do us in earlier in the evening, but succeeded in killing a Dutchman out in the street. It brought one briefly face to face with the hardship and misery of these brave Dutch civilians in this long cruel war.

Left Tilburg early morning and drove in a T.C.V. up to Nijmegen to the Divisional Supply Point, and from there on my last lap into Nijmegen in a battalion truck. It was pleasant in a small way to be back here again. Arrived back to the Squadron in time for lunch. I was beset with congratulations from all sides, and Brown who was particularly pleased, I think, immediately seized my battledress blouse and started sewing bits of ribbon on.

A vast pile of letters awaited and I've been spending ever since trying to answer them. One was from old General Coddy, Colonel of the Regiment, congratulating me and mentioning his association with the family for the last seventy years. "The 'Star' was our senior subaltern when I joined the Regiment – 1st Battalion – about 70 years ago," wrote General Coddy.

Later Comment
Sadly he did not live to know how that association would continue.

Known by the Regiment as The 'Star' my grandfather too had been Colonel of the Regiment through the first world war until on his death he was succeeded by Lt. General Sir Alfred Codrington at the end of that war – General 'Coddy' as he was now universally known.

I walked round the Squadron in the afternoon and saw O.K.H., Oliver Heywood, and Adjutant, only just back from leave himself. I found myself being congratulated on all sides; it is a nice thing to have, I must say. I learnt that on the morning I left Oisterwijk to go on leave, news came through that George Dawnay, Peter Hunt, Sergeant Partridge and myself had been given medals, and that General Allan was coming immediately to present the ribbons. John Sedgwick was despatched poste haste in the jeep to find and bring me back. He reached Tilburg but I had already disappeared without trace.

The news was varied and not unencouraging. The battle of the Reichswald was still very sticky, though masses of ours and Canadian troops were in the sector. As expected the Division had not yet been flung in. 32nd Brigade – we are now back in 5th Brigade – was holding the line somewhere by Gennep, and 3rd Irish had suffered rather heavy casualties, one hundred and seventy, I'm afraid. The Reichswald was cleared now and Cleve had fallen, but there were a large number of troops against us and there was heavy fighting round Goch. However, the air was stonking continually day and night. The flooding and soft-going had curtailed the use of armour during the first part of this huge battle. Infantry and artillery had borne the brunt, akin to the battles of the last war. It appeared we should be sitting here for several days, but soon this was to be refuted when the order to move at first light came through during dinner. Dermot arrived back from England to the Squadron during the day, so we 'stonked' into the champagne, celebrating Jimmy's thirtieth birthday and my 'gong'. Part I Orders stated that "His Majesty had graciously approved the following awards for conspicuous gallantry. . . ."

Gathered my things together for an early start tomorrow.

Friday, 23 February. Did not move off till about ten in the morning. A damp and rainy day, but everyone was in extremely good form at breakfast. I don't quite know why. Rather a chaotic start in my troop, as they were not all present at the time, so we went off without them only to find them running down the street after us. Teach them a lesson. We drove out of Nijmegen down the familiar main road to Mook passing the billets we lived in last November. The roads and streets are packed with vehicles bearing all the div. signs I know, showing that nearly all the British and Canadian troops were in this sector. The rain made things miserable; however, I had an excellent haversack ration of duck given me by Ian. Down as far as Gennep, and from there we drove along the railway to Goch.

All the way the road and fields around were covered with shell craters, showing the size of our opening barrage. We passed over several lines of trenches, part of the Siegfried Line, camouflaged in places but they seemed little affected by the shelling. In the whole way I only saw one dead German, which was rather disappointing from what we had been led to believe. The railway was poor going even for tanks, and we bounced about over the sleepers. It was creditable that only one broke its track. Passed John Yerburgh and Henty Smith. John was working away with a broken-down tank. I believe he is now the Mick Technical Adjutant.

We crossed the German frontier at Hassum and entered Goch, a badly battered small town, mainly shellfire, but few houses left undamaged except the water tower, well camouflaged like a church. Desultory white flags were hanging out of a few of the windows. 6th Guards Brigade H.Q. was in Goch. We turn north of Goch for two miles and the Battalion harboured in a field around two battlestruck farms, a rather dismal place. The luxury of billets is now over once and for all, I'm afraid, and we have to sleep out again under our bivouacs. There was a German P.O.W. cage in a field over the hedge from the Squadron that caused considerable interest. Several people went to listen to the interrogation of the prisoners, stupidly I did not. One who refused to talk was being made to dig his own grave alongside some other graves. However, at the sight of our Padre, he at once started to talk.

I saw the Commander this evening and he came up about my M.C. Brown produced some dinner for us in our cowshed, – very welcome.

I went to bed in the bivouac with my crew; fortunately the weather is mild for February.

Saturday, 24 February. Brown managed to find an excellent egg for my breakfast, after which Ian and I walked to the Reichswald Forest for our daily duty. The end of it was about a mile away, but it was an exceedingly uninteresting pine forest, little signs of German equipment, only some heavy stonking. Dermot did tremendous stuff by building a wonderful fireplace in a cattle shed that made things much better. Guardsmen were rushing in and out collecting the chickens putting them in a pen, and of course the inevitable problem of a number of cattle and pigs left behind, poor things.

Continuous stonking going on all the time from our guns situated all round. The 4.5s in the next field making a beastly row. In the distance we could see the Typhies were stonking away having a good day. The Canadian attack was going well and the 11th Armoured Division were attacking Udem and trying to go as far as the last Siegfried defences. This morning the great American attack towards Cologne started. Already they had several bridgeheads across the Roer.

I tried to polish off some of my letters this afternoon. I had one from Sergeant Brough's sister thanking me for a photograph I sent of my troop in Normandy. She always writes a very nice letter. George also wrote, just back from a weeks leave in Rome. It is strange to see two letters after one's name on the envelope.

Sunday, 25 February. Still in our field at Goch. Rained hard in the night, but fortunately our bivouac held water. A dull day no good for flying, a pity. Saw Drill-Sergeant Robertson this morning, a great friend of mine, and I was pleased he had got a decoration. He had won the C in C's Certificate for Conspicuous Service. Church parade was held this morning, but I missed. Walked through part of the forest with Dermot this afternoon, though saw little signs of warfare and only two dead Germans. A letter from Basil convalescing at home now and will not be coming out again, also one from Val at Pirbright. Went to bed early, but a noisy night due, I think, to an enemy counter-attack quite close, anyhow four hours of continuous stonking on both sides.

Monday, 26 February. No sign of moving yet. Morning routine of maintenance, guncleaning and P.T. This afternoon walked with Jimmy and Dermot to Brigade about three miles away, a long and hard walk. We saw Peter Chance, but he was not very informative except that we should be flung in soon. The German Para Divs seem to be fighting well still. We passed several colossal 7.2 inch Howitzers banging away somewhere. 11th Armoured was due to attack this afternoon.

27 and 28 February. There is excitement in the air. The attack on our front is going well. Udem has fallen and Canadian troops have reached the last Siegfried defences. The Guards Armoured is expected to be thrown in as the final *coup de grâce*. Rumours came in the Americans were advancing on Cologne. Everyone is optimistic about the war. It is rather like last August.

Rather restless that we are not yet called upon. Camouflaged my tanks with a new wire netting. After lunch had a short walk with Ian, and then a bath in a bucket in a cowshed, and felt much better for it. Another heavy lot of stonking this evening.

Thursday, 1 March. After a bad night I retired to bed again for the morning. My inside was extremely ill. I must have one of the bugs flying around, most unlike me, and in the afternoon Johnny Thompson packed me off to hospital. Much to my disgust I was driven off in an ambulance to the Advanced Dressing Station, and from there to the Field Dressing Station, typical Army. I was put in a staff car for Nijmegen and then to bed in a Dutch house. There I remained comfortable and undisturbed save for the drone and thud of the V-Is as they dealt their blows on the town. On the way back we had passed through Cleve, now reminiscent in its destruction of a Norman town, battered beyond recognition.

I spent the next morning in bed, feeling much better and recovered, but stayed in all day as it was trying to snow.

The Yanks have reached the Rhine near Düsseldorf and are shelling Cologne, while only a few miles from our troops moving south. This must be well out of date too, as I only heard it on the nine o'clock news.

I foresee a long and difficult day tomorrow. I am going to get back to the Battalion, somehow or other, and everyone will try and prevent me.

Saturday, 3 March. Set off early from the Doctor's grip, picked up a jeep from the Battalion's 'B' Echelon, most fortuitously just next door, and drove off at great speed to Schaijk, fourteen miles behind to the reinforcement unit. I had to obtain a piece of paper with my name on it just to show I had passed through. A mile or two out of the front line and the real thing, the battle of the red tape, begins. They had no notification I was required by the battalion and, if they had, they would have sent someone up. Until then anyone discharged from hospital must stay put there. One of the reinforcement officers would show me to the mess. I was clearly getting nowhere with the Duty Officer and asked to see the C.O. He was in the mess too, so off we went to a small hut, my driver tailing me close behind. There were a crowd of intensely bored-looking officers sitting round the walls and a stuffy, elderly looking Welsh Guards Major. It was all too much like Anthony Armstrong. I just wanted a piece of paper so that I could get on my way without delay; the Battalion were moving any moment now, could he help me? No, he was sorry he could not. I must join them in the mess; where was my kit?

That was with the Battalion, I said. I was going there in the Squadron jeep and had to pick up another officer on the way. I was sorry I couldn't stay and it was too bad about the piece of paper. He looked at me hard and saw he wasn't going to win. Grumpily he caved in. The others round the walls beamed with delight. Into the jeep outside at the double, my driver couldn't wait to let the clutch in and with a bang, we shot away. Back then to Nijmegen, picked up the 'Colonel', as we called Timmy Smyth-Osbourne, from 'B' Echelon and on up to the Battalion, through the Reichswald and on to Goch, where I found them in precisely the same position. They were at two hours' notice to move. I'd made it.

The Division was to move due south to Kapellen to close in on the diminishing German bridgehead this side of the Rhine opposite Wesel. The Germans were pulling out of the Rhineland as fast as they could.

Sunday, 4 March. Was a cold and wet day. Remained at Goch. A small church service in the evening. Warning came to move at one a.m., so early to bed. 5th Brigade had already moved. We are again in 32nd Brigade, forming with the 5th Battalion the Coldstream Group, fighting as one command, and we would remain thus for the rest of the war, two Groups to each Brigade.

Monday, 5 March. At one a.m. moved south through Goch and Weeze, not too bad a night drive. The road was lit by the reflection from violet-coloured searchlights, 'Monty's moonlight'. Arrived just short of Kapellen village at dawn, cooked breakfast at the side of the road, and expected to have a battle later in the day. The General drove past and took up his Tac H.Q. in a farmhouse just ahead of my troop. We had moved a few yards off the road into this field shared with two batteries of twenty-five pounders. The noise was terrific. Firing at short range, the low angle shells whistled a few feet only above our heads. Beyond Kapellen 5th Brigade were having trouble in some woods, held up by S.P.s and an S.S. Para. Battalion, and the gunners solemnly stonked these woods. We were going to attack, Jimmy gave out preliminary orders and we stood to, but the plan failed to come off; other objectives had not yet been reached. Remained in the field with morale steadily sinking. The Wesel bridgehead is quite small by now, the Canadians are closing in from the north at Xanten, but the para boys are making a stiff fight for it. The Micks had lost about five tanks.

During the morning the Corps Commander, General Jorrocks, arrived in a scout-car to visit our General. Carrying a map case, he leapt out of the top of the scout-car and hurried into the farmhouse. All was a bustle at Div. H.Q. and he was there for some while before he left. One of the Div. staff told me that with the battle for the Rhineland virtually over he was now going back to plan the next move, the breakout across the Rhine. Shortly afterwards Div. H.Q. upped stakes and moved off too.

Later comment

General Horrocks long since described this five-week battle to clear the Germans from the west bank of the Rhine, as "the grimmest battle in which he took part during the war". It took place in appalling weather conditions aided by the widespread flooding the Germans caused by breaching the banks of the Rhine, and soon developed into a mud-churned slogging match. The German defences were in great depth, and their First Parachute Army, under a Hitler order, put up the most stubborn resistance. In consequence the brunt of the fighting fell on the Infantry Divisions, two Canadian and the five British in 30 Corps, of which our friends the 43rd played a conspicuous part at Cleve and Goch. The constrictions of the Reichswald, the extensive flooding and these small towns meant that the opportunity for an armoured breakthrough never came. Thus the Armoured Divisions, as we found, had a severely limited part. Casualties suffered by the Canadian and British Divisions were tragically high, 15,634, two-thirds from 30 Corps, although such figures were never revealed. It appeared there was no other way at this stage of the war, if we were to succeed in forcing the Rhine and beating the Germans quickly.

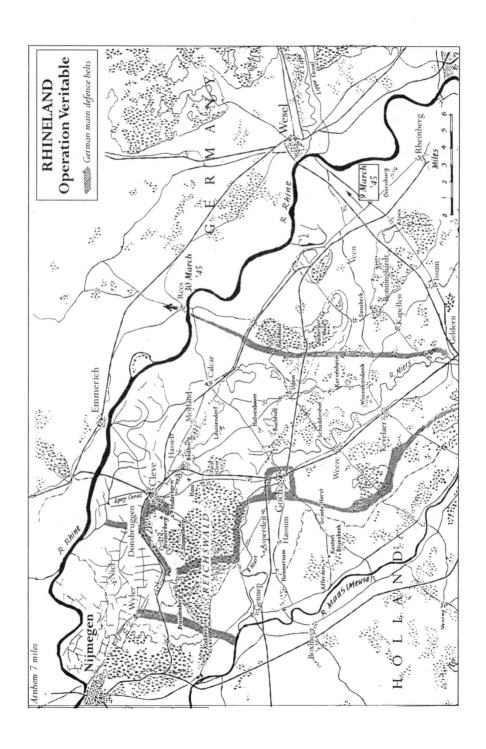

RHINELAND
Operation Veritable

///// German main defence belts

Tuesday, 6 March. Stayed all day in this muddy field at Kapellen, expecting to attack, but by bad luck that caused some ill-feeling afterwards, we were not wanted. The 5th Battalion did a good small attack on the woods beyond Kapellen, after a terrific barrage from some nine field and medium batteries, – two of them in our field. It made a colossal row. They put down fifty rounds 'of gun'. Unfortunately some of these fell short on to our Guardsmen and killed and wounded several of them, I'm afraid. The attack was limited, but went well, though the para boys held out strongly.

My Guardsmen amused themselves by boating on a small lake by our field in punts and canoes. Dermot, of course, fell in, so did most of my crew. I survived, fortunately. Good fun, and helped to keep morale high.

Wednesday, 7 March. Still in this gloomy field, now about two or three miles behind the line, waiting to attack beyond Kapellen. Waiting, always waiting, that's what war is about. Clear day and the 'Typhies' are out and make a good sight. Walked round with Ian and a gun after some duck in the nearby pond. Letters from Edward and Mary arrived this evening. I must write to them soon.

The German civilians round about seem wretches, and mostly Russian labourers, whilst the houses of course have been looted by the Germans themselves. Masses of food, eggs etc. to be had. Earlier two of my crew had been across the fields to obtain eggs from a farmhouse. To their surprise they were well received by an attractive German girl. Later a rumour went around that someone from elsewhere in the Battalion had been there too, supposedly found her willing, and 'had her down'. My troop were shocked and I had heard them discussing this in lowered voices. Later that night it became the topic of our bivouac. Would there be such easy lures amongst the vanquished maidens when we had crossed the Rhine, the dreams of licentious soldiery no doubt since history began? My hopeful crew began to cheer up no end as such vistas opened before them. I had to keep to myself my recurrent forebodings these last few days about the occupation of a hostile, sullen nation, whose hatred of England would have been compounded by years of R.A.F. bombing. Among the white flags I had seen was a tattered sheet strung beneath the windows of a German hovel. It bore crudely written words, '*Nie wieder Krieg.*'* Perhaps such weariness would prevail.

* Never again war.

192

Thursday, 8 March. Still at Kapellen, very boring. Walked with John Sedgwick up towards the front this afternoon, but saw nothing. The Germans are still fighting stiffly in the Wesel pocket. No. 1 Squadron had expected to attack, but it was put off.

Friday, 9 March. The battle to destroy the last pocket this side of the Rhine at Wesel is nearly over. The coup de grace was given by the 5th Battalion, supported by No. 1 Squadron this afternoon in a brilliant attack at Bonninghardt. No more details yet.

This evening we settled in some filthy German houses near our field, while the remainder of the Division streamed back to Holland to wait for the next blow across the Rhine. There was a bridge party started amongst some officers in one of the houses to which some from No. 3 Squadron came. One of them, John Ambler, let out the tragic news that Malcolm Lock had been killed in this afternoon's attack. I felt utterly sick. The affected way Jack Ambler spoke. I suppose he couldn't help it – made the shock that much worse. War always takes the best people. Poor Malcolm, he was a great man. I left them and tried to settle down with a book to pass the time, but could not concentrate.

Saturday, 10 March. The Para troops had blown the Wesel bridge during the night and withdrawn. We were waiting to move back to a more comfortable area. Malcolm's funeral was at a little divisional cemetery on the edge of Kapellen at midday. Nearly all the officers and No. 1 Squadron attended. He had a direct hit by a mortar shell in the turret of his tank, a very unlucky hit. All his crew were seriously wounded. He had already reached his objective.

I realized at this sad event that now Malcolm had gone there were only three of the original Troop Leaders left who began the campaign in Normandy, Ian Jardine, John Sutton and myself, and only a few of the more senior officers as well. I was very sorry about Malcolm, he had always been an old friend, at Sandhurst in the troop ahead of me, and in the Battalion since. A completely fearless officer, he really enjoyed fighting, and as in anything he did, he did well, truly one of those 'the Gods loved'.

It had been a great attack and they had captured a lot of prisoners. Jeff Darell, who commanded No. 1 Squadron, told me the shelling and mortaring when they had reached their objective – the main road crossing their front – was as heavy as ever he could remember. The enemy, 7 Para Division, continued their resistance long after it was taken. As well as Malcolm's tank three more were lost on mines, and casualties in the Group were once again rather heavy.

For the first time since the outbreak of war the BBC were recently allowed to reveal the names of formations immediately after an action. There happened to have been a man from the BBC with No. 1 Squadron, but when he was approached, Jeff, told this 'dreadful little man' where he belonged, in language no doubt all of us who knew Jeff would have been more than proud. The result was that the 5th Battalion received a great splash of well deserved compliments in all the papers, and their armoured comrades none! Jeff and Peter Strutt the latter the only officer left in No. 2 Company covering the Right Flank nearest the enemy-held Hans Loo, were deservedly awarded MCs.

It was Colonel Roddy's great day too. We heard today that the Americans had 'bounced' a bridge across the Rhine at Remagen, thirty miles south of Cologne.

Sunday, 11 March. We left Kapellen, thank goodness, and moved back to Holland. A good run, though dusty, we crossed the Maas on a pontoon bridge at Mook, and the Battalion settled itself in the village of Cujk beside the river. Not a bad billet, and we were extremely comfortable. I found the welcome sight of Brown with all my clean clothes and camp bed. Settled down to clean up and get straight. Leave to Brussels begins again.

Monday, 12 March. Everyone clamouring for ammunition and parts for guns. Round my old haunts in Nijmegen to collect spares and get equipment from the Canadians. The Canadian armoured crews had found a way of making our Browning machine guns spit that much faster, so the Battalion all wanted me to have their guns 'hammered and bent' in the same fashion. Walked along the Maas with Tim this evening. Andy Graham from Division, an extraordinary Welsh Guards character, with an even larger moustache than when I last saw him in Normandy, came to dinner. He was most amusing imitating the General.

Thursday, 15 March. Again go to Nijmegen, this time with Dermot to look for a boat to use on the Maas. We had a good look at the bridge too, a gigantic structure. We spent a happy afternoon wandering amongst the little craft and tugs on the Rhine, but no luck. Michael Fox turned up from Army this evening on his way through, and we had a drink.

Friday, 16 March. From now on 'Rocket' is the key word. Dermot had heard that the Canadians had fitted some Typhoon rockets onto a tank but never taken it up, and had been talking about it for several days. Suddenly he and I hit on the idea of fitting rockets to our Shermans so we went off to a Typhoon aerodrome nearby. Our luck was in; the Wing Commander was only too happy to help and we drove home complete with rockets and rails after lunch with the R.A.F. We immediately set about fixing one on a tank, – very exciting and great fun.

Saturday, 17 March. My birthday, and a lovely day. Spent the morning having a rocket apparatus welded on to my tank and in the afternoon we fired it by remote control from some way away. A thrilling moment when I touched the battery and, with a terrific roar, the rocket moved out slowly at first with a tremendous hiss, sinking almost to the ground, then gathering speed, it exploded on rising ground some three hundred yards away. Most successful. Jimmy was enthusiastic too and we decided to fit the whole Squadron, and if possible the Battalion.

A terrible E.N.S.A. party to dinner tonight after they had given us their show. They tried hard, but were not awfully good.

Sunday, 18 March. More dashing around collecting rockets. In the afternoon we gave a demonstration inside Germany to Colonel Dickie. Very satisfactory, it blew down a damaged house completely. So full speed ahead with production. Each tank was to have one rocket with a sixty-pound explosive warhead fired from rails welded on each side of the turret, the same rails as were slung under the wings of the Typhoons. It was a short-range inaccurate blunderbus, but, in the close-country road-bound advance we could expect, the leading tanks were always vulnerable to an ambush. An immediate and devastating reply against an enemy, more often than not unaimed, was a god-send.

A Guardsmen's dance, organized by them, was held this evening. A good dance, but I never enjoy those evenings.

Monday, 19 March. After a week looking forward to it, and the rockets under way, I set off again for Brussels with John Sutton at nine o'clock. John Baillie's staff car behaved itself well. He is temporarily attached to the Squadron and most astutely brought this car with him from his last posting somewhere in Rear Army. Selfishly I drove the whole way, through Tilburg and Malines. As we reached the outskirts of Brussels, we were greeted by the crump, crump, swish of bombs. It must have been a 'jet-propelled' aircraft dropping 'anti-personnels', and the vehicles two or three ahead in the column ahead were hit. Most disturbing. However, we weren't hit and so could drive on.

Stayed at the Eye Club, but no great friends there, mostly 5th Brigade H.Q. Went to a film with John, *The Way Ahead*, with David Niven, an amusing army film, some of it taken at Pirbright. Dinner with John; it is rather difficult now to find a good restaurant without being 'progged' by M.Ps. The 'Redcaps' were reported to be extremely active in stopping one going to places deemed out of bounds in the city. Whom should I meet there but an old friend, John Poe, in the Rifle Brigade, – in great form, he was. A very good black-market dinner, and then returned to a soft comfortable bed and sank beneath the pillows.

Tuesday, 20 March. A good day. A long lie, one of the major pleasures in life. Returned to the Welfare Centre to see if our friend Jacqueline Demeure was there as she was away yesterday. I had to fight my way past a sergeant into the gift shop. Jacqueline was pleased to see me and congratulated me, to my surprise. I arranged to have tea and settled to do something in the evening. She told me of a good place for lunch in the country near her home to which John and I drove. A lovely drive through the Forêt de Soignes and an excellent lunch in a small restaurant which Jacqueline knew when she ran messages in the Belgian underground movement. John and I then went to Hougoumont Farm at Waterloo quite close. It is one of the most fascinating places, steeped with memories. I could almost feel the battle on, a tremendous atmosphere.

We drove back via Nivelles, badly bombed by the R.A.F. owing to the steel factory there, then round north, and back up the centre line we took on the way into Brussels. It was new to John since No. 3 Squadron had been held back in the afternoon of September 3rd to protect the soft vehicles and to convoy them into the city next morning. This was very interesting to see the places we came through into Brussels. I recognized the way that the battalion actually came right into the Bourse that first night. After a little trouble with the staff car, sped back to meet Jacqueline at four. She arrived smiling and apologetic after half an hour and we had an excellent tea at Le Muscadin. We could not get into a film so went to dinner in the Rue d'Arlon at the enormous house there. Dinner was great fun and a bottle of champagne. Afterwards a night club and back to her home in a taxi where we sat for a while, a lovely evening, and home in a car fortunately.

Wednesday, 21 March. Alas, forty-eight hours was to go too quickly. A busy morning shopping and buying some wine. I saw Greville Chester in Brussels, also Neville Berry. Then I picked Jacqueline up in the staff car and drove down to her home for lunch with her mother near Chapelle St. Lambert. They were more than kind. Walked round the woods for half an hour and she picked some flowers as it was a sunny spring day. We left and drove back to Brussels. She left the car and disappeared behind a tram, – a wonderful lunch. So back to the Battalion once more. I don't see any chance of visiting Brussels again for a long time.

I picked up John and drove back uneventfully, some one hundred and thirty miles, – a lovely holiday.

Thursday, 22 March. Went hard at the rockets all day. To Nijmegen in the morning in the Mercedes with Tim Pearson to borrow a welder, successfully, and back to the aerodrome with Dermot and Watty for more rockets. Not a cloud in the sky, we watched the Typhoons coming in and out on operations. Michael Hamilton came and had a drink with me this evening; afterwards I was painfully inoculated by Johnny Thompson for Typhoid.

The pause at the Rhine is nearly over and the preparations to cross into Germany proper seem nearly ready. South of the Moselle the Germans have collapsed and are reeling back to the Rhine. This will be the last big battle, I feel sure. Then, who knows, the end of the war perhaps by May. I hope May is a month of peace, the best month in the year. Goodness, I hope it is.

A mysterious letter from Edward has just arrived, saying he is in the B.L.A.,* good news, I must try and find him. Later a message came he was in Ghent in 5th Div.

* British Liberation Army

197

Friday, 23 March. We have got the rocket production working well at the L.A.D. The Light Aid Detachment fitters from Brigade had been lent to us and now the Squadron is nearly complete with rockets, while other troops in the Battalion are being fitted. We have now changed over to fitting double rockets and warheads on either side of the turrets. These have a much better trajectory, fly faster, and of course cause a huge explosion. I went off to another aerodrome to get more rockets. The R.A.F. were very helpful to us, really good liaison.

After lunch Dermot and I gave up work and went and lay on the bank of the Meuse in the glorious sun. He told me of the plan; exciting times we live in, great days. We could see the greenish cloud of the smoke-screen hiding the bridge-building preparations towards the Rhine. In the distance that evening could be seen the glow of guns firing and the aircraft attack stepped up. A fine clear night, the weather was at last good.

Saturday, 24 March. By breakfast time the news was out. Last night we had crossed the Rhine. At ten o'clock the Commander briefed all the officers, followed by all the men. 21 Army Group helped by Airborne and Commando troops had crossed at Rees and Wesel. The Guards Armoured Division was to break out from the bridgehead and 'lead on'. Exciting news.

Spent the rest of the morning preparing for the great rocket demonstration we were doing before the Brigadier, George Johnson, this afternoon. A great success. Jimmy did the commentary and we ended up with all six rockets on three tanks fired at once in a sandpit with clouds of dust and an immense bang. The Brigadier was most impressed. Dermot and I drove back on the top of a scout-car feeling very pleased.

Ian arrived back from leave in England this evening. The attack seems going well.

Sunday, 25 March. All day, we prepared to move, a busy day, hot and dusty, with the R.A.F. over all the time. News seemed good, but as yet the bridgehead was a little tricky. The Para boys as usual were holding up the British sector. Dermot, John Baillie, and I had dinner at an Officers' Club in Nijmegen and we 'stonked' the champagne.

Monday, 26 March. Another busy day. Fitted rockets on to Richard Boughey's tanks. No. 2 Troop of 3 Squadron. Ironically his tank was my old tank Cheetah III, refitted with a new engine. All the Division seems to be excited by the idea. Brigadiers and Colonels came round daily and looked at them, even the General came round. Slept all afternoon, as I was exhausted.

The news is excellent. Patton's U.S. Third Army, has broken right through in the south and everywhere is going well.

John Sutton came to dinner with us and we had an amusing dinner. Dermot and I afterwards went for a long walk along the Meuse. A clear cold night.

Tuesday, 27 March. Another rocket demonstration in morning, but not so successful, I'm afraid, in front of the 2nd Irish Guards Battalion.

The feeling is the end of the war is very near, and the front appears to be crumbling. John Yerburgh came to dinner and we had another enjoyable party.

These last days I had a personal problem over Brown. He pleaded with me, each time I saw him, to be allowed to go into action in my tank for the next battle. I would have liked to take him. He is a rough, tough, resolute character, cheerful though rather uncommunicative, and I always found him reliable. Why not? After all a Platoon Commander has his servant up with him as the platoon runner. Unfortunately he could not drive a tank and had no training on the Browning or other trades. If he came he could put other lives in jeopardy and I had to say no. He was terribly disappointed and never gave up asking to join me. I have often wondered since how he feels about my decision now.

Wednesday, 28 March. Fine and lovely. We gave a great rocket demonstration to the Divisional Commander and most of the Division turned up. All the rockets at once. We fired all sixteen rockets from four tanks in one go in the sandpit, the equivalent of a destroyer's broadside. There was a vast explosion and flash, and the General rolled on the ground roaring with laughter. It was a great success, an enterprise that had worked. I saw masses of friends there, including Reggie Gordon Lennox, only out recently from England. We were congratulated by all on the rockets.*

Back for lunch, we found orders to move at four o'clock this afternoon. The news is terrific. I cannot believe it can last much longer, the

* The rockets were given the codename 'Tulips', as they were of that shape.

whole front is crumbling and the armour is on the move. We are keen to be flung in, so as to race across Germany. Lead on. It is a terrific feeling. Really after six years it is coming to an end. My God how wonderful. Lead on. The Germans are collapsing. Roll on victory.

★   ★   ★

This was the last entry in my diary. The rest came from scribbled notes in a black notebook which I always carried in the knee pocket of my battledress. To my amazement this returned to me with my cap star and shoulder stars at home nearly nine months later from GHQ, Effects Section.

★   ★   ★

Wednesday, 28 March. The time having been put off again till eleven, went to sleep in afternoon. We had a large dinner at eight with champagne and brandy and at last set off on our journey from Cujk. Where we should end, who knows? Being a night drive and with the prospect of a long day tomorrow I rode in the co-driver's seat and put Corporal Siddons in command. I dozed off overcoming the noise and roar. Some twenty-eight miles drive. I was awoken by B........, my temporary driver, Daniel being on leave, and told, "We're here, Sir". "Where?" "We're here, Sir", as if everyone knew. We were in fact near Calcar, not far from the Rhine. We filled with petrol and got down to sleep straightaway. That staid old soldier, Sergeant Holland, walked slowly down the line of tanks. "Reveille seven-thirty," he said, "Objective, Hamburg". "F... A.. left of that place, why not Berlin," said a Guardsman; such were the spirits of everyone, as these momentous orders sank in.

Thursday, 29 March. A dull, overcast and damp day. The battalion remained (in a flat gloomy field) drawn up in three close lines just south of Calcar. A bad incident occurred in the morning when one of the squadron trod on a mine, (not far from the tank lines), in a clearly marked minefield. Incredible stupidity, which cost two stretcher bearers very seriously injured trying to get him out, and Sergeant Hathaway wounded in the head. Watty was also hit, but not much damaged.

200

Morale is terrific though, everyone is champing at the bit wondering why we don't move. The rest of the army are pouring across Germany. The reason, we did not know, was the hard fighting going on to enlarge the bridgehead opposite 30 Corps, where the fighting spirit of 7th and 8th Para Divisions showed no signs of giving way.

The news is terrific. The Americans have advanced at incredible speed towards the Russians and are nearing Cassel, some one hundred miles from the Rhine. 6th Guards Brigade are nearing Münster. The crack has come, just as we said it would; quite suddenly, at once, the whole front except in the north is on the move. It is too big a thing to comprehend after six years; everyone seemed to have this opinion.

Orders came at three this afternoon the Guards Armoured Division were to move, 5th Brigade leading, towards Hamburg via Bremen after breaking out of the bridgehead, – the only one still fighting. It was disappointing and infuriating we could not move at once; we thought we may miss the boat.

A long stint of map-folding, giving orders to my N.C.O.s, and a pep talk. My driver, Bland, with Bradbury, co-driver, Hanson and Wright in the turret, we were now complete. As it got dark I wandered down the lines of bivouacs and listened to the Guardsmen talking quietly of the end. That which once seemed impossible has now arrived. What will tomorrow bring? The anticipation is almost unbearable.

Friday, 30 March. Good Friday, dull and overcast. Remained all morning in field. 5th Brigade crossed the Rhine. Good Friday service. Orders. Map-folding. Moved at three across the Rhine at Rees. Not one house standing. Ended up near Dinxperlo. 5th Brigade held up. Sun came out in afternoon. Twenty five miles.

★   ★   ★

This was the last entry. There was nothing more in my notebook. The rest was written down months later in Cornwall.

★   ★   ★

I felt it was a tremendous moment in one's lifetime as we rumbled slowly over the immensely long pontoon bridge the Sappers had built so impressively. Through the shattered town of Rees we went on to harbour at the Dutch frontier village of Dinxperlo. Nearby the German town of Bocholt was reported still strongly held by them. The Grenadier Group, ahead, had met strong opposition, numerous demolished bridges and cratering, and was held up short of Aalten.

Next day we waited all morning, anxious to get a move on, but after midday the Battalion was ordered to advance at the head of 32nd Brigade on a different centre line from that of 5th Brigade on our right. We were back inside Holland again to cross a bulge of their land that pushes out into Germany and contained three industrial towns in a row at right-angles to our centre line, Almelo, Hengelo and Enschede. It was an infuriatingly slow advance and by evening No. 3 Squadron were held up by some opposition short of the village of Neede on the River Berkel. They seemed unable to find a way round. One or two of the Recce Troop tanks under John Rodney were hit by bazookas near a concrete factory. No. 2 Squadron was sent to find a way across. After fussing about in almost darkness we could not find a bridge that looked strong enough, so it was called a day and the Battalion harboured in a field just short of Neede. Although we had advanced about twenty miles and numerous prisoners had been taken, it had been a frustrating and indecisive day, particularly in the evening when we had looked for a bridge that wasn't there. The Squadron officers gathered around Jimmy's tank to discuss these events for a few minutes. We were not uncritical of the slowness up in front. We turned in early, after we filled up and had a meal. It rained hard later in the night.

Sunday, 1 April. Easter Day. The advance continued. No. 2 Squadron was put in the lead. Our objective was to seize the bridge across the canal between Hengelo and Enschede. Both towns were reported to be strongly held, and so to 'bounce' this bridge by surprise and cut the road beyond was clearly important. The Irish Guards Group would advance on the main road to Enschede to our right. Ian's troop was to lead, then mine, followed by Squadron H.Q. At our 'O' Group, I could feel the excitement at this chance for the Squadron, and especially for Ian, to capture a bridge. Nothing would stop us. Sergeant Shipley pressed me again for his tank to be allowed to lead the Troop for once instead of mine. Normally his, with the 17-pounder, would move last, but such was the morale and enthusiasm of the men to push on, I had to say yes. Sergeant Reading's tank was behind mine and Sergeant Bastone's with another 17-pounder in the rear. We started soon after seven, and rushed along for about ten miles on minor roads in wooded country and through one or two straggling villages, so as to avoid the main opposition.* The route twisted about and we made a number of sharp turns. At one point there was a long wood, set back a few hundred yards on the right of the road, from which it appeared we had come under slight enemy fire. My Troop was deployed to deal with this and I moved across a field so as to use my seventy-fives and Brownings on a few houses in the trees.† We set them ablaze and the 5th Battalion quickly moved up from behind to mop up and take a number of prisoners, while on we went. Ian dealt with similar opposition ahead when we entered a village, possibly Beckum,‡ but he quickly brushed it aside with a few rounds of seventy-five H.E. into the suspect house that left it ablaze. A number of Germans appeared along the route showing no fight, while a few Dutch civilians waved and cheered. There were too the inevitable

---

* In March 1984 Adrie Roding, the Archivist of the town of Enschede, first wrote to me that he was involved in writing a history of the liberation of this town on 1 April 1945 by the British Army, especially the action near the bridge over the Twente Canal between Enschede and Hengelo. Only a very small number of Dutch documents were available, and hitherto there had been many rumours about what happened there, but nobody knew the real story: "I should like to hear from you your experiences on this day near the bridge." From then on we corresponded and met in London prior to nine of us who were present in the battle being invited with our wives to commemorate with the people of Enschede their Liberation and VE-day, 40 years earlier on May 4 and 5, 1985. By then Adrie Roding had obtained a great deal of information about our battle and some Dutch eyewitness accounts of what happened around our bridge on 1 April 1945. He presented us with copies of *The Liberation of Enschede*, gave us a tour of the battle and our route that morning, and introduced us to the eyewitnesses. According to this, we first went back to cross the only intact bridge over the Berkel on the main road to Haakshergen and Enschede at Eibergen and then moved north-west onto our own route via Rietmolen where we reported at 0750 hours.

† We made a sharp left turn shortly afterwards towards St. Isidorushoeve and this is where we came under fire from the houses in the trees on the right.

‡ We had passed through Beckum and passed Boekelo by then and this house was at the farm of Gerink which is described by one of the eyewitnesses as being held by bazookamen. We were then quite close to the bridge although we did not know it, and, instead of going via Twekkelo towards it, we turned right, one road too early, towards Enschede, since the maps we had did not show that way, along the Strootsweg. One of the eyewitnesses, Mr Dam, saw our tanks from the bridge itself and saw the battery of guns defending it open fire on us apparently along the Strootsweg, but none of us re-alized this. The Strootsweg runs about 1200 yards from the battery. I do, however, recall a short burst of heavy gunfire about this time. This was about 0850 hours. By now the Squadron was miles ahead of all our troops advancing in this area.

pathetic refugees, women and children, struggling along with bundles of belongings.

Unfortunately Sergeant Shipley missed a turning and fell behind us. He tried frantically to regain his place in the lead, and took a short cut across the corner of a field to our left. His driver failed to see the ditch half-way in time. I saw his tank bury its nose down in this and I knew we should not see him again that morning.*

There were one or two armoured cars of the Household Cavalry close in front of us. We were in some confusion as to where the bridge was. Ian had tried without success to ask a civilian but the roads were most complicated with some detached houses and the map did not help, when we suddenly found the canal ahead.† The road rose slightly and the canal appeared ahead of us at right-angles, with a high bank on the opposite side. There, too, was the bridge half a mile or less to the left, and a road along the canal bank ran towards it. The armoured cars were being rather useless‡ and we had come upon the bridge from the wrong direction. A Dutchman ran out in front of my tank shouting at me the bridge was "kaput" and some more I could not understand. It was too late to do anything but rush the bridge. We saw the bridge clearly, a steel bow span, about a quarter of a mile down with a crowd of Germans standing on it. We charged towards it, in front of me were Ian's three tanks and close behind me Sergeant Reading's and Sergeant Bastone's, then Jimmy and Dermot with the H.Q. tanks. We scattered the Germans with long bursts of M.G. fire from the Brownings on top of our tanks. I was aware of some trees on our left and a small black gasometer beside the bridge on the far bank, – I thought it might explode.

---

* Shipley's tank had become ditched, I think, shortly after we turned right at Gerink and not far from the bridge.
† This was borne out by Adrie Roding's research that we were nearly into Enschede itself before we reached the canal and turned back towards the bridge.
‡ My stricture about the armoured cars was most unfair. The truth was we were not used to having them work so close in front of us. They had had a very trying night in pouring rain in order to reach our startline on time. The troop of two armoured cars and one scout car under the Troop Leader, Bill Allen, acted with great gallantry once across the bridge. He was severely wounded, after dismounting so as to try and pull the fuse wires from the bombs on the bridge, and the remainder of his troop were killed or taken prisoner.

204

Ian rushed over the bridge with the armoured cars, his second tank close behind. I was just turning right on to the approach ramp to cross it when Caulfield's tank in front of me stopped across the road. He was firing his 17-pounder to the left.

My driver halted and I found myself broadside on looking down the barrels of four 88 mms,* beside the bridge, the place seething with Germans. The flak battery, each gun protected by earth mounds, lay just the other side of the road beyond the ramp up to the bridge.

A short fight followed. I hit one 88 with my seventy-five straightaway, my Browning belt emptied so I let the rockets off. They flew towards the 88s. The bridge blew, I felt it go. Caulfield was the last across. I saw the 88 shots flying up at me, there was a whoof and the turret was engulfed from below in a whirlwind of flame.

I eventually broke free from the flames and threw myself into the ditch. It was dry, but something said to me, "You're all right, get up and go on." Bland and I stumbled back for some two hundred yards to safety. The rest were trapped or shot down before reaching it. Another crew was running back near me and someone beat out the flames.†

I climbed up the back of Sergeant-Major Greenwell's tank somehow

---

* This was a heavy flak battery of four 105 m.m. guns, not 88 m.m. as I always believed, and were identified clearly from later photographs and from an instruction book found on the gunsite.

† Mr Olink, who lives at the farm De Veldgeuver, about 150 yards from the flak battery and which has a clear view of the approach right up to the bridge, saw all this happen. His account so long after the event, resembling so closely my own, is both fascinating and moving. Sitting with his family in his cellar, watching the things that developed through a small window just above the soil, he saw "something I will never forget and what gave me for a long time afterwards sleepless nights. After two or three tanks had passed I saw another tank coming up, firing constantly at the German positions. When it reached the turning of the road towards the bridge, I saw that this tank got a direct hit and I saw a ball of fire rising from it. Almost immediately I saw some burning beings coming out of this tank, half falling, half rolling, but still burning. It was a terrible sight for me, because I could do nothing to help. Very heavy firing from all directions was going on, and the German battery directed its fire at our farm, so we hid at the bottom of our cellar now. At the same moment we felt a shock and heard a dull sound of an explosion. 'There the bridge goes,' said my father. Later, when the Germans had retreated to the north bank of the canal, we buried the three crew members from this vehicle with the help of some British soldiers near our barn". This was my crew.

and was joined almost immediately by Dermot. The rest is best told in letters from Dermot some time later.

To give the full story, interspersed in the letter Dermot wrote to me, are extracts from that written to my mother the same day and to Val Hermon six weeks later.

1st (Armd.) Bn.
Coldstream Guards
B.L.A.

April 12

My dear Bob,

A letter came from your Mother today saying you are in goodish order – which has *delighted* everyone in No. 2. We had not heard a word.

[To my mother he wrote, "Till your letter arrived today we knew nothing and we were all a bit worried about him, it was a ghastly experience. . . ."]

No doubt you would like to know what happened at Enschede. Ian got across – the bridge blew up and all No. 1 Troop went off the air. Our position was completely untenable and we all withdrew.

I saw you get out – but was so busy trying to produce smoke and get myself out of the way that I can't remember much else! We drove through a small house backwards and an A.P. hit a tree two yards away – just to hurry us up. Then there was a bang and my track came off and we baled out.* The Sergeant-Major and you on board came charging through the wood and off we went – being chased by air bursts and eventually arrived at a house where you remained for an hour. (Guardsman) Montgomery made an expert nurse!

---

* Another eyewitness in a farm "wondered seeing a tank crew leaving their vehicle 'as calmly as if they were on a sightseeing tour' after it had received a blow on its track, 'while firing was going on like hell'. Later on, one of this crew helped the farmer finish off his horse; its leg had been shot off by a German flak shell, which exploded in his barn. One of the attacking tanks drove right through his small barn completely demolishing it." This was Dermot's tank and crew and bears close resemblance to Dermot's account immediately afterwards.

Letter to R.B. from A. Roding. 10 May 1984.

[Here the letter to Val Hermon of 20 May gives a fuller account. "Bob was extremely lucky to get away with his life. We were trying to rush a bridge at Enschede. It was a canal bridge with a large bank on the far side, stuffed with Germans. We had to go down a concrete road alongside the canal for ¾s of a mile, then turn across.

"We roared flat-out down the concrete firing at the bank opposite. Unfortunately the huns had laid a nice little trap. Ian Jardine who was leading got across the bridge just as it went up. Four 88 flak guns then opened up on us from 150 yards. They scored one hit, Bob's petrol tank. His tank and the next, Sergeant Reading's, were enveloped in flames. Jimmy gave the order to withdraw, which we did at 3 m.p.h. I think each gun fired 5 or 6 rounds and the A.P. wasn't half getting around. Trees falling in all directions, tanks charging about firing, people burning from head to foot running all over the place and airbursts going off just over our heads from other guns over the canal. I saw Bob running down the road, burning, but did not know it was him of course. My track came off for some reason and we had to get out. We ran through a small wood which was definitely unhealthy, then Sergeant-Major Greenwell came crashing along, trees going in all directions. I got up on the back and found Bob there, unrecognizable except for his pips and M.C. We got away by great luck having a shower of sh.. bursting over our heads for half a mile as the huns could see us. B. was in a dreadful state but making perfect sense and incredibly tough about the whole thing. We did furious i.a. on him in a cellar and blew for medics. They were with Bn. H.Q. and out of wireless touch. It was an hour before he could be moved. Johnny Thompson said he did not think he would make it – but he has, thank God."]

Returning to the letter to me:

Meanwhile Ian was in severe trouble the other side. Scores of Krauts with Bazookas and an 88 or two. He rushed on half a mile, the bridge blew, so he turned round and came back. Incidentally he saw four huge bombs wired up on the bridge as he went over!

Sergeant Caulfield was hit in the head and killed. His crew got away into a house. Sergeant Lyon, Ian's second tank, turned sharp right over the bridge and came along the rear side of the embankment and got back complete with tank through Enschede.* A magnificent effort. Ian meanwhile was hit by three bazookas and an 88 which removed his track and the tank fell over an embankment. They got out O.K. and removed their clothes before swimming back over the canal. They arrived stark naked and very cold in our lines half an hour later – none the worse though he is a bit shaken understandably.† The squadron made its name in a big way though, which is excellent. Altogether we lost five tanks and six killed. Bradbury, Wright and Hanson failed to make it I'm afraid." The third tank, Sergeant Bastone's, got away by turning down to the left behind a few farm buildings. He received a serious head wound from an airburst shell at Berge beyond the River Ems a week later.

To my mother Dermot wrote "There has been no news of Bland. He was not very bad and will undoubtedly recover." Bland was badly burnt in the legs. For a week or more he was in the same hospital close to me and was more than kind.

I went up next morning, Dermot continued to me, and had a look round. There were four 88s within 200 yards of you. Sergeant Bastone knocked out one, and someone got another, possibly your 'tulips'? I was delighted to see you had fired them. Your tank was hit. A sketch showed the hole immediately behind the turret and right through the top of the petrol tanks and engine.

Very unlucky – six inches higher and it would have missed. The guns were manned by paratroops of 7 Para, the flak blokes having been

---

* Guardsman K. Hurworth I met for the first time since these events at the Commemoration of the Liberation of Enschede, May 1985, with Trooper McNinley, Household Cavalry, two of the few survivors from those who had crossed the bridge before it blew. Hurworth told me his story how he drove Sergeant Lyon's tank back round the end of the canal in Enschede. After Ian's tank had been hit by bazookas, Hurworth reversed their tank straight back into Sergeant Caulfield's knocked-out tank behind to push it out of the way, so that Lyon could take the track running down to the right along the enemy bank of the canal. They were under heavy fire from Germans along the embankment above them but ploughed their way along and smashed through an iron gate to where there were two huge cranes near the end of the Canal. He squeezed the tank underneath the legs of one of these cranes. They stopped and went into a house where the Dutch people contacted the Resistance who told them how to get back to the Squadron. The cranes were still there in 1985.
† Ian Jardine's letter to General Sir Colin and Lady Jardine written next day describes his escape vividly. Priscilla Jardine who came to the Commemoration made this letter available to Adrie Roding.

'Typhooned' the day before and left. They were incredibly bad shots and did not score another hit – four guns at 150 – 250 yards!! They must have been bobbing in a big way. Long after, I learnt there were about thirty German dead left behind at this bridge.

That evening Jeff Darell and our footed friends took the town and got on another five miles. . . .*

Yours, Dermot

In a later letter Dermot wrote:

"Tim Smyth Osbourne, The Young Colonel, took over your troop and we had another bad go when Shipley and Lyon were both hit and killed by bazookas, and Corporal Siddons badly wounded, the rest got out. . . . After leaving Holland we had six weeks' non-stop fighting. The Squadron was fighting about every third day and we ended up sadly deficient of many of the best N.C.O.s. Shipley, Green, Taswell, Lyon and Caulfield all dead, and about 35 Guardsmen killed and missing. Bob was the only Officer casualty. No. 2 was most unlucky and took all the knocks,[†] eleven tanks knocked out in all. . . . Jimmy and Ian both got M.C.s. . . . We took the surrender of 7 Para. Div. on Cuxhaven aerodrome on V.E. Day. They were very good and behaved themselves O.K. They had a few f...... great guns and quite a lot of transport but only 9 AFVs and those tiddlers. . . . However, *enough of it all*, the Squadron is about due for a rest."

---

* None of us in the Squadron knew at the time that the Twente Canal ended in a small basin a few yards to our right when we turned left towards the bridge alongside the canal. Jimmy Priestley has confirmed several times since that his Orders from the Commanding Officer, Colonel Dicky, that morning were emphatic, you must take the bridge. The maps of this area by the canal were not very clear, but had we known the canal ended there, as Sergeant Lyon was to discover, things might have been quite different. The bridge really wasn't that important. Indeed in the early afternoon, 1415 hours, No. 1 Squadron under Jeff Darell went round the end of the canal and through the eastern part of Enschede encountering light opposition at roadblocks to reach the crossroads on the Hengelo Oldenzaal main road. Here they spent 'a very lonely but successful night', capturing surprised male and female prisoners and vehicles escaping from Holland to Germany. Fifty years later one of the tracks of my tank was discovered in the ditch leading up to the bridge and is now in the Town Museum!

† Jimmy Priestley contends that it was all due to No. 2 having the 'tulips' that they were so often required for the stickiest places.

209

The final entry in the Battalion War Diary described the scene at Cuxhaven.

'At six o-clock on the 8th May the Coldstream Group accepted the surrender of 7th Parachute division. . . . Under the guns of our tanks the paratroopers were marshalled into regiments, 7,000 in all. . . . This was a great honour. We had been fighting these men all the way from the Rhine and they had given us some of the toughest battles we had ever had. They were the elite of the German Army and one of the very few divisions that still had a coherent organization. They had refused to surrender to any but the Guards Armoured Division. . . .

Our Commanding Officers then went round the Division . . . and Colonel Roddy Hill took the salute. Two hundred and thirty of their officers were then separated and marched away . . . five deep, resplendent in their best uniforms, led by our Commanding Officer. This . . . gave one a curiously moving sense of triumph and achievement.'

Enough of it all is right. For, to reach this triumphal end the enormity of the cost in individual lives and suffering can never be told nor words describe; virtually all existence everywhere had had to be turned upside down and much of it destroyed. The road to recovery would be long and momentous, and for another world.

Meanwhile on 6th May, 1945, unable to see as yet and for months to come, I heard over the wireless in Hospital in England that Germany had surrendered unconditionally and shared in the relief of all that the war was won.

SEQUEL

'We got away by great good luck,' wrote Dermot Musker, describing the moment he had found me on the back of Sergeant Major Greenwell's tank, when the curtain had come down for me on any further part I was going to play. He had given me a shot of morphine from his pocket to deaden the pain, thank God. For me it was over, for most of my friends in the Squadron and the Battalion the costly, cruel and senseless war would go on for a few more weeks. Not on our front was there much sign of a demoralized and beaten Army. The German Para divisions would be fighting to the bitter end, for they knew there could be no unconditional surrender for them. I was aware that the two poor Guardsmen in the turret of the tank below me, Hanson and Wright, could not have survived more than a few moments. I hoped Bradbury might just have escaped, as I knew Bland had leapt out of the driver's hatch by a hair's breadth. The heat and pain were unbelievably intense. It seemed an age while I fought my way out of the cauldron of flame surrounding the tank. I knew I was terribly burnt, but from the moment I picked myself up something told me I was going to be all right, to get up and go on.

By the time the MO had arrived from Battalion HQ I could no longer see anything. Dermot says it was about an hour before they could get me off to the Field Dressing Station and Johnny Thompson gave his instructions to get me there as fast as they could on a stretcher laid on the top of their scout car. I had remained fully conscious throughout it all, but there was to be one more moment of alarm when I could just overhear the conversation between the driver and his mate below me. They were hopelessly lost along the route back to the Rhine. Knowing how many enemy we had seen still around the area when we raced through that morning, I was prepared for anything to

211

happen. A despatch rider was at length spotted, and stopped, they spoke and all was well.

The quiet efficiency of everyone thereafter at the Field Dressing Station and then at long last at the 21st Army Base Hospital, near Brussels, gave me courage. Fifty years later I was singled out by one of the Senior Nursing Sisters at that hospital. This was after the dinner given in Portsmouth City Hall to commemorate the landings in Normandy. She wanted to tell me how much worry I had caused them when I was brought in there. It was very remarkable that she should have recalled my name.

I told her it was there that the staff and the Padre boosted my morale no end by saying that my eyesight would be all right. Most kind and encouraging too was my driver, Bland, in a bed close by. Evidently his legs were not too badly burned. Sadly, he told me, Bradbury did not make it with the others.

Then to England – by Dakota aircraft – a slow and painful flight. The relief to be back home was wonderful. I was flown to Swindon Transit Hospital, where my mother and father first came to visit me, with my brother George too; a complete surprise, he was back from Italy. From there I was dispersed to Derby City by Hospital train, most uncomfortable and the pain was pretty dreadful. The war still dragged on, of course. I had heard President Roosevelt had died, but all the talk seemed to be about victory celebrations and nothing much about the ceaseless, bitter fighting in Germany that might still have to be done to achieve it. I wondered often what reception my friends in the Armoured Division were having to face after I left. It would be a long while before I could hear anything about them.

After a week or so a Red Cross Ambulance arrived to take me by road south again to Sussex to the Hospital where the RAF pilots and crews had been treated throughout the war, when shot down in flames with serious burns.

I had never heard of it myself until then, but to anyone else the fame of the Emergency Medical Service Hospital with the Canadian Wing at East Grinstead was already a legend. The two great surgeons were of course Archie Macindoe, who originally came from New Zealand and became Consultant to the RAF when war began, and Ben Tilley, in charge of the Canadian Wing from Ottawa. They led a remarkable team of senior doctors and civilians, and dedicated girls and male nurses, British and Canadian, presided over by the magnificent Matron, Cherry Hall. By now they had achieved with practised expertise the restoration of many pilots and crew members of the British Empire and Allied Air Forces to a renewed existence. High morale is what they understood and aimed for – for a few airmen this even meant getting them fit again for operational flying. So for this team, at the close of six years of aerial combat, I was just another patient, and an Army wallah at that. For them all in the day's work. The Hospital had been one of the very first too, late in the war, to be allocated the remarkable drug, penicillin, so necessary and effective to counter infection in such wounds.

It was then to be endless penicillin for me, and saline baths for weeks on end, the treatment that had emerged from the better recovery trend made by pilots who had parachuted into the sea. Even if I had a small share of the literary talents of the Australian-born Spitfire pilot, Richard Hillary, let alone a Siegfrid Sassoon, to write of the countless operations or mental torment that were theirs, I would hate to recall my treatment after more than fifty years, or inflict such memories on anyone today. Hillary has written his story of recovery at East Grinstead and elsewhere after being shot down in the North Sea in his book *The Last Enemy*. He went back to flying after his treatment, only then to die on active service.

Within a few days of my arrival in the Canadian Wing Hitler was dead. Those in hospital at the time were not to be deprived of their share of savouring the Victory in Europe celebrations. For days they were stocking up the wards, hiding bottles where they could, down the ends of all our beds, to avoid the eagle eye of Cherry Hall. Then the great day came at last and those young men of our generation who had done so much to bring it about made the very best of it they could, with all the girls on the hospital strength that could be enticed along to join the fun. VE day apart, I soon learned there was a totally different approach to discipline in the RAF wards from what would have been the case in an Army hospital. We were all on Christian name terms with staff and patients alike, but when it came to medical requirements that mattered they were rightly as strict as anywhere.

The road to recovery, I knew by now, was bound to be long. I heard Macindoe tell those of the staff around him that my eyes would be attended to first, but they all impressed on me that I could not expect the dressings to be removed for many weeks. I was fortunate, I knew, to be in such good hands, even if I did not feel so at times.

Most of all the part my mother played in my recovery was wonderful. She visited me from London, evening after evening, pushing her bicycle into the guards van of the train from Victoria and bicycling up from the station at Three Bridges near East Grinstead to the Hospital. She was exceedingly busy at the Headquarters of the British Red Cross in Belgrave Square, where she was in charge of all the Civilian Relief teams being sent to the former enemy territories that were occupied by British forces. There were millions of displaced persons, DPs as they were called, in the British Zones of Germany and Austria, Nazi slave workers, concentration camp survivors and civilian prisoners, from all over Europe and beyond. There was no United Nations to organize things in those early days and only the British voluntary societies were there to do the welfare work amongst them in our occupied zones. It was a huge job, yet she came as often as she could to tell me about the outside world and help me come to terms with boredom and discomfort. My father came too when he could. As a temporary civil servant in the Ministry of Home Security, he was involved in advising on limiting the damage done to buildings, factories and services in the Blitz. The kindness of local volunteers and others was great too. They came to read books and correspondence to me and write some letters to my friends. I learned the extreme importance of the human voice to those who cannot see the source. The tone, the expression, even the accent, gave one the only insight and enabled one to assess or guess the sort of person standing near one. Surrounded as I was and kept in my place by hosts of Canadian girls and their expressions and instructions, my prejudices on one occasion unwittingly escaped. I heard a sweet, low, voice beside my bed asking how I was feeling, and out it came. "Thank God for an English voice," I exclaimed too loudly, and it became a standing joke in the Canadian Wing. The voice came from the hospital's Chief Physiotherapist, as English a source as anyone could wish for, Miss Anne Harvey. She was to become a long-time friend and confidante whose skills did so much to get me on the road to normal life again in the coming months. She knew a great deal about the effects of war, having looked after many of the airmen from the Battle of Britain since the earlier days of the Macindoe team. Her heart was with the RAF although her elder brother had served in the Irish Guards, earning an MC in the mud and trenches of 1917.

As the end in Germany approached, news from the Battalion, which I had been so impatient for, started to arrive. As I feared, they had been in action almost continually right up to the end of April. I was particularly sad to hear that No. 2 Troop had lost Sergeant Shipley and Sergeant Lyon who joined them after Enschede. Both were killed by bazookas fired by the Paras from windows of the houses at Berge, a strongly held village about 20 miles east of the frontier. Corporal Siddons, Shipley's operator, was badly wounded too. Shipley had achieved his last wish to be the leading tank in the Squadron attack. His action, and that of Ian Liddell, rather belies the suggestion that officers and men showed less courage when the end of the fighting was obviously so close. It was also a tragedy that our tanks could be so easily destroyed and their crews killed by such small hand-held weapons as the Panzerfaust. Commanding Officers must have had some difficult decisions near the end in reaching their objectives when everyone naturally wanted to keep casualties as low as possible. The last grievous loss was when a tank of No. 2 Squadron was blown into small pieces by a sea mine placed under the road, killing Sergeant Green and all his crew on 1st May, just three days before the Germans surrendered. I could not help feeling that just retribution had been realized somewhat when letters told me that in these last battles the rockets instigated by No. 2 Squadron had killed many more Germans. Sergeant Fawcett recalled that after one of these fights, probably that near Lingen, a German officer had complained like mad that our rockets were against the Geneva Convention and were not allowed! Dermot Musker, now our Second-in-Command, had written that between leaving Holland and the end of hostilities, although I was their only Officer casualty, No. 2 Squadron had lost five of the best NCOs, all dead, and about thirty-five Guardsmen killed, wounded or missing. Of those who served with me in No. 2 Troop since we crossed, nineteen strong, to Normandy, thirteen men had died and eight or nine were wounded.

Soon after the German surrender was complete, it was learned that the Guards Armoured Division was to lose its armour. The enemy had been disarmed and the priority was to carry forward the huge policing job needed for an army of occupation. Val Hermon wrote to me from Pirbright on 11 June, "You are probably aware the Division has now

215

reverted to Infantry and I see by the papers that it is referred to as 'the cream of the Infantry'. No doubt we were just rather gassy milkshakes before!" He sounded his cheerful self once again and said he would be coming to see me soon. A great ceremonial parade with massed Bands, called 'Farewell to Armour', was held at Rotenburg Airfield on 9 June before the Field Marshal. Then the tanks, spruced up to the last, were driven off into obscurity.

Although sometimes questioned, the high standard of discipline and appearance of Officers and Guardsmen in Armour had proved every bit as essential to the success of the Armoured Battalions and the Division as a whole, indeed to the survival of individual tank crews, as in any other formation. The Regular Officers and remarkable Warrant Officers understood this well. That wars and battles are lost by those who make the most mistakes is the truism drummed into us, but without this discipline our mistakes would have been many more.

The longed-for moment had arrived – leave was stepped up, some of our long-serving friends were to be 'demobbed'. One of the first out, Bill Gray, 'retired from the Army on V+1,' Val wrote to me in his letter, "to pursue his nefarious calling of MP", and some were able to come and visit me at East Grinstead.

Perhaps the extent of our wounds in this hospital may have taken some aback at first, but the remarkable state of morale engendered by the staff and others soon got across to visitors. One of the first Coldstreamers to visit was Major Bill Harris, whose home was close to East Grinstead. When I first joined the Regiment he was the extremely smart Adjutant at Pirbright, and later became a Company Commander through the campaign in Italy. He was a solid friend to us all and a tremendously enthusiastic supporter of the Regiment. Henry Graham Vivian, badly wounded by a machine gun near Caen with the 5th Battalion and now at Regimental Headquarters, came full of news to cheer me up.

Another great event as the summer wore on was the visit to the Hospital of the Queen, now the Queen Mother. She came round and talked individually to us in our beds on the ward. I could not see her, but I was asked in such a friendly voice what I wanted to do when I escaped from their clutches. I did not really know of course, but said I would like to go sailing again. She made it clear that this was not a favourite pastime of hers, and she recalled she was not very comfortable

216

or happy when "off the Needles". I have not forgotten, since this conversation has returned to me many times when I have been in that very area. Her visit was enormously cheering to all.

My progress had been slowed down because of an unpleasant go of jaundice, but then at last Macindoe allowed the dressings over my eyes to be removed in July. Gradually daylight and faces reappeared and life took a new turn. By August when I could move about on a stick, I was sent home for a month or so and my mother was able to take me in a train back to Cornwall, provided I had someone to come and treat me from the local hospital. I received a great welcome when I reached home in Cornwall, but I knew it was a bit of a shock when they saw how wobbly I was at first. Some precious petrol had been acquired, we could not ask how, so that we could go around by car.

Almost the day we arrived we heard the announcement that the whole of the BBC news bulletin that evening would be devoted to one subject, the Atomic bomb. So we hovered over the wireless. The first Atomic bomb had been dropped that morning, 6 August, over Japan and its devastating power had destroyed the city of Hiroshima in a vast fireball. Casualties were expected to be enormous. My mother's reaction was, what a dreadful thing, directly opposite from mine which was how wonderful, it must stop the war! A second bomb was dropped and by the 14th Japan had surrendered unconditionally and World War II was finally at an end. Thousands of British Servicemen were in training for the invasion of Japan. It would never happen now. The dozens of ships of all sorts moored in the River Fal below us, many of them damaged by enemy action, sounded their sirens far into the night. I could not sleep and kept asking myself – how can we and our allies stop this bloody stupid thing ever happening again? We owed it to all the millions that had died to find the answer.

The General Election had taken place while I was unable to read and a charming voiced VAD came to explain my voting papers and told me what each candidate for Penryn and Falmouth had to say. It was of course the first vote for millions of us, there having been no such election since 1935. I voted against a Colonel Evelyn King, largely because his address said, "Vote for King and Country" at least so my VAD read out! A generation later I found myself sitting alongside this Honourable and Gallant Member on the green benches and I pulled his leg mercilessly for such an indiscretion. "Never," he replied, "it must have been

217

something dreamed up by my Agent!" The result was announced weeks later, a clean sweep for Labour – and Winston Churchill had gone. "Vote for us. We'll get you home quicker" had clearly done the trick with the millions in uniform.

I returned to East Grinstead in the autumn after a Medical Board in Brighton of all places had pronounced I was in the lowest category, E, and unfit for any duty. The Canadians had returned home by then, and I was put in the main Service Ward III, most of the hospital returning to civilian use. I asked Archie Macindoe if he could do something to my hands then, so that I could fire my shotgun again before the winter. I think he rather wondered who I was going to use it on. However, he and the team did a remarkable job, helped by Anne Harvey, and I was duly able to go out shooting at Christmas in Cornwall, so life was turning greatly for the better. I had been to Birdcage Walk after the Medical Board wearing uniform and received a warm welcome from Major John Chandos-Pole, then Regimental Adjutant. With the 5th Battalion he himself was seriously wounded in the same attack for that horrible village of Heppen near the Albert Canal in Belgium, where No. 2 Squadron lost many tanks, including Sergeant Brough's in the evening of 8 September.

Well versed in handling the medical authorities in the War Office, he was immensely helpful to me in negotiating that, rather than being invalided out, I should remain in the Army until I had had the hospital treatment that I needed. Thus they would take account of all medical expenses and keep me on full pay. No visit to Regimental Headquarters was possible without being put properly in one's place. Next day I received a letter, full of medal ribbons and the comment, "It was noticed you were not wearing the proper ribbons of your campaign stars"! I was amused by the consequence. The young nurses in Ward III had a rack on which hung the uniforms of those inside. Here they showed off to any visitors a row of dazzling medal ribbons of great distinction belonging to the RAF patients of the Ward. One of my visitors was now confronted by a lone Coldstreamer's in the middle – he thought it very funny that I should be in such company.

Among the very great of our generation, a Spitfire and Hurricane Pilot, shot down at least three times from the Battle of Britain to Arnhem who lay in the next bed to mine being rebuilt in the same way as I, was Geoffrey Page. A frequent attender at the Hospital, he had certainly not lost his humour nor his deft way of handling of the hospital staff, even Cherry Hall, I learnt from him a little how the Luftwaffe never stood a chance. No one of course wanted in such a hospital to talk about their exploits that brought them there, but it soon became clear to me what we owed to such remarkable men and what fun they were to be with, even in our dismal circumstances.

Enough's enough. It was many more months of much discomfort before I could return to normal life again. I feel it should be said, however, that this country should be proud of the Private and Emergency Hospital system that existed in wartime to mend the severely wounded, military and no doubt the many civilian casualties too, long before the State-run National Health Service had been brought into being. They did a fantastic job. At the end of the summer of 1946, I had asked my mother to see if I could join one of the many Civilian Relief Teams. Under the Joint War organization of the Red Cross and St. John, with other well known charities under the umbrella, they provided the only civilian outside aid to the British zones of Occupied Territories. She agreed to arrange this and the Army did not object. I was still in their lowest category, so to have some interesting work to occupy myself with for a time outside England was going to be a great help to me.

Meanwhile in the early summer I began sailing again with my brother George, although our Hospital Matron clearly did not approve, so I had to paint quite a different picture for her benefit. We had a splendid trip in a beautiful old black cutter, *Varuna*, which belonged since pre-war to Mervyn Varnon; he had been serving with the Grenadiers from well before and wanted to bring her up from Cowes to the Clyde where he was now living. Others on board included John Nelson and Peter Thorne, our cousin, both long-serving Grenadiers too. It was a hilarious party, and, although foggy in the Channel, we had a spanking good sail up the Irish Sea.

This was to be no brief interlude of the post-war world for me, since, as well as whetting my appetite for sailing once again, it had another long-lasting consequence. Among the genuine war-prizes of the British Forces were the sailing yachts built on the orders of Hermann Goering for the Luftwaffe's recreation in the Baltic about the time the Germans were playing host to the 1936 Olympics. The RAF had organized a flotilla of the best of them to be sailed to the UK ten years later as fair 'loot'. The War Office subsequently allotted them to each of the

219

Services' various Yacht Clubs, and the Household Division received two. One was to become the renowned yacht *Gladeye*, fittingly named after our former Divisional sign. Many of us former Guardmen had a lot of fun in her in the years to come.

Jumping forward by a couple of years, and on another of the Division's yachts *Farewell*, we had, by way of ensuring that the quality of the food was of the best for the crew while crossing the Channel, invited two very attractive cooks. The cuisine was indeed much better than we bargained for, and two of the crew decided the cooks should be taken on on a more permanent basis. Without more ado Peter Heneage, one of my oldest friends, and a wartime Gunner, was promptly engaged to marry Jean Douglas, the first of them.

By amazing chance the other of the cooks has already featured in my story. She was none other than the Wren who had driven through our lines day after day in the streets of Brighton. She had attracted the soldiers' greetings as she went by when we were preparing to move towards the invasion beaches in 1944. I had not taken her name then, but she was not to get away that easily again. Mary Codrington and I had the great privilege of being married in the Chapel Royal, St. James's, later in the year.

After that digression, September 1946 was when I joined one of the Red Cross teams in Hamburg. Their prime purpose was to bring aid to the hundreds of thousands of Displaced Persons who had ended up inside the British Zone of Germany and, for a multitude of reasons, could never return to their homes. The team looked after an area from Hamburg to Flensburg on the Danish border. With fifteen or so dedicated individuals, some with nursing, medical or community service backgrounds, and others retired from the Forces, they were an impressive crowd under an able leader, Maurice Belton. The task facing them and the other teams was prodigious. Some of these brave ladies had worked very early on in the indescribable horror of Belsen concentration camp within a few days of the British reaching it, where disease and starvation was claiming thousands before they could be rescued and saved. The DPs were now housed and fed in the vast solidly-built Hitler barracks that abounded in the area around Hamburg. The buildings were regularly visited by us to see that hospital supplies and medical attention were getting through where most required, but the shortages of essentials such as clothing, shoes and basic drugs, were chronic.

Some of them could talk a little English, I found. They looked forward only for the day when the United States and Canada would take them as refugees, which for a huge number eventually occurred.

Hamburg itself had suffered as much – or worse – destruction as any city in the war in Europe. The fire-storm, as it was known there, of July 1943, had set alight many wooden buildings and caused the horrendous wind that fanned the heat and flame with three-quarters of the city being totally destroyed. Thousands had fled into the two great lakes in the centre and where many hundreds must have drowned. By 1946 large numbers were living still in mile upon mile of rubble, which was revealed only after dark by little twinkling lights appearing out of the ground.

The British Army gave up one day's ration a week during the winter, so that German children living in these conditions in the city could have one meal of hot soup, which the Relief teams were to hand out to them. It was to be one of the coldest winters this century. I can still see the smiles on their little faces when they found a lump of meat in the bowls we had filled for them. One feels so totally different when the enemy is beaten to the ground and they are faced by the consequences of their action. The least we can do is to help those who can bear no responsibility. I think the Army did very well. It was well known that none of the German population in our zone had ever had anything to do with the Nazi party!

As a contrast I was taken by some of the team to a session of a War Crimes trial of the guards in one of the concentration camps, and I saw the odious faces of those men and women who had perpetrated some of the worst of the mass evils.

A planned expedition by the Red Cross Foreign Relations Team, whose prime job was searching for missing prisoners of war, to enter the Russian Zone and, among other tasks, to try and obtain surgical instruments for the hospitals in our zone, was taking place. No combatant or DP drivers were allowed, so I was asked if I could drive one of the cars. Under the team leader Brigadier Henry Hawtry we set off via Berlin to Leipzig, displaying our Red Cross designations. We were escorted by Russians from Berlin, and the destruction and poverty in their zone looked no different from ours. Because of the desperate shortages there too, the factory in Leipzig could not release any of the instruments they made and we came back empty-handed. There was, it seemed, a tremendous shortage of these instruments everywhere and none could be spared, even from Britain.

In Berlin I visited the Reich Chancellery and saw the vast rooms Hitler used and the entrance to the bunker in the garden, guarded by bored-looking Russian sentries. The sufferings one saw inside Germany, compounded with all the horrors we had seen and been through, brought one back again to what every civilized human must feel. It must never be allowed to happen again.

It so happened that Winston Churchill, who had recently in Zurich, made his first call that France should lead Germany by the hand, and with full British co-operation rally her to the west. Received at first with official hostility, not by any means by all, including those who had seen the vast scale of reconstruction in Europe that had to take place, we were hearing the first seeds sewn on fertile ground for his early ideas of a United Europe, which would become the stuff of politics for the next fifty years. When he first used these words he included Soviet Russia in the hope they might too sponsor the New Europe.

It was very good to hear that those who understood what caused the evil and perverted ideologies that had brought so much death and destruction over two generations had begun to wrestle with how to prevent this madness ever occurring again. It made one feel one wanted to join in whatever modest way one could their efforts to find the right way forward if only in respect for our friends who never made it.

There was an occasion that autumn that gave me the opportunity to meet the 1st Coldstream once more and to provide a poignant and fitting moment to bring this tale to an end. A visit to a large camp of Polish displaced persons near Lübeck enabled me to do so. Not far north on the coast of the Baltic at Travemünde the Battalion were in a quiet sector guarding the border with the Russian zone across the river. It was about eighteen months to the day since I had left them. I found one old friend, Greville Chester, now the Adjutant, who gave me a great welcome. Almost all I had known had by now been demobbed or transferred to more senior jobs in the Army, or to other battalions. Regimental soldiering was not much catch these days for some of my friends, and as the Regiment was now reduced to three battalions, it was a different world from what I had known. They did not have an awful lot to do anyhow there just now, guards or fatigues seemed to be the order of the day, but they were greatly looking forward to returning to

London quite soon, where peacetime public duties would prevail. There were new faces, but the spirit and their good cheer had not changed. It never will. They were immensely proud of what their Battalion had done over the past six years, and that was something I most certainly shared.

INDEX

Note: Page numbers in bold refer to
  maps

Aachen, 156, 158, 164
Adair, Maj Gen Allan, 26, 97, 115, 185
Adeane, Michael, 164, 172
Aircraft
  Normandy landings, 22
  Typhoons, 48–9, 113, 127
Albert Canal, Belgium, 117, 118, 121,
  173
Allen, Bill, 204
Allsopp, Henry, 28, 91, 93, 97, 99, 164
  advance to Holland,
  in Brussels, 116
  Flers, 102
  Operation Market Garden, 131
Althorp, John, 23
Ambler, John, 193
Amiens, liberation of, 107
Anstruther-Gray, Bill, Captain, 6, 8–9,
  101, 105–6, 176, 216
  Bemmel, 143
  in Brussels, 116, 117
  at Estry, 64
  Giberville, 49
  in Normandy, 21, 24, 27, 96
  Normandy landings, 13
  Operation Goodwood, 42–3
  Sourdevalle, 68, 69, 71, 76–7, 79, 80,
    81, 84, 89–90
Antwerp, 115, 155–6
Ardennes offensive, 175, 176, 177
Argentan, 102
Arnhem, 127, 130, 135, 147, 156
  airborne landings, 124, 125

bridge, 130
Arnold, Lance Sgt S., 9, 42, 66, 67, 80,
  81, 96
Arras, battle for, 108–11, 115
Arromanches, 22
Avranches, 52, 67, 92

Bachy, Belgium, 113
Baddeley, John, 82, 91, 123, 143
Bailey, Cpl W., 89
Baillie, John, 195–6, 198
Banks, Sgt, 82, 91
Bastone, Sgt, 90, 91, 169
  at Enschede, 202–3, 204, 208
Bates, Corporal S, VC, 68
Batt, Reggie, 55
Baxendale, David, 5, 42
  death, 44
  in Normandy, 13, 15, 18, 24
Bayeux, 21, 50
BBC, 194
Beauvais, 106–7
Beckum, 203
Belgium, advance into, 113–14
Belton, Maurice, 220
Bemmel, Netherlands, 148
  orchard near, 134, 136, 137–44
Beny Bocage, 52, 53
Beresford, Guardsman, 118
Beringen, Belgium, 118, 119
Berlin, 221, 222
  Russian advance on, 178, 179
Berry, Guardsman, 49, 67, 75
Berry, Neville, 197
Biddlecombe, John, 174
Bingham, Nigel, 91, 104, 138

Birch, Simon, 157
Bland, Guardsman, 137, 201, 212
   Enschede, 205, 208, 211
Bodley, Miles, 102–3, 119, 122, 131
Bodsworth, Cpl, 77, 78–80, 81
Bonninghardt, 193
Boscawen, Edward, Royal Engineers, 1,
   14, 67, 154, 197
Boscawen, Evelyn, 1
Boscawen, George, Coldstream Guards,
   1, 43, 154, 212, 219
Boscawen, Mary, 183
   letters from, 24, 83, 154
Boughey, Richard, 177–9, 182, 198–9
Bourg Leopold, 122, 173, 176
Bourgebus, 26
Bradbury, Guardsman, 134, 201, 208,
   211, 212
Bradley, General Omar, 172
Bretteville L'Orgueilleuse, 21
Briscoe, Cpl, 39
British Army
   21st Army Group, 117, 175, 198
   armies, Second Army, 10, 20, 117,
      126, 130, 157, 162, 175
   brigades
      4th Armoured, 23
      5th Guards, 7, 123, 185, 190, 201,
         202
      6th Guards Tank, 51, 52, 59, 66,
         156, 201
      8th Rifle, 56
      29th Armoured, 62
      32nd Guards, 8, 21, 52, 59, 123,
         185, 189, 202
      231st Infantry, 133, 142
   corps
      8 Corps, 8, 26, 49–50, 51, 62, 92, 93
      12 Corps, 26
      30 Corps, 26, 104, 117, 175, 181
      Geilenkirchen, 162
      Operation Market Garden, 123,
         129, 130–1, 147, 148–9
      Operation Veritable, 190
   divisions
      1st Airborne, 127, 128, 130, 147
      3rd Infantry, 26, 62

      6th Airborne, 171
      7th Armoured, 26, 40, 129
      11th Armoured, 26, 29, 40, 51–2,
         56, 98, 187
         advance into Holland, 104, 106,
            107, 115
         Dinant, 167
         Estry-Vire, 62–3
      15th Scottish, 51, 59, 62, 64
      43rd Infantry, 104, 128, 152, 162,
         190
      50th Infantry, 104, 131, 133
      51st Highland, 26
      Guards Armoured, 26, 46, 98, 104,
         175, 198
         formation, 3–4, 6
         Operation Market Garden, 123–4,
            126, 147
         reversion to infantry, 215–16
         towards Hamburg, 201
   regiments
      23rd Hussars, 52, 56
      Coldstream Guards, 4, 105, 113,
         115, 123, 189, 210
         1st Battalion, 26, 104, 126, 132,
            222–3 and *passim*
         5th Battalion, 21, 39, 59, 60, 83,
            104, 179
           Beringen, 118
           Bonninghardt, 193
           Chênedollé, 90
           Hillensberg, 160
           Namur, 167
           near Beckum, 203
         Arras, 108–11
         Operation Market Garden, 131,
            147
      Devonshire, 2nd Battalion, 136
      Dorset, 1st Battalion, 136, 147
      Durham Light Infantry, 141
      Fife and Forfar Yeomanry, 30, 56, 62
      Grenadier Guards
         1st Motor Battalion, 31–3, 74, 104
         2nd Battalion, 26, 30, 46, 74, 104
         4th Battalion, 57, 64
         advance to Holland, 106, 112,
            113–14, 115

regiments *(continued)*
  Nijmegen, 147
  Hampshire, 1st Battalion, 134, 136, 141
  Household Cavalry Regiment, 111, 121, 204
    2nd Battalion, 52, 106
  Irish Guards, 112, 123, 147, 202
    2nd Battalion, 26, 41, 59, 83, 121, 133
    3rd Battalion, 52, 59, 61–4, 104, 121, 185
      Sourdevalle, 67–8, 72, 76–7, 81, 83, 86, 89
  Irish Infantry regiment, 55
  King's Own Scottish Borderers, 64
  Leicester Yeomanry, 30, 152
  Monmouthshire Regiment, 3rd Battalion, 52, 56, 62, 67–8
  Northants Yeomanry, 52
  Queen's Regiment, 165
  Royal Norfolk Regiment, 62, 68
  Scots Guards, 59, 83
  Welsh Guards, 31, 90, 106, 112, 118, 167
    1st Battalion, 52, 59, 65, 83, 104
    2nd Battalion, 104
  Royal Engineers, 3rd Training Battalion, 1–2
  Light Aid Detachment, 197
  Pioneer Corps, 175
  German yachts requisitioned, 219–20
  supply dump, 175
British Liberation Army, 197
Brooke, Field Marshal Sir Alan, Monty's letter to, 93
Brough, Miss May, 154, 187
Brough, Sgt F., 8, 21, 27, 29, 61, 96
  advance to Holland, 107
  at Arras, 110–11, 112
  in Brussels, 116
  killed, 119, 120–1, 124, 126
  at Sourdevalle, 66–7, 69, 72–3, 75, 77, 79, 81–2, 84, 88, 89
Brown, Guardsman, 117, 149, 161, 166, 174, 182, 186–7, 194, 199
Browning, General 'Boy', 97

Brussels, 112, 113–18
  21st Army Group Base Hospital, 212
  delay near, 117–18
  Eye Club, 151, 157, 178, 180, 196
  leave in, 150–2, 157–8, 162, 177–8, 195–6
Burcy, 71
Buxton, Peter, 30

Caen, 17, 20, 22, 25, 50
  Faubourg de Vaucelles, 45
  Operation Goodwood, 28–45, **37**
Cagny, battle for, 32, 33–4, **35**, 36
Cahan, 101
Calcar, Germany, 200
Callow, Sgt, 5
Cambridge, 2–4
Cambridge, Lord Frederick, 126
Canadian Army
  1st Army, 10, 49
  Antwerp, 155–6
  at Caen, 22, 26, 46, 47
  at Falaise, 93
  Nijmegen, 181, 186, 187, 188
  Operation Veritable, 190
Carew-Pole, John, Colonel, 136
Carrington, Peter, 134
Carver, Michael, Brigadier, 23
Cathéolles, bridge at, 52, 55, 57
Caulfield, Lance Sgt R., 21, 34, 54, 61, 96
  Enschede, 205, 207, 208
  Sourdevalle, 69, 72, 73–4, 77, 79, 84, 86–7, 89
Caumont, 49–50, 51
Champagne, liberated, 116–17
Chance, Peter, 19, 187–8
Chandos-Pole, John, Major, 218
Channon, Cpl, 67, 133
  at Sourdevalle, 75, 77, 78–9, 80–1
Chaumont, 105
Chênedollé, 75, 83, **85**
Cherbourg, 17, 20, 49
Chester, Greville, 122, 168, 197, 222
  at Namur, 169–70, 171, 172
Chisendale-Marsh, Hugo, 5
  Giberville, 49
  in Normandy, 24, 27

Normandy landings, 13–15
  Sourdevalle, 68, 71, 82, 84
Churchill, W.S., Prime Minister, 9, 48,
  156, 218, 222
Civilian Relief Teams, 214, 219
Clark, Bob, 152, 153, 155
Cleve, Netherlands, 185, 190
Clifford, Freddie, 178
Coates, Jimmy, Colonel, 176
Cobbold, Ralph, 23
Codrington, Lt General Sir Alfred, 184–5
Codrington, Mary, 11
  marriage to author, 220
Collin, Nico, 97, 140, 164
Cologne, 188
Corbould, John, 67
Cornwall
  convalescence in, 217
  leave in, 183
Cox, Cpl, 119, 127
Crerar, General, 177
Cuverville, 29, 30
Cuxhaven, 209, 210

Dam, Mr, eyewitness at Enschede, 203
Daniel, Guardsman, 137
Darell, Jeff, 103, 106, 145, 193–4, 209
Dawnay, George, 8, 16, 24, 27, 50, 61,
  96, 97, 164, 180
  advance from Seine, 103
  Brussels, 153–4
  MC award, 185
  Operation Market Garden, 134, 138
  Sourdevalle, 68, 79, 82, 84, 87, 91
  Squadron leader, 101, 106
De Cröy family, 167–8
De Vinq, Baron Jose, 157
Demeure, Jacqueline, 162, 178, 196, 197
Demouville, 29, 30
Dempsey, General Sir Miles, 48, 128, 177
Denbigh, Billy (Earl of), 93, 94, 119,
  124, 151
Diest, 118
Dinant, 167
Dinxperlo, Germany, 201, 202
Displaced Persons, Hamburg, 220–1
Dorman, Tony, 177

Dormer, Hugh, 95
Douai, 111, 112
Doughty, George, 159
Douglas, Jean, 220
D'Outremont, Comte de, 166, 172,
  173–4
Doyle, Peter, Irish Guards, 72, 76, 84
Driscoll, Cpl, 182
Dyle, River, 126

Eardley Wilmot, Anthony, 84, 92
East Grinstead, Emergency Medical
  Service Hospital, 212–14, 215–19
Eastman, Derek, 109–10
Eberbach, General, 107
Eindhoven, 127–8
Elizabeth, Queen (now Queen Mother),
  216–17
Emmerson, Lance Sgt N., 8, 21, 61, 67,
  96
  Operation Goodwood, 27, 29, 32, 34
  Sourdevalle, 69, 74, 75–6, 77–8, 80
England, leave in, 180, 181, 182–4
ENSA, 178, 195
Enschede, author's tank hit at, 204–9,
  211
Entwistle, Cpl, 80
Escaut Canal, 121, 123–4
Esemael, Mayor of, 171–2
Esquay-sur-Seulles, 17
Estry-Vire ridge, 61–2, 63–5, 66
Europe, reconstruction in, 222

Falaise, Canadian advance on, 93
Falaise Gap, 100, 101
Falmouth, Lady (author's mother), 183,
  214
  with Red Cross in Cairo, 24, 67
Falmouth, Lord (author's father), 183,
  214
  letters from, 67, 145, 176
Farewell (yacht), 220
Fawcett, Sgt T., 5, 133, 140–1, 142–3,
  215
Finch, Cpl, 89
Fitzalan Howard, Michael, 162, 173
Fitzmaurice, Lord Edward, 92

227

Fitzroy, Captain Oliver, RN, 19
Fitzroy, Oliver, 64
Flers, 101–2
Fox, Michael, Major, 5, 8, 63, 94, 118,
   175
  Nijmegen, 194–5
  Operation Market Garden, 124, 129
France, South of, 98
French Army, to Rhine at Strasbourg, 162
Frénouville, 38, 41

Game shooting, 150, 154, 159, 166,
   181–2
Gascoigne, Humphrey, Grenadier
   Guards, 121, 131
Gavin, General, US Army, 132
Geilenkirchen, 162
Gell, Anthony, 68–9, 84, 87, 89, 95,
   147, 160, 173
General Election (1945), 217–18
German Army, 65, 122, 147–8, 188, 210
  armies
    1st Parachute Army, 190
    7th Army, 48, 92, 95
  divisions
    3rd Parachute, 56, 86
    5th Parachute, 86
    7th Parachute, 194, 209, 210
    9th SS Panzer, 54, 56, 62, 86, 130
    10th SS Panzer, 62, 86, 130
    21st Panzer, 29, 54, 56
  regiment, 125 Panzer Grenadier, 32
  counter-attack at Aachen, 164
  horse transport, 102
Germany
  civilians, 192
  surrender of, 210, 213, 215
Giberville, 45–51
Gisors, 105
Goch, 186–8, 189, 190
Gooch, Dickie, Lt Col, 97, 102, 106,
   108, 115, 195
  advance to Holland, 118
  Brussels, 152–3, 161
  Operation Market Garden, 131, 145
  and Twente Canal, 209
Gordon Lennox, Reggie, 199

Gorman, John, 95
Graham, Andy, 194
Graham-Vivian, Harry, 24, 95, 144, 216
Grant, Sir Arthur, 31
Grave, 124, 130, 131
Green, Gavin, 167
Green, Sgt, 209, 215
Greenwell, Sgt Major, at Enschede,
   205–6, 207, 211
Griffiths, Hugh, 124
Grigg, P.J., Minister of War, 9
Gull, Johnny, 38, 39, 91, 106, 107, 132,
   160
Gwatkin, Norman, Brigadier, 27, 94

Hall, Cherry, Matron at East Grinstead,
   213, 219
Hamburg, 201
  Displaced Persons, 220–1
Hamilton, Michael, 22, 54, 98, 149, 182,
   197
  advance from Seine, 104, 107
  advance to Holland, 119, 122, 126
  in Brussels, 178
Hanson, Guardsman, 46, 201, 208, 211
Hardwicke, Jock, 144
Hardy, William, Irish Guards, 83
Harricourt, 104
Harrington, Bill, 5, 94
Harris, Bill, Major, 216
Harris, Guardsman, 126, 173, 174
Hartington, Billy (Marquess of), 60, 122,
   126
Harvey, Miss Anne, Chief
   Physiotherapist at East Grinstead,
   214–15, 218
Harvey-Kelly, William, Irish Guards, 83,
   84, 89
Hathaway, Sgt, 200
Hawtry, Brigadier Henry, 221
Haydock, Dennis, 84
Hechtel, Belgium, 119, 121–2
Hèdauville, 108
Helmsley, N. Yorks, 8
Heneage, Peter, 95, 220
Heppen, Belgium, 119–20, 122
Herent, Belgium, 126

Hermon, Val, 6, 13, 14, 95, 187, 215–16
  in Bocage, 56
  Dermot Musker's letter to, 207
  in Normandy, 24
  Operation Goodwood, 32, 45
  Sourdevalle, 68, 71, 83, 84, 89
Heywood, Oliver, 17, 29, 50, 95, 101, 176
  advance to Holland, 105, 107, 111, 122
  in Brussels, 117
  Nijmegen, 185
  Operation Market Garden, 131
Higgins, James, 57
Hill, Col Roddy, 56, 62, 194, 210
Hillensberg, 158
Hiroshima, 217
Hitler, Adolf
  attempt to assassinate, 48
  death, 213
Holland, advance into, 104–18
Holland, Sgt, 200
Holmes, Sgt, 90
Horn, Allen, 144
Horrocks, General Sir Brian, 104,
    117–18, 128, 175
  on Operation Market Garden, 147–9
  Rhine offensive, 190
Hospitals
  Private and Emergency system, 219
  see also East Grinstead
Houtakker farm (Nijmegen), orchard at,
    134–43
Hove, 10–11
Howard, Mark, 21
Howitt, Dick, 132
Humphrey, Frank, Welsh Guards, 174,
    178
Hunt, Peter, 14, 28, 185
Hurworth, Guardsman K., 91, 208
Jabeek, Netherlands, 162
Jardine, General Sir Colin and Lady, 208
Jardine, Ian, 24, 28, 43, 63, 91, 96, 97,
    181
  Arras, 112
  birthday, 149
  Brussels, 157, 161, 181
  Brussels leave, 150–2
  at Enschede, 202, 204–5, 207–8, 209

Giberville, 49
Mont St Michel, 98–100
  at Namur, 169
  Neerheylissem, 166, 172, 173
  Operation Market Garden, 131, 132,
    145
  Tirlemont, 179
Jardine, Priscilla, 208
Jepson, Guardsman R., 5, 34, 41, 43, 49
Johnson, George, Brigadier, 198
Jones, Tony, RE, 2, 39, 134

Kapellen, 189–90, 192, 193, 194
Kennard, David, 122, 159, 160, 167, 179
  Namur, 168, 169–70
Kershaw, Guardsman, 46, 91, 97, 153
Kilmany, Lord see Anstruther-Gray, Bill
King, Evelyn, Colonel, MP, 217–18
Kingsford, Desmond, 74, 76, 81
Kluge, Field Marshal G. von, 48, 67
Knowles, RSM, 17

Larkin, CSM, 88, 92
Lawson-Tancred, Christopher, 2
Le Mans, 93
Le Prieure farm, Cagny, 33, 39
Lee, Joe, 150, 174
Leetham, Tony, 129
Leipzig, 221–2
Lens, 113
Les Escoublets, 61
Lessines, 113
Liddell, Ian, Captain, VC, 159, 160, 215
Liddle, Cpl, 27, 34, 42, 67
  Sourdevalle, 74, 75, 80
Liège, 162
Lille, 113
Lillingston, Luke, 94
Lingèvres, 18
Lock, Malcolm, 31, 119, 157, 175–6, 193
Lommel, 173, 176–7
Longueville, Reggie, 96–7, 154
Looker, Guardsman, 45, 90
Louvain, 115, 164
Loyd, General Budget, 97
Loyd, Peter, 116, 162, 169, 171
Lulworth, gunnery course, 8, 9

Lyon, Sgt, 215
  at Enschede, 207–8, 209

Maas (Meuse), River, 156, 162, 165–6, 167–8, 169–71, 194
Maastricht, 158
Macindoe, Archie, consultant surgeon to RAF, 212, 213–14, 218
McNinley, Trooper, 208
Maguire, Kevin, 95
Mahillon, Monsieur, 151, 157
Maquis, 99, 100, 106, 107, 110, 111
Marshall-Cornwall, Jim, 64
Martyn, David, 57, 95
Maxted, Stanley, journalist, 130
Meadows, Cpl, 67, 75, 133
Metz, 162
Meuse, River *see* Maas
Middleditch, Sydney, 131
Military Cross, awarded to author, 183, 185
Miller, Corporal, 2
Mont Cerisi, 100–1
Mont St Michel, 98–9
Montchamp, 68
Montgomery, General Sir Bernard, 19–20, 48, 93, 148, 156, 172, 178
Montgomery, Guardsman, 206
Morgan, Sgt, 5
Mortain, 67, 92, 93
Münster, 201
Musker, Dermot, 19, 32, 94, 164, 183, 185, 215
  account of author's wounding at Enschede, 206–9, 211
  Brussels, 153, 155
  Giberville, 49
  Goch, 187
  Nijmegen, 194
  in Normandy, 21
  and rockets, 197, 198
  at Twente Canal, 204
Myddelton, Ririd, Lt Col, 8, 25, 54, 63, 97, 101, 102

Namur, 166, 167–71
  photograph of author, 169
Neary, Guardsman, 20

Neerheylissem, 165, 166, 171
Nelson, John, 219
Netherlands, 127–8, 145, 146
Neville, Sandy, 136, 139, 144
Newton, Sgt, 89, 96, 111
Nijmegen, 127, 130, 133–4, 146–7, 181, 184, 185–6, 194–5
  airborne landings, 124
  the Island, **135**, 146, 148
Nijnsel, 128, 129
Nivelles, 196
Normandy, 17, 20
  the Bocage, 25, 51–66
  Operation Goodwood, 26–7, 28–45, **37**
Normandy Landings, 10–11, **12**, 13–17

O'Connor, General Dick, 51
Oisterwijk, 182
Olink, Mr, eyewitness at Enschede, 205
Operation Goodwood, 26–7, 28–45, **37**
Operation Market Garden, 123–4, **125**, 126–31
Operation Pepperpot, 152, 153
Operation Veritable (Rhine Offensive), 181, 190, **191**
Opheylissem, 165

Page, Geoffrey, RAF, 218–19
Paris, liberation of, 98
Partridge, Sgt, 185
Patton, General, 149, 156, 199
Pavée-Perriers ridge, 62–3, 69
Pearson, Timothy, 164, 197
Pegasus bridge, 29
Pemberton, Alan, 159, 167, 169–70, 179
Pereira, Jocelyn, 110
Peter, King of Yugoslavia, 3
Pirbright, Guards Training Battalion, 5
Poe, John, 196
Pollock, Patrick, Irish Guards, 9
Pratt, Nigel, 8, 44, 65, 97
  in Bocage, 56
  death, 87, 88, 90, 93–4
  Giberville, 47, 49
  in Normany, 17, 18, 19, 21, 24
  Operation Goodwood, 29, 32, 33, 34, 40
Sourdevalle, 68–9, 71, 73, 76, 82, 84

Priestley, Jimmy, 164, 169, 180, 181, 185
  at Enschede, 204, 207, 209
  and rockets, 198
Priestly, Tony, 90
'Prinz' (dog), 158, 159

Rasch, David, 51
Reading, Sgt, at Enschede, 202, 204, 207
Red Cross, 214, 219
  Foreign Relations Team, 221
Rees, Rhine crossing, 201
Refugees, 167
Reichswald Forest, 152, 153, 181, 182
  Battle of, 185, 190
Reid, Desmond, Irish Guards, 81, 84, 92
Rennes, 99–100
Rhine, River
  advance to, 162, 181
  crossing of, 198
  Operation Veritable, 190, **191**
Ridley, Matthew, 166, 176, 181
Roberts, HMS, 17
Robertson, Drill-Sgt, 187
Robertson, Sgt-Maj P., 24
Robertson, SSM, 18
Robinson, Sgt, 134
Rockets, 195, 197, 198–9
Roding, Adrie, archivist of Enschede,
  203, 204
Rodney, HMS, 15, 19–20
Rodney, John, 26, 99, 131, 133, 149, 202
  Brussels, 157
Roer, River, 163, 181
Royal Air Force, 98, 197, 218–19
  see also Aircraft
Rundstedt, General, 164, 172, 177
Russia, 177, 178
Russian Zone, post-war, 221–2
Ryder, David, 86, 130

Sailing, 219–20
St Aubin-sur-Mer, 8th Corps Rest
  Camp, 95
St Charles de Percy (Courteil), 53, 57,
  58, 59, 60
  British Military Cemetery, 59
St Clair, Murray, 97, 119
St Oedenrode, Netherlands, 128

Salisbury Plain, exercises, 6
Sandhurst, Royal Military Academy, 4–5
Schaijk, 188
Scheldt estuary, 156
Schilling, Herr, 154
Schreiber, Dick, 116
Sedgwick, John, 144, 149, 179, 180,
  181, 185, 193
Seine, River
  advance from, 101–7
  crossing at Vernon, 103–4
Shipley, Sgt, 90, 133, 137, 139, 171, 215
  at Enschede, 202, 203, 209
Shoreham Harbour, 10–11
Shotguns, 151, 154–5
Siddons, Cpl, 171, 200, 209, 215
Siegfried Line, 122, 152, 181, 187
Sittard, 164–5
Smith, Henty, Welsh Guards, 128, 129,
  186
Smyth-Osbourne, Tim, 180, 189, 209
Snaith, Cpl, 141
Somme, River, 107
Son, Netherlands, 128
Sourdevalle, 63, 66–9, **70**, 71–82, 92–3,
  97
  Hill 242, 75, 83, 87, 90
  La Jarrière farm, 88–9, 90
  Sourdevalle-Perrier ridge, **85**, 90–2
Sparrow, Basil, 105, 108, 109, 162, 164,
  176, 181, 187
Stanier, Brigadier Sir Alexander, 18n, 142
Stanley, Harry, 31, 36
Stewart-Fotheringham, Patrick, 59, 63, 90
Strasbourg, 162
Strutt, Peter, 194
Student, General Kurt, 122, 129
Style, Gerald, 132
Sutton, John, 14, 28, 63, 91, 96, 97, 157
  Arras, 112
  Bemmel, 140, 145
  birthday, 154
  Brussels, 151, 152, 161, 195–6
  in Esmael, 177

Tanks, 5
  Churchill, 57

Cromwell, 106
Crusader (Mark VI), 4, 7–8
Jagd-Panther, 124
Panther (German), 18, 31, 80
Sherman M4, 7, 9, 18, 106
  loss of confidence in, 40, 41, 47–8
  rockets fitted to, 195, 197, 198–9
Tiger (German), 9, 21, 31
Taswell, Sgt, 209
Thompson, Bob, 172, 174
Thompson, Johnny, 91, 111, 159, 178,
  188, 197
  on author's wounds, 207, 211
Thorne, Peter, 219
Thornton, TQMS, 118
Tibble, Guardsman, 137
Tilburg, 184
Tilley, Ben, consultant surgeon, 212
Tilly-sur-Seulles, 18
Tirlemont, 179
Tomlinson, Sgt Major, 166
Tournai, 113
Towers-Clarke, Peter, 54–5, 177
Training, 5, 6, 7–8
Tryon, Aylmer, 111
Twente Canal, author's tank hit at, 202,
  204–9

Udal, Eric, 84, 86
Udem, 187, 188
United States Army, 20, 67
  armies
    1st Army, 17, 20, 104
    3rd Army, 117, 199
    7th Army, 166
  army groups
    12th Army Group, 93
    21st Army Group, 117
  corps
    15 Corps, 93
    19 Corps, 56
  divisions
    82nd Airborne, 132, 145–6
    84th, 162
    101st Airborne, 128
  advance to Cologne, 188
  advance to Rhine, 162

and liberation of Paris, 98
and Normandy bridgehead, 25, 49, 60
at Cassel, 201
Avranches, 51–2, 92

V-1 flying bombs, 11
V-2 rockets, 155
Vandeleur, Col Joe, 60, 82, 84, 86, 92
Varnon, Mervyn, 219
Varuna (cutter), 219
Venlo, 156
Ver-sur-Mer, Gold beach, 15–16
Verneuil, Ecole de Roche, 102
Vernon, 103–4
Verson, 23
Victory in Europe celebrations, 213
Villers Bocage, 60
Vimont, 26, 40
Vire, 54, 56, 60

Waal, River, 131, 133
Waterloo, 162, 180
  Hougoumont Farm, 180, 196
Watkins, Tony, 6, 127, 128, 129, 131,
  136, 137, 164, 200
  in Brussels, 178
  at Hillensberg, 160
  and rockets, 197
Wehr, 160, 161, 164
Weigall, Tony, 22, 116
Wesel bridgehead, 190, 193
Whistler, Rex, 23
White, Sgt, 39, 79
Whittle, Cpl, 29, 43, 66
Wicking, Cpl, 97, 158
Wigan, Derek, 22, 147
Williams, Guardsman, 119
Wilson, Brian, Irish Guards, 84
Wilson, Cpl, 89
Wood, Cpl, 119
Wright, Guardsman, 201, 208, 211
Wynne Finch, John, Lt Col, 4

Xanten, 190

Yardley, Cpl, 119, 127
Yerburgh, John, Irish Guards, 19, 94,
  186, 199